The Nazi Religion and the Rise of the French Christian Resistance

The Nazi Religion and the Rise of the French Christian Resistance

Kathleen Burton

ROWMAN & LITTLEFIELD
Lanham • Boulder • New York • London

Published by Rowman & Littlefield
An imprint of The Rowman & Littlefield Publishing Group, Inc.
4501 Forbes Boulevard, Suite 200, Lanham, Maryland 20706
www.rowman.com

86-90 Paul Street, London EC2A 4NE

Copyright © 2022 by Kathleen Burton

All rights reserved. No part of this book may be reproduced in any form or by any electronic or mechanical means, including information storage and retrieval systems, without written permission from the publisher, except by a reviewer who may quote passages in a review.

British Library Cataloguing in Publication Information Available

Library of Congress Cataloging-in-Publication Data

Names: Burton, Kathleen, 1957– author.
Title: The Nazi religion and the rise of the French Christian resistance / Kathleen Burton.
Other titles: Nazisme comme religion. English
Description: Lanham : Rowman & Littlefield, [2022] | Translation of author's thesis (Ph.D.—Laval University, Quebec City, 2007), orignally published as: Le nazisme comme religion : quatre théologiens déchiffrent le code religieux nazi, 1932–1945. | Includes bibliographical references and index.
Identifiers: LCCN 2022030183 (print) | LCCN 2022030184 (ebook) | ISBN 9781538171400 (cloth) | ISBN 9781538171417 (paperback) | ISBN 9781538171424 (epub)
Subjects: LCSH: National socialism—Religious aspects. | National socialism and religion. | Christianity and politics—Germany—History—20th century. | Church and state—Germany—History—1933–1945. | World War, 1939–1945—Religious aspects—Christianity. | Germany—Religion—1933–1945.
Classification: LCC BR856 .H25713 2006 (print) | LCC BR856 (ebook) | DDC 274.3—dc23/eng/20220725
LC record available at https://lccn.loc.gov/2022030183
LC ebook record available at https://lccn.loc.gov/2022030184

I dedicate this book to those who survived the Nazi occupation of France, Jew and gentile alike, thanks to the efforts of the French Christian resistance, and to those who gave their lives so that their survival might testify to a great love—that of Christian unity.

Contents

Preface ix

Acknowledgments xvii

PART I: THE NAZI RELIGION: HIDING IN PLAIN SIGHT 1

Chapter 1: Point 24 of the Nazi Political Party Platform 5

Chapter 2: The Myth of the Twentieth Century 9

Chapter 3: Alfred Rosenberg and Positive Christianity 23

Chapter 4: Religious References in *Mein Kampf* 39

Chapter 5: Rosenberg's Early Writings and Friends of Europe Publications 55

PART II: DUPED CHRISTIANITY: HITLER'S PROPAGANDA COUP 69

Chapter 6: A Weak Christian Shield in Germany 79

Chapter 7: Disunity in Germany's Protestant Voice 95

PART III: THE RISE OF THE CHRISTIAN RESISTANCE IN FRANCE 113

Chapter 8: The French Churches Confront Nazism 115

Chapter 9: The French Christian Resistance 129

Chapter 10: Témoignage Chrétien (The Christian Witness) 143

Chapter 11: L'Amitié chrétienne (Christian Friendship) 165

Afterword: What Needs to Be Done?	175
Appendix A: The Program of the National Socialist German Workers' Party	181
Appendix B: Paul Tillich's "Ten Theses on National Socialism"	185
Appendix C: Friends of Europe Publications	187
Index	193
About the Author	203

Preface

THE HYPOTHESIS

Nazism contained, from its inception and in its scope, a religious objective which was in fact to bring about the disappearance of traditional Christianity and to replace it with "Positive Christianity," a Nazi version to serve as the spiritual guiding light of the Third Reich. Furthermore, actual physical proof exists in Germany today.

THE GOAL OF THIS BOOK IS TO ELUCIDATE

Who knew and understood this?
Where is the proof that this is true?
Who fought against it?
Who was defeated in their attempts?
Who feigned attempts?
Who brought victories in the end?
Why are their victories as yet unknown?
Why is it relevant today?

IMPETUS FOR THE BOOK

I am sure the salesclerk wondered what I had found so fascinating in the history corner of the used-book store in Caen, France, that hot summer day in 1998. I was spending three weeks at the University of Caen for a course on World War II during my graduate studies, and I had just found the book that would begin my passionate journey of more than twenty years. That passion—the drive to make known a missing puzzle piece of one of the greatest enigmas of the twentieth century—is finally in English, fulfilled. It seeks to clearly raise the question as well as boldly present a partial answer to the following: *How could such a monumental aberration as Nazism emerge out of the cradle of the scholarly Christian world?*

The book I encountered in Caen encapsulated the areas of this personal passion: the French-language and modern European history, both Christian and political. I was spellbound. This book, Paul Tillich's *Écrits contre les nazis, 1932–1935* (*Writings against the Nazis, 1932–1935*), resounded with the flair and vigor of Martin Luther's theses at Wittenberg in 1517, nailing his objections to the cathedral door, and thus beginning the Protestant Reformation. Tillich was facing down the rising tide of Nazism in his native country. His book contained ten theses, for which he was exiled to the United States in 1932, and that reverberated with a battle cry to the Christian world against the German "wolf in sheep's clothing" gaining political ground in the chaotic freedom of the Weimar Republic.

Tillich's book led me to *The Myth of the Twentieth Century*, the religious source of the Third Reich, commissioned by Hitler and written by Alfred Rosenberg, a founding member of the Party, who will be explored thoroughly in part I. This book, published in 1930, coupled with Hitler's own *Mein Kampf*, elucidates the enigmatic nature of the Nazi visceral hatred of Jews. The two stand together, as does their content, without which a clear picture of the German vision of the thousand-year Reich remains elusive.

In the early days of the Nazi regime, Tillich was not the only Christian theologian concerned and active, as we will come to realize. However, it is a travesty of historic proportions that the religious element of Nazi ideology and those that fought against it are still unknown. On the floor of that used-book store in Caen began my passion to begin the work to fill this intellectual void and shine the light necessary in the twenty-first century to avoid the calamitous breach of understanding of the twentieth century in neglecting such an essential element to the worldview of Hitler and the Third Reich. In my research, three concrete references to physical proof in Germany have been uncovered, the most recent only translated in the last few years. Yet this journey that began in Normandy, France, was only the beginning.

Tillich's book that I found in Caen (and that now rests in a place of honor in my bookcase at Yale) was translated into French from German by a team of scholars at Laval University in Quebec City, Canada, led by Dr. Jean Richard, a Jesuit scholar. I, being only a day's drive away in New Haven, Connecticut, set out to meet the leader of the team. I wrote to him and was invited to visit. I received a cordial welcome and an ardent interest in my graduate thesis. A mentorship began then that I can only define as sublime. Father Richard, after having perused my initial work on the topic, announced to me that I was to do my doctoral work under his supervision there at Laval University in Quebec City, and he would return in a few minutes with the necessary application and paperwork to get things under way! He informed me, as a matter of fact, that there was the opportunity at Laval for native English-language students to apply for a scholarship to complete their doctoral work at Laval (a strictly French-speaking university) if they had the language skills. He was impressed with mine and took care of researching the details.

Counting myself fortunate to have received such an amiable reception in his office, I was dumbstruck by his offer of tutelage and possible scholarship. He was the former head of the theology department at Laval and had only just become emeritus. Doors opened as he personally escorted me to administrative offices, and even government bureaucratic interviews for my necessary visas. I owe a prodigious debt of gratitude to him and to the country of Canada, not only for my doctorate, but for seeing the value of my work to the extent of publishing my thesis *Le Nazisme comme religion, quatre théologiens déchiffrent le code religieux nazi (1932–1945)* in 2006.

The book, while in French and in a format tailored to an academic and theological community, was a satisfying endeavor and a gratifying accomplishment. It is for this reason, furthermore, that many of the primary sources cited are from French-language works. However, my deep desire remained to reach a general educated public in my native English so as to ignite interest from a variety of social and cultural spheres. Education, as to all the pieces of the enigmatic Nazi puzzle, must be of paramount importance as we begin, with trepidation, this twenty-first century. The content may surprise you, may shock you, may inspire you, but most of all, the desire is to inform you. Of what, one may ask?

First, the fact that Nazism is a self-defined religious movement with a well-defined religion. It is true, and, under the name of "Positive Christianity" (think what you will, they had a very clear idea of what they meant by this term, and a very savvy way of letting you interpret it as you wished, in the short term), there is proof. It is here in research and in physical evidence not yet revealed but hiding in plain sight.

Second, to gain recognition for the courageous ones who fought the battle against the Nazi religion in Germany and in France, who, albeit indirectly, were completely verifiably responsible for saving three-quarters of French Jews, yet have hitherto received no public appreciation either by their respective countries or by the Vatican.

These are the clear and passionate goals to which this book is devoted. In so doing, I will endeavor to shine the light of the Christian Resistance, reveal the proof that exists still today in Germany, and bring recognition of the heroes of this resistance to the Vatican and to their respective countries. Finally, the desire for American academic research in the various fields upon which this book will touch will allow for continuing clarity about a period of a century so laden with loss.

OBJECT OF THE BOOK

The following assumption will be presented and defended: Nazism was a spiritual movement whose goal was to replace traditional Christianity by a Nazi version of "Positive Christianity," an element of the overall design of the Third Reich. It is by including and understanding this religious element of Nazism and by expanding the research of this neglected perspective that I will clearly demonstrate the method of hiding in plain sight.

Hitler had developed a theology within the very center of his ideology. The essence of the Nazi faith is held in the book commissioned by Hitler, written by the designated spiritual and ideological leader of the Nazi Party, Alfred Rosenberg, *The Myth of the Twentieth Century*. Furthermore, the present work will provide new information as to its importance in Nazi ideology by the discovery of Rosenberg's personal diary and its subsequent publication by the United States Holocaust Memorial Museum in 2015.

The present volume will follow a spiritual perspective of Nazism and will endeavor to clarify its meaning and purpose. Additionally, it will address the necessary questions of who and why that emerge from these clarifications. It will lead us to the substantial proof of this hypothesis still in Germany today. Finally, this treatise hopes to bring recognition to the unsung heroes of the Christian Resistance, primarily in France, while recognizing as well the initial efforts in Germany.

STRUCTURE OF THE BOOK

Part I relates to the two pillars which form the base of Nazism—*Mein Kampf* by Adolf Hitler and *The Myth of the Twentieth Century* by Alfred Rosenberg. This last work is little known, the French translation available to the general public only since 1986. It was initially published, however, in 1930 on commission from Hitler, and contains the key ideas of "Positive Christianity," which constitute the theological base of Nazism. It will, therefore, be treated first. Religious references in Hitler's *Mein Kampf* constitute the external source of the Nazi religion, *The Myth of the Twentieth Century* serving as the clear internal source. One finds here in this combined analysis the origin of the visceral anti-Semitism of Nazism, which leads to a comprehensive understanding of Nazism's spiritual base.

To conclude this first part, a little-known collection of publications addressing, in English, the dire religious situation engulfing Germany will be studied. It has been thought that little was written in English during the 1930s in this regard; however, the publications of the Friends of Europe prove that both England and the United States had scholars and theologians analyzing the Nazi Party's religious plans for their thousand-year reign. Even Winston Churchill when still a member of parliament in the 1930s was published in volume 19 of this unknown collection. This series (over seventy volumes in all) merits an in-depth study, beyond the breadth of this publication, yet their very emergence in the early 1930s validates their importance.

Part II introduces two German-language theologians, Paul Tillich and Karl Barth, who, together in Protestant Germany, faced the theological quagmire of Positive Christianity. *Ten Theses against the Nazis* by Paul Tillich, the book that was my initial inspiration, is an essential resource in understanding German Christian dissent in this period. The second religious scholar is the Swiss theologian Karl Barth. His contribution against Nazism is here recognized for its unceasing efforts to keep Protestants throughout Europe informed of Nazi Christian persecution and Jewish oppression. However, we will study this pivotal theologian's refusal to address the Nazi movement as a religious one, contrary to Tillich, and see how this led to the impotence of a united Christian offensive against Positive Christianity. Despite Barth's tardive volte-face of his indirect strategy against Nazism, it will come too late and be too little as the weakened Protestant shield is passed to predominantly Catholic France.

Part III is devoted to the work of Pierre Chaillet, a Jesuit visionary, who quickly understood the danger of European Christianity facing the spiritual forces of Nazism and spearheaded the French Christian resistance. This ecumenical resistance, combining efforts of Protestants and Catholics alike, was a true phenomenon almost without precedent in the long, blood-soaked religious history of France. This Christian cooperation bore its fruit in the publication, the distribution, and the influence of the clandestine newspaper, founded by Pierre Chaillet, *Témoignage Chrétien* (*The Christian Witness*). It also bore fruit in the joint Christian efforts of the CIMADE (Comité Inter-Mouvements Auprès des Évacués—Inter-Movement Committee for Assistance to Refugees) and L'Amitié chrétienne (Christian Friendship), two benevolent organizations founded by Chaillet working in the concentration camps in France.

The conclusion of part III affirms that the French Christian Resistance, led by Pierre Chaillet, was responsible, albeit indirectly, for the rescue of three-quarters of French Jews, one of the highest percentages in Europe. How so? By the constant pressure *The Christian Witness* newspaper put upon the French Catholic hierarchy to begin hiding the Jews. Dangerous monthly distribution of the publication to the archbishops of France finally bore fruit after the horrors of the Vélodrome d'Hiver Jewish roundups in Paris of 1942.

Finally, in the afterword, the question "What Needs to be Done?" is asked and solutions are proposed. There is much to consider. The purpose of this book is twofold. First, the missing puzzle piece of Nazism as a religion must be clarified: Who knew about the religious agenda of the Party, who understood it, and who fought against it? However, it is also a goal of this book to bring to light unexplored territory and encourage future research. The collection of the Friends of Europe publications, virtually unheard of, is very pertinent to this topic. With several independently cited references in this book to the contents of the cornerstone of the Nazi Congress Hall in Nuremberg, it is still unknown if *The Myth of the Twentieth Century* alongside *Mein Kampf* is interred there. What of the contents of the other many cornerstones laid by Hitler? Pierre Chaillet's efforts are still unsung in France and unrecognized by the Catholic Church. It is certainly advantageous to have a Jesuit priest as Pope for the first time in Vatican history, encouraging at least some recognition of the heroes of the Christian Resistance, most Jesuits, where none has been given. Fortuitous timing in publication is evident, as well, by exploiting the recent discoveries explained below.

RECENT MILESTONES AND RELEVANT DISCOVERIES

It is of particular interest to conclude this preface by mentioning both a milestone for the postwar era in Germany and an incredible discovery recently here in the United States. For the first time since the end of World War II, in January 2016, Hitler's two-volume *Mein Kampf* (*My Struggle*), which will be discussed for its religious content in part I, was published in Germany and available for purchase in German bookstores. Reportedly, four thousand copies sold in the first week of publication.

Regarding recent and relevant discoveries, it is important to bring to the reader's attention an extraordinary find made in 2013. Special agents of Homeland Security Investigations from Delaware found Alfred Rosenberg's personal journals in an apartment in New York State, a remarkable document that contains more than four hundred pages, written in longhand. These journals are now in the archives of the United States Holocaust Memorial Museum in Washington, DC.

Their translation into English was published in 2015 by Rowman & Littlefield under the title *The Political Diary of Alfred Rosenberg and the Onset of the Holocaust*, and has given rise to other publications, such as *The Devil's Diary: Alfred Rosenberg and the Stolen Secrets of the Third Reich*,

An extraordinary find: Four hundred pages of Rosenberg's personal diary were found in 2013 by Homeland Security. (United States Holocaust Memorial Museum)

written in 2016 by Robert Wittman and David Kinney and published by HarperCollins the following year.

The importance of these journals to the present work is the notoriety brought to Rosenberg, who has been considered until now to be a less pivotal member of Hitler's inner circle. Yet new discoveries are yet to be made. The cornerstone ceremonies during the Third Reich have been validated by this new diary, as well as corroborated by two other references. The contents will be historical in validation of *The Myth of the Twentieth Century*'s importance to the thousand-year Reich dream, and are set forth here.

After reading the present work, it will be more than obvious that this very regrettable historical mistake needs ardent attention in order to correctly and meticulously place "one puzzle piece more" into the enigmatic puzzle of Nazism.

Acknowledgments

While personal passion has driven the publication of this book, first in French and now in English, it never could have been accomplished without the help of many. I am grateful to all who supported my vision to see these two publications through the twenty-one-year journey.

There are a few supporters that I would like to particularly thank. First, Dr. Jean Richard, professor emeritus from the theology department at Laval University in Quebec: without his personal encouragement for my doctoral studies, neither book would have ever been completed. Dr. Marie-Claire Rohinsky was an editor *extraordinaire* for the French version of the book, published in 2007. The pages returned from her, awash with red ink, always kept me humble in my love affair with the French language. I owe a debt of gratitude to Beth Davey, my literary agent; she never stopped supporting me, as she has always believed this is a story that must be told.

Finally, it is with the utmost gratitude that I thank my husband, Dr. David Burton. The long drives to Quebec and his technological support were constant throughout the extensive and arduous journey to publication. I owe him a special thanks for his faith in me.

PART I

The Nazi Religion: Hiding in Plain Sight

Heed what is written, not what is said.
A Case in Point: The Words of Hitler's Architect, Albert Speer

The commonsense concept of investigation and conclusion was grossly lacking in many who joined the Nazi Party, even early on. One of these, self-admittedly, was Albert Speer, an upper-middle-class architect who, having willingly admitted his share of guilt at the Nuremberg trials after the war (the only one to do so), served a twenty-year sentence, during which time he wrote *Inside the Third Reich: Memoirs*. In the following quote from his autobiography, it is interesting to note his self-avowed frivolity in joining the Nazi Party, not even reading the crucial works of Hitler and Rosenberg (author of *The Myth of the Twentieth Century*). This certainly proves the point of the propaganda ploy in Nazi planning: hiding in plain sight.

> Quite often even the most important step in a man's life, his choice of vocation, is taken quite frivolously.... My decision to enter Hitler's party was no less frivolous. Why, for example, was I willing to abide by the almost hypnotic impression Hitler's speech had made upon me? Why did I not undertake a thorough, systematic investigation of, say, the value or worthlessness of the ideologies of *all* the parties? Why did I not read the various party programs, or at least Hitler's *Mein Kampf* and Rosenberg's *Myth of the Twentieth Century*? ... For had I only wanted to, I could have found out even then that Hitler was proclaiming expansion of the Reich to the east; that he was a rank anti-Semite; that he was committed to a system of authoritarian rule; that after attaining power he intended to eliminate democratic procedures and would thereafter yield only to force. Not to have worked that out for myself; not, given my education, to have

read books, magazines, and newspapers of various viewpoints; not to have tried to see through the whole apparatus of mystification—was already criminal. At this initial stage my guilt was as grave as, at the end, my work for Hitler.[1]

Heed what is reported but not believed.
Reports from William Dodd, US Ambassador to Nazi Germany

Another introductory religious reference to the oncoming storm of the Third Reich comes from a vigilant American source within Nazi Germany. In a translated copy of a 1938 edition of *The Nazi Primer*, a volume used for the education of the Hitler Youth, a commentary is made by William E. Dodd, the American ambassador to Nazi Germany. His story was superbly told in the best-selling novel by Erik Larson, *In the Garden of Beasts: Love, Terror and an American Family in Hitler's Berlin* (Broadway Paperbacks, 2011).

The following are excerpts from this commentary, *The Bible of a Political Church*. It gives a rare, on-the-spot assessment of the Reich's early religious efforts.

The children belong to the state and party, not to families.[2]

. . . and before the end of 1936, sixteen hundred and thirty professors and teachers had been dismissed.[3]

Under this pressure from Hitler and Goebbels, operating through Rosenberg, hundreds of professors and teachers of the highest standing fled the country.[4]

. . . a distinguished thinker said once that the whole German people will be made over in a few more years. Nor was this all. As Hitler demanded absolute unity of the German people and a close relationship of all Germans who lived in other countries, he counted himself a sort of spokesman of God Almighty, and his chiefs often proclaimed him a "greater leader than Jesus Christ."[5]

A meeting was called by the Hitler Party in 1934 at Wittenberg. Preachers and others were to attend and shout the praise of the new Führer and of the ancient Aryan religion, which was being restored and elaborated by the curious Rosenberg, who was also doing so much to control education. The book contains no reference to any mistakes of the past.[6]

The central idea behind it is to make the rising generation worship their chief and get ready to "save civilization" from the Jews, from Communism, and from democracy.[7]

Ambassador Dodd's reporting failed to communicate the all-encompassing nature of the Nazi goal and hence remained unheeded. In contemporary scholarship, this emphasis on the totality of the hold that the Nazi Party commanded on the German people mentioned above by Dodd is captured by the eminent professor Thomas Childers of the University of Pennsylvania in his audio series *A History of Hitler's Empire*, in which he states that the goal of the Party was to have dominion over the entire person, the total person: at home, at work, at social gatherings. It was the complete Nazi Aryan identity that was sought.[8]

Heed what is not written.
Lessons from Sir Ian Kershaw's Book, *What Is Nazism?*

A third element to introduce the religious dimension of Nazism is found in the eminent scholar Sir Ian Kershaw's *What Is Nazism?* In his book, he identifies the Nazi desire for "a revolution in mentalities." Kershaw explains here that, for the National Socialists, this mentality was the essential problem of the Third Reich. It is important to grasp this Nazi preoccupation, even though it's not clearly defined. For the purposes of this book, it can be synopsized in the warning to "heed what is not written." Kershaw elaborates:

> According to their diagnosis, the problem of Germany lay fundamentally in attitudes, values and mentalities; it was therefore they that the Nazis tried to modify, by replacing class, religious and regional affiliations with an exacerbated national conscience capable of galvanizing the German people for the coming battle and to mobilize them when war broke out.[9]

To implement this revolution of mentalities, Hitler follows a plan explained in *Mein Kampf,* and in the Nazi 25-point program. According to historian Karl Dietrich Bracher, "There was a planned, controlled and 'rational' progression to preconceived goals, an argument he consistently reformulated in his major works."[10]

It is interesting to note that Kershaw, throughout his book, emphasizes the need for a moral dimension in any serious interpretation of Nazism. On the penultimate page of the book he emphasizes this essential aspect:

> The Nazi past arouses in those who face it, passionate reactions of moral condemnation. It is good that it is so. However justified, and even necessary, it may be, moral condemnation cannot suffice in the long term and risks favoring the legend, instead of true knowledge. Moral indignation and repulsion must be constantly nurtured by authentic historical research and knowledge.[11]

To overcome this enigma of Nazism, a certain moralism is essential. A new theological perspective presented here can add to the moral aspect called for by this famed historian and add a puzzle piece to the ever-emerging picture of the Nazi enigma.

To end this introduction of Part I, it is imperative to mention the importance of the clarity of terms in the context of this book. Regarding the use of the word *theology*, the concept of a theological analysis of Nazism seems contradictory. Given the most widespread definition of the term *theology* as "the science of divine things or of the Christian religion: the science which treats of God and man in all their known relations with one another,"[12] the question arises: What definition will be given to a study of religious questions based mainly on texts which, first of all, question the fundamental bases of the sacred biblical texts and the foundations of the Christian faith, and, second, seek to replace them with another interpretation of Christianity? The answer to this question is found in the clarification here of the word *theology*.

The religious elements of Nazism, although inane when analyzed from the point of view of traditional Christianity, are a source to which this book will refer using the words *theology* and *theological*, because *Mein Kampf* and *The Myth of the Twentieth Century* make their own analysis of Christianity, refer to biblical texts, and require the use of the term *theology* to clarify their beliefs and reasoning, no matter how inane. It is in this context that these terms will be applied.

NOTES

1. Albert Speer, *Inside the Third Reich* (New York: Macmillan, 1970), 18–19.
2. William E. Dodd, commentary published in *The Nazi Primer: Official Handbook for Schooling the Hitler Youth* (New York, London: Harper & Brothers, 1938), 268.
3. Ibid., 270.
4. Ibid., 271.
5. Ibid., 272–73.
6. Ibid., 274.
7. Ibid., 280.
8. Thomas Childers, *A History of Hitler's Empire*, The Great Courses (Chantilly, VA: The Teaching Company, 2001), disc 1, track 4.
9. Martin Broszat, *Der Staat Hitlers*, Munich, 1969; trans. by Patrick Moreau, *The Hitlerite State: The Origin and Evolution of the Structures of the Third Reich* (Paris, France: Fayard, 1985), quoted by Ian Kershaw in his book, *What Is Nazism?* (Paris, France: Folio, 1997), 271.
10. Kershaw, *What Is Nazism?*, 62.
11. Ibid., 426–27.
12. *The New Webster Encyclopedic Dictionary of the English Language* (Chicago: Consolidated Book Publishers, 1980).

Chapter 1

Point 24 of the Nazi Political Party Platform

"IN THE BEGINNING"

In the Beginning Was the Word. Disregarding most biblical content, Nazi propaganda still exploited biblical innuendo in this painting by Hermann Hoyer. (Army Art Collection, US Army Center of Military History)

In the Beginning Was the Word. This painting by Hermann Hoyer is a good example of the realistic style of genre painting favored by Hitler and the Nazi regime. A straightforward portrait of Hitler addressing his followers has been given a dramatic biblically inspired title.

Albert Speer's regrets give insight into the superficiality of many political activists in 1930s Munich. Many were the parties, many were the platforms, and many were the political views during the short-lived Weimar Republic in postwar Germany. However, by including the religious beliefs of the Nazi Party clearly declared in the founding 25-point platform, one can affirm that "hiding in plain sight" was a significant objective. One can also surmise that the desire to remain obscure as to the meaning of Positive Christianity was also a propaganda objective, leaving each prospective member to draw his own conclusions as to its meaning. Its meaning and its centrality to the present work puts it squarely in this brief introductory chapter of part I, so as not in any way to be obfuscated or lost in what follows. Hitler was able, unhindered, to advance his religious agenda for the thousand-year Reich through Rosenberg's writings while duping the established churches as to the clarity of its meaning. What does point 24 actually say? The text reads as follows:

> We demand liberty for all religious confessions in the State, in so far as they do not in any way endanger its existence or do not offend the moral sentiment and the customs of the Germanic race. The party as such represents the standpoint of "positive Christianity" without binding itself confessionally to a particular faith. It opposes the Jewish materialistic spirit within and without, and is convinced that permanent recovery of our people is possible only from within and on the basis of the principle: General Welfare Before Individual Welfare.[1]

In what direction does this new terminology wish to take the German people of the new Third Reich? This question will presently be answered, but its central importance in Nazi ideology is undeniable in the founding beliefs of the National Socialist Party introduced by Hitler in 1920.

It is significant to know that the Nazi Party had a precise idea of Positive Christianity in its political program. However, it took ten more years, until the publication of *The Myth*, and thirteen more years, until Hitler's rise to power in 1933, to effectively see the clear threat to Christianity in Germany. In 1920, the Nazi Party was only one among many. After the imprisonment of Hitler in 1923—a result of the infamous Beer Hall Putsch, when the Nazi Party attempted to gain power by force—his influence further decreased. It is only with Hitler's rise to power, the evolution of the ideas of the German Christian Movement (referred to below), and the increasing popularity of the NSDAP (the official name of the Nazi Party is the National Socialist German Workers' Party), that the Christian churches started to consider this idea of

Positive Christianity found in point 24 of the Nazi program. Unfortunately, as will be shown, they will interpret it in various ways according to their own priorities. Presuming that a political movement was in no position to interpret theological ideas, nor would wish to do so, they supposed that this reference, although of theological connotation, was no real threat.

Positive Christianity is the central idea in any theological analysis of Nazism. Before approaching its fundamental beliefs as established in *The Myth*, it is a logical step a priori to ask the following question: Where are the roots of Positive Christianity to be found? In his seminal book, *Une Église à croix gammée?* (*A Swastika Church?*), Swiss theologian Bernard Reymond traces the roots of Positive Christianity in the evolution of German Christianity and the German faith:

> It is indeed in the context of the academic and liberal theology of the [nineteenth] century that the first research is found on the characteristics suitable for a religious faith which would be typically German. Schleiermacher, in his first Speech on the religion (1799), then Fichte in his sixth discourse to the German nation (1808), had already insisted on affinities of Christianity clashing with the Germanic character.... One had begun research on the religion of Germany.... Consequently, a question became inevitable: how had the meeting of Christianity taken place with the German world?... Or (but it was a frightening question!) had the evangelization of Germany denatured their character and was it not advisable to reconcile a former Germanity to its Christianization?[2]

Bernard Reymond continues his explanation by quoting the name of university personalities like Paul de Lagarde (1827–1891), who considered a transformation of the German Protestant Christian churches, in their practices and their theologies, by carrying out a Germanic and "degasified" Christian piety.[3] Reymond also speaks about *pasteur* Artur Bonus (1846–1941) who in 1911 wrote *Contributions to the Germanization of Christianity*. But, finally, Reymond affirms that the true danger arises when these ideas, which in the academic world remain inoffensive, become the ideological sources of political actions.

> Thus, it was ... in particular when the incendiary and nationalist ideas of Stewart Chamberlain, the son-in-law of Richard Wagner, were taken up by the populist movement (Völkische Bewegung) and started to feed what was going to become the Nazi movement. Consequently, the reflections born around the topic "Christianity and Germanity" gave rise to two distinct currents: a) a Christian current, which sometimes ended in resolutely racial theses ... [and] b) The German faith movement ... which claimed to disencumber the ancestral and authentic faith of Germany from "foreign" influences, Eastern or Latin, whose Christianization had made it suffer.[4]

This German Christian Movement was positioned to easily recognize elements of their belief system in point 24, bringing essential support to the Nazi Party's successful political position in the 1933 elections.

In the early years of Nazi power, the Roman Catholic Church and an obscure English-language group by the name of the Friends of Europe began to take notice of Rosenberg's writings. As his publications continued to elaborate the aspects of point 24's Positive Christianity, the Roman Catholic Church focused its concern on the publication of *The Myth of the Twentieth Century*, while the Friends of Europe focused its analyses on Rosenberg's early publications. The Roman Catholic Church's reaction to Hitler's regime and Rosenberg's writings will be explored in chapters 3 and 4, whereas the publications of the Friends of Europe will be analyzed as a secondary source in chapter 5.

NOTES

1. The 25 points of the Program of the National Socialist German Workers' Party are in Ernst Jeuerlein, ed., *Der Aufstieg DER NSDAP in Augenzeugenberichten* (Dusseldorf, 1968). They are published in English in an appendix in Arthur C. Cochrane, *The Church's Confession Under Hitler* (Philadelphia: Westminster Press, 1962), 219–22. (They are found in appendix A of this book.)

2. Bernard Reymond, *Une Église à croix gammée? (A Swastika Church?)* (Genève: L'âge de l'homme, 1980), 45–46 (author's translation).

3. Ibid., 46.

4. Ibid., 46–47.

Chapter 2

The Myth of the Twentieth Century

"EXPECT THE UNEXPECTED"

Looking back on the research for this book, it has become clear that we need to expect the unexpected. Initially, however, the straightforwardness of checking out books at Yale's esteemed Sterling Memorial Library did not seem to be the place for the surprise I found concerning *The Myth of the Twentieth Century*. Perusing the shelves, I struggled to find the only copy in all of Yale's vast libraries. Even more surprising was the fact that it was only a bound photocopy. Shocked that such a pivotal Nazi source should be so meagerly represented at Yale, I was reminded of a comment made by a German colleague's wife at Laval University. She was surprised that I had emphasized Rosenberg's work in my book, since most writers of the Nazi period had written him off as odd in his ideas and insignificant in his influence (refer to the previous Albert Speer quote). My doubts regarding this cursory view of Rosenberg were affirmed early on when it was evident that from the very start, Positive Christianity figured in the founding principles of the Party. Furthermore, France had not permitted *The Myth of the Twentieth Century* to be translated or published in France until 1989. These two facts alone supported my research and bolstered my belief that I had a story to tell; in fact, by connecting the dots of the Nazi's words themselves, the story would nearly tell itself. Therefore, to complete this brief introduction to this pivotal chapter, it is appropriate to reveal here another unknown and neglected fact.

There is irrefutable proof existing in Germany today of the value of what has heretofore been considered an obscure and irrelevant Nazi publication. The proof lies in the cornerstones of the still-existing buildings constructed by Hitler during the Third Reich. During the groundbreaking ceremonies of the cornerstones, as mentioned in the preface, Hitler placed copies of both *Mein Kampf* and *The Myth of the Twentieth Century* together into the cornerstones themselves, to mark the importance of the occasion in Third Reich history. The most famous of these cornerstones was placed for the monumental construction of the Nuremberg Congress Hall stadium, which is still standing today. Part of the Nuremberg Party Rally grounds, it has been under consideration for demolition since 2016.[1]

There are three clear validating references to this yet-to-be-discovered truth. The first is from Rosenberg's own unequivocal words in his diary, discovered in 2013 and published in 2015. He writes:

Nuremberg: Germany's dilemma over the Nazis' field of dreams

Some want the Nuremburg complex where Hitler spoke to be left to crumble, others want it preserved as a warning from history, says Tony Paterson

Tony Paterson • Friday 01 January 2016 19:18 • Comments

The Nuremberg Congress Hall completed by Hitler in 1936 still stands, now in ruins. (Independent Digital News & Media Ltd.)

And finally, in Nuremberg, the largest congress hall in the world is being built. In all the coming years and centuries, the declaration of commitment to eternal Germany is to be sworn there. And two works—*Mein Kampf* and *The Myth*—are bricked into the cornerstone of this gigantic building for all time.[2]

The second reference is also recent, found in the 2017 publication *The Devil's Diary*, written by Robert Wittman and David Kinney after the discovery of Rosenberg's diary and its subsequent publication.

That week, Rosenberg was not just another speaker at the rallies. He was a guest of honor. Eighteen years after first turning up at a regular meeting of a tiny band of beer-hall anti-Semites in Munich, he was being hailed as the man who'd laid the ideological foundations of National Socialism. His masterwork, *The Myth of the Twentieth Century*, already rested beside *Mein Kampf* in the cornerstone of Nuremberg's Congress Hall, the monumental arena rising in the middle of the rally grounds. When finished, it would be larger than the colosseum in Rome.[3]

Finally, the third reference comes from the French Christian Resistance clandestine publication, *The Christian Witness*.[4] This extraordinary underground newspaper will be featured in part III. It is in one of their early editions, *Racists: A Self-Portrait* (*Les racistes peints par eux-mêmes*), that the proof can be found. The reference here, written in March 1942, is the same as that of the other two, November 11, 1935, on the day of the laying of the cornerstone marking the construction of the immense congress hall.

Two books dominate and inspired the abundant literature of the III Reich on racism. These are truly the official sources of the racist Revelation . . . millions of copies, commented on religiously in the Party ceremonies . . . they are the Bible of the national-socialist conception of the world: Hitler's *Mein Kampf* and Rosenberg's *The Myth of the XXth Century*. During the National Days of Nuremberg, November 11, 1935, they were placed, one next to the other, in the cement of the foundations of the Congressional Palace Hall, giving in this way a symbolic consecration to the New German Home.[5]

To conclude this irrefutable proof of the centrality of *The Myth* for the vision of the thousand-year Reich, in Speer's autobiography, although he doesn't mention the two volumes themselves, he discusses the construction of the grandiose Nuremberg Congress Hall and its meaning for the Reich.

Hitler's demand for huge dimensions, however, involved more than he was willing to admit to the workers. He wanted the biggest of everything to glorify his works and magnify his pride. These monuments were an assertion of his claim to world domination long before he dared to voice any such intention even to his closest associates. I, too, was intoxicated by the idea of using drawings, money, and construction firms to create stone witnesses to history, and thus affirm our claim that our works would survive for a thousand years. . . . At the same Party Rally of 1937 at which Hitler laid the cornerstone of the stadium, his last speech ended with the ringing words: "The German nation has after all acquired its Germanic Reich."[6]

It comes as no surprise that, in Rosenberg's *Myth*, the Germanic race is perceived as the dominant race in history. Indeed, one can say that this view of race is presupposed in all aspects of Nazi ideology. In this work, however, Rosenberg does not defend only this idea of superiority. He presents the Germanic race (his references also include "Scandinavian" or "Aryan") as the original chosen race. This belief is supported by a long study of world history, which seeks to prove that all the great empires and dynasties had their origins in the Aryan people.

We will reconsider this point, because it is fundamental to understanding this guiding principle of the chosen people. This exceeds the idea of a simple national superiority. This enters the field of faith, because according to Rosenberg and the tenets of Positive Christianity in point 24, God chose the Germanic people to realize His providence. It is, finally, after the multitudinous attempts throughout history to gain its proper position, that the Aryan race is to reject Negative Christianity (traditional Christianity) and realize without delay or failure the true Christianity never seen or experienced before at this time in the twentieth century.

Rosenberg emphasizes this Germanic destiny in a conversation with Hermann Göring, who was an intimate of Hitler's from the days of the Beer Hall Putsch in 1923, president of the Reichstag, and, after the French Armistice in 1940, the *Reichsmarschall*—supreme commander over all of Germany's armed forces. Rosenberg assures Göring in this conversation of the demise of Negative Christianity and the triumph of Positive Christianity of the Nazi program's point 24, recorded in his recently discovered diary:

> The day before yesterday I was in Göring's office for three hours. He had read my essay about ideology and religion and suddenly launched into an extensive discussion of religion.
>
> Göring: Next to the Führer you are the only one who has dealt with these questions in a cogent way, and I would like to know what you think. . . . Do you believe that Christianity is thus drawing to an end, and later on a new form determined by us will emerge?
>
> Rosenberg: Absolutely! After the crumbling away occurs in all sorts of ways, the churches' *value* system will no longer be inwardly acknowledged.

Göring: *That* is what I want to know. I will have to ask the Führer in private what he wants in *his heart of hearts.* You know he has said some accommodating things.[7]

As to the first part of the title of Rosenberg's book, what does the author wish to say when speaking about "myth"? The definition here does not reflect merely the popular definition of a fabulous fictional story. It is more obscure and restricted, having been chosen for that purpose. The *New Oxford American Dictionary* (Oxford Press, 2001) cites the first meaning of *myth* as "a traditional story, especially one concerning the early history of a people." This definition corresponds to Aryan Germany's expression of the community of the chosen people. The Aryan race will be able to carry out this "myth," which remained unrealized throughout history, but which, in the twentieth century, will see its fruition in the Third Reich.

It is of equal importance to add that the full title of Rosenberg's book is *The Myth of the Twentieth Century: An Evaluation of the Spiritual-Intellectual Confrontations of Our Age.* This full title explains why Rosenberg traverses so much of human history to discover and emphasize the myth of an Aryan diaspora in the world, bringing the reader to the importance of the Nazi vision. More significant still is the fact that this Nazi vision of race impregnates the theological analysis.

BELIEF IN THE GERMANIC RACE AS "THE CHOSEN PEOPLE"

The Germanic people constitute the chosen people of God. This belief ipso facto denies the possibility of a chosen Jewish people, since the theological concept of an Aryan chosen people leaves no place for competition. It is thus necessary to eliminate any other interpretation of the existence of another chosen people. All of Rosenberg's theology depends upon this belief. When we analyze his book from this point of view, we seize the veritable root of Nazi anti-Semitism in one fundamental ideological belief. Hitler always insisted on the expression "Jewish race," refusing any interpretation of Judaism as a simple religion. The Jewish people are the usurping race pretentiously claiming to be the elect of God. This usurpation throughout history thwarted the Aryan race's efforts to achieve God's will and must not, at any cost, achieve that same fate in the twentieth-century efforts of Nazism. Even the false economic hegemony of Russian bolshevism is seen as a conspiratorial Jewish effort to once again gain historical ground to stop the true chosen people from achieving their rightful place in God's plan. We will see in the next sections that, for this same reason, Positive Christianity seeks to eliminate all Jewish biblical associations as well as to deny the Jewish origin of Jesus.

With this vision of the Germanic chosen people, it becomes obvious why Rosenberg attacks traditional Christianity and particularly the Catholic Church so savagely. It is a consequence of the same principle. The Roman Catholic Church defends the doctrines of the universality of salvation by Christ, and it maintains its center in Rome with a central figure in the Pope of an infallible power on questions of faith. These two fundamental principles of Catholicism are rejected categorically by Positive Christianity.

First of all, the central idea of the universality of salvation in Christ—that all people are equal in faith in the resurrected Christ Jesus—is problematic for the Aryan concept of a chosen people. Furthermore, the recognition of the Pope—the representative of this faith on Earth until the second advent of Christ—also proves problematic. A different view of the chosen people is confronted by Rosenberg, as we will see more closely in his early writings, in chapter 6. These are, of course, those Christian people saved in their faith in Christ and, in the case of the Catholic Church's representative, the Pope. This competition in the Christian concept of a chosen people is unacceptable for Positive Christianity—even more so when considering the role of the Pope. This is because, by his very existence, the Pope creates an obstacle to a messianism of the Aryan people in the twentieth century, fulfilled in Hitler, *Führer* of the Third Reich.

This explains the open aggressiveness of Rosenberg toward the Catholic Church, the Jesuits, and the Pope. There can be only one chosen people. Since the beginning of creation, according to Rosenberg, these people were always the people of the North, with Viking blood, the Scandinavian race which, throughout history, tried to achieve its divine role: to spread throughout the world the hegemony of pure blood, and to thus found the dominion of the Germanic people, chosen by the providence of God to reign on Earth. This is what emerges out of a theological study of the work of Rosenberg. References to the text that follow will confirm the validity of this interpretation and substantiate the importance of *The Myth*.

From the first section of the first book of *The Myth*, Rosenberg makes known his intention: to prove the rightful place of the Germanic people. He introduces his historical overview by proclaiming the divine role of Scandinavian blood, which he accompanies by a warning against any obstacles to the realization of this destiny:

> None who have disregarded the religion of the blood have escaped this nemesis—neither Hindus, neither the Indians nor the Persians, neither the Greeks, nor the Romans. Nor will Nordic Europe escape if it does not call a halt, turning away from bloodless absolutes and spiritually empty delusions, and begin to

hearken trustingly once again to the subtle welling up of the ancient sap of life and values. . . . The solar myth, with all its ramifications, did not arise spontaneously as a stage of general development, but was born where the appearance of the sun must have been a cosmic event of profoundest significance, that is, in the far north. . . . And so today the long derived hypotheses becomes a probability, namely that from a northern center of creation which, without postulating an actual submerged Atlantic continent, we may call Atlantis, swarms of warriors once fanned out in obedience to the ever-renewed and incarnate Nordic longing for the distance to conquer and space to shape.[8]

THE GERMANIC RACE AS THE ORIGIN OF CIVILIZATION

When speaking of "all the directions," Rosenberg refers to the historical framework which *The Myth* undertakes in order to defend his idea of the chosen Aryan people. It evokes the presence of Nordic blood throughout history and emphasizes that civilization is prosperous when it defends Germanic racial purity and that it weakens when it is contaminated by the mixture of blood, i.e., "the retrogression." Its study starts with the Nordic influence in Hindustan, where it locates the origin of Aryan blood, just as it begins its decline because of the latter's mixture with a lower blood source.

> When the first great Nordic wave rolled over the high mountains into India, it had already passed through many hostile races. Instinctively, as it were, the Indo-Aryan separated themselves from the dark alien peoples they encountered. The institution of caste was the outcome of this instinctive aversion. . . . The fair Aryans thus linked themselves to an acceptable image of the human type, and created a gulf between themselves as conquerors and the black brown natives of pre-Aryan India. According to this opposition of blood and blood, the Aryans evolved a worldview which, for depth and range, cannot be surpassed by any philosophy even today. . . . Soon the rich, blood-based meaning of Varna was entirely lost. Today it is only a division between technical, professional, and other classes, and has degenerated into the vilest travesty of the wisest idea in world history. The later Indian did not comprehend the threefold significance of blood, self, and universe. He saw only the last two. . . . The only reality for him is the world soul (Brahman) and its eternal reoccurrence in the individual soul (Atman). . . . If the only reality is the world soul, and if Atman is essentially one with it, then individuality vanishes and an undifferentiated universal oneness is achieved. . . . Thus was destroyed the original concept of the identity of caste and race. Bastardization was inevitable. . . . Aryan blood flowed out and trickled away.[9]

After this failure of Aryan blood in India, Rosenberg continues the journey in Iran, to sixth-century Persia, where it finds antecedents of Jewish and Christian universalism in the religious concept of Zarathustra, which, in spite of its Aryan genius, did not manage to protect Aryan blood from the Asian invasion.

> From the sixth century BC on, Iran underwent a vast expansion by the Aryan Persians. Under Arshama, there arose one of the greatest personalities of Indo-European history, Spitama (Zoroaster, or Zarathustra). Concerned about the fate of the Aryan minority, he developed an idea which is only now beginning to revive in the Nordic west—protecting the race by endogamy within kin. But since the Aryan ruling aristocracy were sparsely scattered, Zoroaster tried to reinforce this imperative by creating an ideological bound community of faith. Ahura Mazda, the eternal god of light, became a cosmic idea—the divine protector of Aryans everywhere. . . . His enemy is the dark Ahriman who is locked in struggle with him for world domination. This is a truly Nordic Aryan concept of Zoroaster. . . . But struggling man is surrounded by evil and temptation. To be able to oppose these forces successfully, Zoroaster invokes the Aryan blood which calls upon every Persian to serve the god of light. After death, good and evil are separated forever. In a final struggle, Ahura Mazda defeats Ahriman and constructs his kingdom of peace. For a time, the Persians derived great strength from this splendid religious epic. But in spite of such a heroic attempt, the dilution of Aryan blood in Asia could not be stemmed, and the great kingdom of the Persians declined.[10]

We will return to his study of Persia when we speak about the doctrines of Positive Christianity and Rosenberg's theory regarding the influence of Persian religious thought on Judeo-Christian beliefs.

The Aryan blood saga, according to Rosenberg, continues in ancient Greece and the Roman Empire, both founded, in his opinion, by the elected people of the North, who came to establish the chosen race in fertile ground.

> Most beautifully of all was the dream of Nordic man made manifest in Hellas. . . . As sturdy masters and warriors, the Hellenic tribes supplanted the decaying civilization of the Levantine traders, and with the labor of the subjugated races, constructed an incomparable creative culture. . . . A true, aristocratic constitution proscribed any miscegenation. . . . The Nordic's absolute rejection of magical forms is never more clearly shown than in the religious values of Greece. . . . But it was in the earlier age of Homeros, confident in its destiny, which was a period of true religion. . . . The figures of Apollo, Pallas Athena, sky father Zeus, were deifications of the truest religious feeling. Golden-haired Apollo was the guardian and preserver of everything noble and inspired—order, harmony, artistic balance. Apollo was the dawn of day, at once the protector of inner vision and of the gift of sight. . . . But this yearning for a hero was in

vain; money, and with it the subhuman's, had already triumphed over blood. . . . Sons no longer respected their fathers; slaves from all over the world agitated for freedom; sexual equality was proclaimed. . . . As warfare depleted the race, newcomers were admitted to citizenship. Foreign barbarians became Athenians, much as in our era eastern Jews become German.[11]

This passage is extremely significant. It is obvious that Rosenberg retells this story to prove the reality of the myth of the chosen status of Germanic blood, thereby enhancing the Aryan racial success, this time under the Third Reich. It is to this end that it establishes a parallel between ancient Greece and its time. Indeed, this belief in the idea of the chosen Aryan people, who failed in their many historical attempts at world domination, is at the source of Nazi decisions to expel foreigners from the country. With stronger reason, Nazi ideology insists on its inherent duty of *Lebensraum* (expansion of living space, found in point 17 of the Nazi political program) for the Germanic people. One should not, at any price, repeat the faults of all former attempts of establishing the hegemony of the Aryan race. This becomes thoroughly apparent when we study the Roman Empire according to the Rosenbergian theological interpretation of the chosen people.

The grandeur of Ancient Rome, according to *The Myth*, was a Germanic creation: "Rome, too, was established by a Nordic folkish wave which poured into the fertile valleys to the south of the Alps long before the Gauls and the Teutons. It broke the dominion of the Etruscans, that mysterious and alien near eastern people."[12]

Two imperative lessons for the Third Reich emerge from Roman history, as told by Rosenberg: the first is the example of the installation of a racist nationalist State (*Völkisch*); the second is the threat coming from the East. The initial victory of Carthage did not prevent the Eastern forces (of course, Jewish forces, in Rosenberg's thought) from overcoming long-established Rome:

> Ancient Rome, about which history tells us little, became a true folkish state through sound breeding, and was united in the struggle against the whole of orientalism. . . . The three hundred ruling noble families supplied the three hundred senators and from them came also the provincial governors and the senior army officers. . . . The destruction of Carthage was a deed of superlative import in racial history: by it even the later cultures of central and Western Europe were spared the infection of this Phoenician pestilence. World history might well have taken a very different course had the obliteration of Carthage been accompanied by a total annihilation of all the other Semitic Jewish centers in the near east.[13]

If Rosenberg's premises are to be believed—those of the historical origins of the providential Aryan people—it will be imperative that the Third Reich's educational system (also included in the Nazi political program, in point 20) closely studies the successes and failures of Ancient Greece and the Roman Empire. For example, Nazi ideology compares the "Roman *Völkisch* people," who reigned by a senatorial system, and the Nazi Party's "Germanic *Völkisch* people," who came to power through a parliamentary method. Rosenberg perceives a parallel there. A second example is the glorious Roman victory over Carthage, finding its corollary in Hitler's triumphal victory in 1933.

THE MYTH AND THE BOLSHEVIK THREAT TO NAZISM

The debate between Rosenberg and Hitler on Bolshevik Russia could have originated with their two divergent standpoints concerning the interpretation of the Roman antecedent, where Rome was finally conquered by the East ("the East" being synonymous with Semito-Jewish for the Nazis). The USSR was nothing more for Hitler than one more Jewish aggression, threatening, this time, his own victory in Europe, and accentuated by the fact that the fall of Rome was caused by forces from the East. Hitler did not want to fall into the same trap, at any cost. Such a deduction can shed light on the brutality of the Nazis against the Eastern European countries during the war.

On the contrary, Rosenberg saw in the Russians a dichotomy of spirit because of their mixture of original blood from Viking sources (i.e., Scandinavian) and Mongolian blood:

> Originally Russia was the creation of Vikings. Germanic elements brought order to the chaos of the Russian steppes and formed the inhabitants into a political entity which made possible the development of a culture. When the Viking strain died out, the role was assumed by Germans of the Hanse, and by western immigrants generally. . . . But in Russia under the upper classes bearing culture, there always persisted the yearning for boundless expansion. . . . The partially Mongol blood, even if considerably diluted, asserted itself during all the upheavals in Russian history, and impelled men into actions which have often seemed incomprehensible even to those who participated in them.[14]

It is for this reason, says Rosenberg, that an interior fight often appears in the characters of Russian literature. It should not be forgotten that Rosenberg completed his higher education in Moscow and came to Munich only after the Bolshevik Revolution. His vision of the Russian people and Bolshevism is translated here to be an interior combat between Viking blood and Mongolian blood:

> The sudden inversion of all moral and social norms which is a recurring feature in Russian life (and in Russian literature from Chaadayev to Dostoyevsky and Gorki) is a sign that hostile bloodstreams contend with one another, and that

this struggle will not be resolved until the strength of one has triumphed over the other. Bolshevism is the result of the Mongol strain against the Nordic cultural forms.[15]

Rosenberg did not share Hitler's point of view when it came to the total destruction of Bolshevik forces by the invasion of Russia. Himself of German race and born in the Baltic States, he saw the possibility of eliminating this dichotomy inherent in the Russian spirit, but only after the Nordic race had ensured its hegemony in Europe.

> The eastern Baltic race, which has many poetic gifts, shows itself, mixed as it is with a Mongol element, to be pliant clay either in the hands of Nordic leadership or under Jewish and Mongol tyrants. . . . If anywhere, it is in the east that the profound truths of racially based historical interpretation are to be found. But also revealed is the great hour of peril in which the Nordic essence now finds itself.[16]

Perhaps that explains why Rosenberg could not agree with Hitler on Operation Barbarossa, the code name for the Nazi invasion of the Soviet Union, and why he tried to establish autonomous territories in the East before the end of the war.

ROSENBERG'S *THE MYTH* AND THE SPECIAL CASE OF FRANCE

This central idea of the chosen Aryan people in *The Myth* is not limited to antiquity. Without resuming a lengthy historical study, it is certainly relevant to mention Rosenberg's commentary concerning this concept of the providential Nordic race and its relationship to France.

To Rosenberg, the Huguenot movement represented the strength of the Germanic race among the French. By the intelligence of its leaders, by the faith of its members, and by its attempts at seizure of political power, this movement expressed what Rosenberg calls the "primal Germanic idea of inner freedom."[17] Its failure would have had irrevocable racial repercussions and even produced radical changes in the French national character. France, by rejecting the Huguenot Protestant movement in the sixteenth century and the monarchy in the eighteenth century, lost its "interior freedom" and thus its pride and its nobility. Rosenberg affirms:

> The decisive fact that emerged from all this bloodletting is, however, the deterioration of the character of the French nation. That true pride, that unbending resolution, that nobility of mind that the early Huguenot leaders epitomized

Alfred Rosenberg shakes hands outside the French National Assembly. (United States Holocaust Memorial Museum, courtesy of Robert Kempner)

was lost. . . . Expressed in terms of racial history, with the destruction of the Huguenots, the Nordic racial strength in France was, if not absolutely eliminated, at least seriously weakened.[18]

Rosenberg explains that the French people had racially mixed to such a degree that it presented a danger in Germany, and that the common borders brought a considerable risk of racial contamination. He advises that they should be closed until the moment of a later purification. This solution suggested by Rosenberg shows a continuity of belief in the unshakable determination required by the Nazi movement to protect the chosen Nordic blood. According to Rosenberg, France failed this test and underwent the consequences of it.

Today, the very last few drops of the valuable blood are finally trickling away. Over vast stretches of the south, it has entirely disappeared and is now being replaced by African elements, as was once the fate of Rome. The port cities of Toulon and Marseilles transmit unceasingly the germs of bastardization throughout the land. . . . Negroes and mulattos stroll about on arms of white women. An exclusively Jewish quarter has arisen with new synagogues. . . . It is a modern repetition of the tragedy which long overtook Persepolis, Athens, and Rome. This is why a close alliance with France, quite apart from the military and political aspects, would be racially dangerous. On the contrary, what is needed is a clarion call for defense against African infiltration, for the closing of frontiers on the basis of anthropological considerations, and the establishment of a Nordic European coalition for the object of cleansing Mother Europe of the filth of Africa and the Levant. This would be in the true interests of the French themselves.[19]

NOTES

1. News stories on this possibility can be found at the following website: https://www.independent.co.uk/news/world/europe/nuremberg-germany-s-dilemma-over-the-nazis-field-of-dreams-a6793276.html.
2. *The Political Diary of Alfred Rosenberg and the Onset of the Holocaust*, Jürgen Matthäus and Frank Bajohr, eds. (Lanham, MD: Rowman & Littlefield, in association with the United States Holocaust Memorial Museum, 2015), 83.
3. Robert K. Wittman and David Kinney, *The Devil's Diary: Alfred Rosenberg and the Stolen Secrets of the Third Reich* (New York: HarperCollins, 2017), 210.
4. The direct translation of *Le Témoignage Chrétien* is "The Christian Testimony." In this book, it will be translated as *The Christian Witness* in order to convey the active sense of the reality and the urgency of events reported in this publication during the war.
5. Pierre Chaillet, *Les racistes peints par eux-mêmes* (*Racists: A Self-Portrait*) (Paris, France: Cahiers et courriers du Témoignage Chrétien, Éditions du Témoignage Chrétien, 1979), 89.
6. Speer, 69–70.
7. Ibid., 157.
8. Alfred Rosenberg, *The Myth of the Twentieth Century: An Evaluation of the Spiritual-Intellectual Confrontations of Our Age* (Wentzville, MO: Invictus Books, 2011), 18–19.
9. Ibid., 21–24.
10. Ibid., 24–25.
11. Ibid., 25–37.
12. Ibid., 38–39.
13. Ibid., 39.
14. Ibid., 77–78.
15. Ibid., 78.
16. Ibid.
17. Ibid., 67.
18. Ibid., 70.
19. Ibid., 71–72.

Chapter 3

Alfred Rosenberg and Positive Christianity

The Myth of the Twentieth Century was published in 1930, but it does not represent the beginning of Rosenberg's writings; it is rather the apogee. This is evident in the following excerpt from the summary of the writings of Rosenberg by Thilo von Trotha, at the time of the publication of Rosenberg's *Blut und Ehre* (*Blood and Honor*):

> Alfred Rosenberg is, par excellence, the father of National-Socialist literature. From 1919 onward, he had written various texts on Bolshevism, freemasonry and the Jewish question. . . . Already in 1922, he had published the text: *Wesen, Grundsätze und Ziele DER NSDAP* (*Essence, Bases and Objectives of the NSDAP*), the first writing of the party! With *Der Zukunft einer deutschen Aussenpolitik* (*The Future of German Foreign Policy*) and *Das Wesengefüge of Nationalsozialismus* (*The Essence of National Socialism*), [he] gave to the movement two of its greatest reference works.[1]

Alfred Rosenberg, though of German origin, was born in Estonia and studied in Moscow until the Bolshevik Revolution in 1917, when he left for Munich. The question often arises as to the etymology of the name Rosenberg. Its meaning is "rose mountain," and it is a common name in both Germany and Sweden, although it is, ironically for this core Nazi Party member, a Jewish surname as well. Obvious as it might seem that Hitler would never allow a Jew into the Nazi Party, let alone into his close entourage, it is still a wise notation to make from the start.

We can trace Rosenberg's political career to his joining the Nazi Party in 1919 and the emergence of Positive Christianity from his early writings. In addition to his writings cited by von Trotha above, in 1920 Rosenberg published his first brochure in Munich, *The Trace of the Jews in World History*. Three years later, in 1923, he published *The Protocols of the Elder Men of Zion and Jewish World Politics* during the period when Hitler was in prison, and in 1927, he became head of foreign affairs for the NSDAP. *The Myth of the Twentieth Century* was first published in 1930. Three years later he was appointed by Hitler as deputy for the supervision of the ideological and spiritual formation of the National Socialist Party. Finally, in 1937, on the occasion of the Oxford Christian World Conference, he presented his book *Protestant Pilgrims to Rome: The Betrayal of Luther*,[2] and at the outbreak of war he was appointed to a government post with the potential to make him the most important man after Hitler, because he would have been responsible for all the territories occupied in the East as minister of the Reich.[3]

Rosenberg also served as editor of the Party newspaper, *Völkischer Beobachter*, replacing his friend, Dietrich Eckart. Both men belonged to the NSDAP from its inception, and their friendship is often mentioned by Rosenberg in *The Myth*. It is interesting to note that these Party members were also closely allied with the secret group known as the Thule Society, founded in 1918. Bavaria under the Weimar Republic offered a harbor to many *Völkisch* nationalist groups. The Thule Society borrowed its racial philosophy from a former priest, Adolf Josef Lanz, who called himself Lanz von Liebenfels. He had founded an order of quasi monks, "the Order of The New Templars," which Hitler knew about, having researched them when working for the newspaper, *The Ostara*, during his years in Vienna.[4] It is significant to note that it was during these years, from 1908 to 1913, that Hitler formulated fragments of his *Weltanschauung*, his "design of the world," from which he would never deviate.[5]

What is the essential idea of von Liebenfels's racial philosophy, known as "Ariosophy"? In the fourth edition of his book, *Hitler and Nazi Germany: A History*, Jackson Spielvogel explains. "That philosophy was based on the supposed superiority of the Ario-Germans. The Aryan was an exalted spiritual being. . . . The Jews, as well as other inferior races, were characterized as 'animal-men' who must one day be eliminated by genetic selection, sterilization, deportations, forced labor, or even direct liquidation."[6] In a work by Wilfried Daim, *Der Mann, der Hitler die Ideen Gab*, Spielvogel cites Daim's appraisal of this philosophy, which declares that "the Aryan hero is on this planet the most complete incarnation of God and of the Spirit."[7]

The Thule Society combined this ariosophical Aryan supremacy with a belief in militant action.[8] Dietrich Eckart was a member of this society. It was he who Hitler called the cofounder of Nazism,[9] and to whom Hitler dedicated *Mein Kampf*.[10] Eckart introduced Rosenberg to Hitler in 1919, and it was Eckart who prepared Hitler for his entry into Munich society.[11] In the foreword of *The Myth*, the translator explains that if Rosenberg and Master Eckart were the originators of National Socialism, it is because they followed a certain orientation of the "*Thule Gesellschaft.*"[12]

That same year, Eckart prophesied the arrival of a savior for Germany, and in 1920, he proclaimed that this prophecy would be carried out in the person of Adolf Hitler.[13] All of this indicates that these three militant members were closely bound by thought, affiliation, and action. The ideas of Rosenberg, expressed in his writings, constitute the veritable essence of Nazism.[14] These two men, Hitler and Rosenberg, were the ideologists par excellence of Nazism. The influence of Eckart on the advanced beliefs of *The Myth* will become apparent in what follows, as will the close link between *Mein Kampf* and this work.

Before plunging into the theological principles of *The Myth*, it is advisable to provide some background of the Hitler–Rosenberg relations before and after the beginning of the war. From the very start of their friendship, Rosenberg supported and defended Hitler as well as the Nazi Party in his articles in *Völkischer Beobachter*. This support grew after the failure of the Putsch of 1923, which constituted the Nazis' only attempt to take power by force, and for which Hitler was condemned to five years of prison (serving only one year). Rosenberg received accolades for his leading articles during this dark time of the Nazi movement:

Alfred Rosenberg (United States Holocaust Memorial Museum, courtesy of Robert Kempner)

Alfred Rosenberg was to speak in a German city. The head of a local section, himself a veteran of the movement, said in his introduction that from 1925 to 1927, whereas criticism arose against Adolf Hitler, the leading articles of Rosenberg in *Völkischer Beobachter* were for a long time the only support of the Führer after Munich.[15]

Hitler thus created a tight circle around him, based on personal honesty. "The loyalty principle, a feature of Party management before 1933 in binding leaders as well as ordinary members to the person of the Führer, was carried over after 1933 into the practice of governing the Reich."[16] Moreover, Hitler rewarded Rosenberg for his fidelity. He appointed him head of the Party during his imprisonment. This gesture is often interpreted as Hitler's way of ensuring his hegemony, since he knew that Rosenberg did not have the gift of being a leader.[17] However, Hitler's total confidence in Rosenberg was evident in April 1933, when he named Rosenberg head of the service of foreign policy for the NSDAP (Nazi Party), only one month after becoming chancellor. This nomination did not fail to impress the political world. The *NS Funk* wrote on this subject: "All that [Rosenberg] touched became for him even more profound, and in this way did he become, in even the most minute of details, the spiritual father of the National-Socialist movement."[18]

After writing *The Myth*, which was published in 1930, Rosenberg would be greeted by Hitler as the ideologist of Nazism.[19] Furthermore, Rosenberg explains in his memoirs that he gave Hitler the manuscript of his work, which he called *My Myth* before sending it to the publishers.[20] More copies would be printed, exceeding 150,000 in 1934, and then a half-million by 1936. It would go up to two million by the end of the war.[21] This high volume does beg the question: For whom were they being produced? A good answer to that question came in the quotes from Ambassador Dodd in the introduction, with his commentary on the Nazi view that children belong to the State and the Party; in like fashion, so then does the educational system.

Seconding this line of reasoning was the Archbishop of Liverpool, writing in 1935 for the Friends of Europe publication *Rosenberg's Positive Christianity* (discussed in depth in chapter 5). He writes in his foreword:

> In February 1934, by decree of the Holy Office, Herr Rosenberg's notorious book, *The Myth of the 20th Century*, was placed upon the Index of Forbidden Books. A feature of the decree was the added statement that "The book condemns and utterly rejects all the dogmas of the Catholic Church and the very foundations of the Christian faith . . . " Such condemnation would usually cause but little stir. Its author, however, happens to be a person of position in the Nazi regime, a man entrusted, says the official *Völkischer Beobachter* [the official Nazi newspaper], "with the entire spiritual and philosophic instruction

of the party and all allied associations," a Minister of Education whose *Myth* is included in the list of books to be studied in German schools.[22]

The content of *The Myth* viscerally attacks the Catholic Church. As we have seen in our study in chapter 2, "Universal Salvation" and the "centrality of the Pope's power" were anathema to Positive Christianity. The Pope stood as the central figure to one-third of the Christians in Germany and to the entire Roman Catholic Church worldwide. Hitler knew he quickly needed a treaty with Rome (called a "concordat," when negotiations are with the Vatican) in order to lend credence to his newly founded Third Reich. Hitler approached the Holy See only months after he became chancellor in January 1933. Two systematic analyses of Hitler's model of dominance over Christian denominations will be presented in this book: one in the next chapter, where Swiss theologian Bernard Reymond explains the "Three-Step Hitlerian Process"; and the second analysis will be that of the French Jesuit, Gaston Fessard, in part III, with the first publication of the underground newspaper, *The Christian Witness*, titled "France, Beware of Losing Your Soul." Suffice it to say here that they both clearly delineate the first step: *Seduce and gain the confidence (we might add, at any cost) of the Christian denominations.*

The Catholic Church protested in various ways. One of the earliest is noted in Rabbi David G. Dalin's book, *The Myth of Hitler's Pope*. He cites a pastoral letter with a surprisingly early date of February 10, 1931 (Rosenberg's *The Myth of the Twentieth Century* was published only the year before). The letter was requested by the Vatican and was drafted by eight dioceses of Bavaria. It expresses understanding and concern regarding the content of Rosenberg's writings and its threat to Christianity.

> In a pastoral letter of February 10, 1931, prepared at the behest of the Vatican and addressed to the Catholic clergy of Germany, the bishops of eight Bavarian dioceses stated that the rising National Socialist party of Adolf Hitler rejects "the basic premises" of Catholic teaching.[23]

Dalin continues his presentation of early Catholic protests of Nazi anti-Catholicism, this time by citing Pope Pius XI himself. "As the 1930s progressed, Pius came to regard Hitler as "the greatest enemy of Christ and of the Church in modern times," and compared Hitler to an "Antichrist."[24]

Finally, pontifical representatives made direct complaints against Rosenberg during meetings with Hitler. This was during the time of the negotiations of the Concordat, the signed agreement with the Vatican. Due to the minority situation of Catholicism in Germany, the Roman Catholic Church, functioning within the *Länder* political system, signed agreements with Bavaria (1924), Prussia (1929), and the country of Baden (1932). The influence and presence of the Church grew in the interwar years—politically, by establishing political parties; academically, by the expansion of educational institutions on all levels, including higher learning; and socially, by issuing publications for the twenty million Catholics throughout the *Länders*. What was the purpose of this treaty between the Reich and the Holy See? Here is the introductory text of the treaty[25] itself to explain:

> His Holiness Pope Pius XI and the President of the German Reich, moved by a common desire to consolidate and promote the friendly relations existing between the Holy See and the German Reich, wish to permanently regulate the relations between the Catholic Church and the state for the whole territory of the German Reich in a way acceptable to both parties. They have decided to conclude a solemn agreement, which will supplement the Concordats already concluded with [five] individual German states [*Länders*], and will ensure for the remaining states [*Länders*] fundamentally uniform treatment of their respective problems.[26]

The words themselves give pause when compared to the warnings about Rosenberg's Positive Christianity in *The Myth of the Twentieth Century*; the book's study by Bavarian clergy as requested by the Vatican in 1931; and the words of the Pope himself about Hitler. The Church had its reasons not to want to jeopardize the negotiations for the Concordat of 1933, in progress between the Vatican and the new regime, which will be discussed in the introduction to part II. The analyses cited above, however, can lead us to a perception of overconfidence concerning the power of the Vatican as compared to a newly elected, inexperienced German chancellor. In that vein, it is sobering that the ecclesiastical authorities directed all of their complaints to Hitler directly, and solely against Rosenberg personally.

Rosenberg—who had served as the head of the Nazi Party when Hitler was in prison, and whose book *The Myth of the Twentieth Century* was being printed in ever-higher numbers in Germany—was an influential social and political force in the new Third Reich. He should have been addressed as such, but regrettably, that was not the case. That is to say, to avert a more fundamental clash of religious views directly with the Führer himself, and not wanting to give the impression they were calling into question the policy of the government during this delicate period, the papacy relinquished the power of the Vatican in its duty to protect the Catholic population from the Nazi religious threat before them. Hitler was able to easily follow the personal line of attack perpetrated by the pontiff's representatives with his own propaganda ploy. Here, choosing the ploy of understatement, Hitler even said to Bishop Wilhelm Berning and Monseigneur Steinmann, on April 26, 1933, that *The Myth* was just one personal publication.[27]

At a time when the Pope's spokesmen should have done precisely the opposite—by addressing directly the religious goals and vision of the Nazi regime—instead, they equivocated and kept the complaints on a merely personal level. Regrettably, the motto to "Heed what is written, not what is said" could not overcome an overconfidence of the power of the Holy See when faced with the inexperienced new chancellor. However, the stick fell quickly after the carrot was consumed. Barely three months after the legal settlement between the Catholic Church and the Third Reich was signed, in July 1933, to the amazement of the Catholic hierarchy, Hitler appointed Alfred Rosenberg as the ideological and spiritual head of the National Socialist Party.[28]

It is important to recognize Rosenberg's appointment here, as Rosenberg's impact has been marginalized by saying that *The Myth of the Twentieth Century* was only a personal opinion, reinforced by the preceding quotation from Hitler. The study of Hitler's propaganda genius has been previously presented. It has been shown to heed what the Nazi leader did and wrote rather than what he said. Nazism always knew how to choose its moment, and as we have shown previously, Hitler was informed of the exact moment of the publication of *The Myth*. Rosenberg himself explains the relationship between *The Myth*, the Concordat, and the Catholic centrist party in his *Memoirs*. His explanation resonates with the expertise of Hitler's propaganda genius in discussing the Nazi political program:

> I must confess, however, that I never bothered to learn in detail if and when the Führer broke the concordat because I was aware of the fact that, after the initial revolutionary surge had passed, bishops had begun a rather remarkable counterpropaganda campaign against the basic laws of the New Reich. . . . That they sorely missed their "worldly arm, the Centrist Party, was quite obvious. . . . The concordat was primarily intended to help break through the foreign moral-political boycott ring.[29]

This admission certainly lends credence to "the ends justify the means" interpretation of the Nazi motivation to expeditiously "seal the deal" with the Concordat. In so doing, Hitler received in return the propaganda victory of papal representatives accompanying Nazi officials at ceremonies in the Third Reich *Länders* throughout the 1930s and after the war, throughout Europe. We will return to the Concordat of 1933 in part III, when discussing the tragic repercussions of this papal treaty in France after the beginning of the war.

Returning to the relationship of Hitler and Rosenberg, after the war began in earnest, and more particularly, after the invasion of the Soviet Union (Operation Barbarossa), it became evident that they did not see eye to eye on foreign politics in the East, and especially in the Ukraine. "When Operation Barbarossa was considered, the Baltic writer tried to dissuade the persons in charge from them."[30] Rosenberg held a more lenient policy, but the Führer wanted nothing of it. In spite of the fact that the Ukrainians saw initially in the Germans the liberators from Stalinist oppression, the decisions of Hitler with respect to the Soviet Union were among the most brutal of the first years of the war.[31] Rosenberg and Hitler's relations were never the same. Toward the end of the war, in 1944, Rosenberg tried to institute his plans for the occupied territories, to no avail.[32] Having studied the basic racial premises upon which Rosenberg wrote *The Myth*, it is imperative that an understanding of the religious tenets follows.

Positive Christianity is cited in point 24 of the Nazi Party Program of 1920, as already mentioned. Hitler held to these 25 points to the extreme, allowing no tampering with them, as they "were the foundation of our religion, our ideology. To tamper with it would constitute treason to those who died believing in our Idea."[33] Rosenberg uses the terms *positive* and *negative* in relation to Christianity in a clear and unequivocal way. This will be apparent further on in our study of his writing. It is beneficial to refer to dictionary definitions of the term *positive*, taking into account that Nazi propaganda often chose obscure dictionary meanings of words that were typically used differently. An example from Hitler's writing will be forthcoming.

In the case of *positive*, in both English and German dictionaries, the word carries at least seven different definitions. This being said, it is clear that the usage in both languages refers to educational parlance, meaning that which is verifiable and factual. A direct translation from the *Duden German Dictionary* states in meaning number 7(a), in terms of both education and theology, that *positive* means:

> Positive: Latin *positivus*, assuming, given, in due course: 7(a) (Education) real, concrete: positive knowledge, results; positive theology (theology which only concerns itself with the positive sources of revelations, historical facts, with the tradition and the teachings of the church); positive right (legal right versus a natural right; (b) certain, definite, actual.

With what was certainly a clear reference point for Rosenberg and Hitler in their terminology, the definition of Positive Christianity remained open to interpretation until the publication of *The Myth* in 1930, when it was clearly elucidated by Rosenberg at the behest of Hitler. This Nazi ploy succeeded in affecting religious protests: In the case of Protestant attempts, they were too late to produce any significant effects; and in the case of Catholic attempts, they were too apprehensive and hubristic, because of the negotiations of the Concordat of 1933.

The term *Positive Christianity* should have prompted the question, What did the Nazis regard as "negative"? What did Rosenberg have to say of

"Negative Christianity"? It is the term referring to the traditional Christian faith and its fundamental doctrines. In fact, one can learn much about Positive Christianity by studying what the Nazis rejected of traditional Christianity. These dichotomies emphasize the fundamental principles of this Nazi faith. Rosenberg elucidates in *The Myth*:

> Negative and Positive Christianity were locked in conflict from the beginning, and that conflict is today being waged with ever more bitterness. The negative type emphasizes its Levantine Etruscan tradition, its abstract dogmas and hoary old customs; the positive consciously calls upon the Nordic bold to awaken, just as in the simple innocence the first Teutons did when they pressed into Italy, bringing renewed vigor to that sick land. . . . The collapse of 1918 tore apart our very vitals, but at the same time laid bare to the searching soul the threads which had woven their fabric of mixed blessings. . . . There is born today, as the greatest flowering of the German soul, a racially based folkish consciousness. On the basis of this experience we hail as the religion of the German future the fact that, though lying now politically prostrate, humiliated and persecuted, we have found the roots of our strength.[34]

Rosenberg refutes traditional Christian beliefs, regarding them as dogmatic deviations which prevented the true emergence of Christianity throughout history, which he traces in his book. This explains the subtext to the rather obscure main title of *The Myth of the Twentieth Century*. Rosenberg expands his title with the subtitle "An Evaluation of the Spiritual-Intellectual Confrontations of Our Age." It is the mission of the Nazi Third Reich to establish, at long last, the tenets of Positive Christianity as the spiritual foundation of the Aryan culture.

Initially, the origins of this "Negative Christianity" will be studied by presenting what Rosenberg estimates to be the dogmatic deviations from the true Christian faith. These began, according to *The Myth*, from the time of Jesus's death. Rosenberg purports:

> The great personality of Jesus Christ, whatever form it might have taken originally, was distorted and confused immediately after his death with all the rubbish of Jewish and African life.[35]

The origins are multiple, but to begin, it is most significant to underscore the Pauline influence, and then that of the Catholic Church. The criticism of Rosenberg toward the character of Paul of Tarsus and his writings is categorical: It completely rejects his person, his evangelic mission, and his epistles. In *The Myth*, Paul is treated as an opportunist wishing to exploit the birth of Christianity to advance the Jewish cause on the international level. Rosenberg writes:

The Christian movement, disrupting old forms, seemed to the Pharisee Saul to hold great promise of practical usefulness. In a sudden decision he joined its ranks and, possessed by an unrestrained fanaticism, he preached international revolution against the Roman Empire. In spite of all subsequent attempts at reform, his teachings still remain the Jewish spiritual basis, the Talmudic oriental aspect of both the Catholic and Lutheran churches. Paul accomplished something which is never admitted in churchly circles. He made the suppressed Jewish national rebellion internationally effective, thus paving the way for the further spread of racial chaos in the ancient world.[36]

According to Rosenberg, Paul is responsible for the destruction of the racial values developed within the Greek and Roman cultures. The concept of the Scandinavian race, elected for its noble blood as organically superior, dies under the concept of universal salvation advanced by Paul and the Roman Church. Rosenberg quotes the epistle of Paul to the Galatians to clarify his view: "Here, there is neither Jew, nor Greek, there is neither slave, nor free man, neither man, nor woman." Shown to have blocked the success of a Nordic racial domination at his time, Paul will be the object of Rosenberg's criticism. However, there remains to consider the other origin of negative Christianity, i.e., the Catholic Church. Rosenberg defends the idea that, if Paul spread the concept of universal salvation in Christ from the very start of Christianity, disavowing the paramount importance of sacred Nordic blood, the Catholic Church, in the Middle Ages, succeeded in killing the spirit of freedom of the Nordic people. Rosenberg's principle of freedom is essential to the formation of Positive Christianity in Europe. Rosenberg maintains the idea that, because of the dogmas of hell and the image of the life after death established in the Middle Ages, the Roman Church destroyed the free Nordic spirit. He explains:

> Only when we have learned to recognize the utterly alien origins of these concepts and muster the resolution to rid ourselves of this diabolism will we have cast off the middle ages. But with our emancipation, the Roman church, which is inextricably linked with the sadistic visions of the Etruscan hell, will collapse from within.
> The whole mystagogy of Dante's Inferno consists of a hideous marriage of Etruscan demonology and Christianity. . . . Such are the two worlds that tore apart the Nordic man in the middle ages. On the one hand was the idea of a hideous hell which the church adopted; on the other, the longing to be free, upright and healthy. Only insofar as he is free can the Teuton be creative. Only where the insane terrors of witchcraft did not hold sway could great centers of European culture flourish. Into this raceless stew which was not Rome came Christianity.[37]

Having criticized the Catholic Pauline bases of Christianity, Rosenberg continues his criticism of traditional Christian doctrines. Rosenberg's definition of "Negative Christianity" ipso facto differs innately from the Catholic and Protestant traditional doctrines. What are the fundamental criticisms of the Christian dogmas upon which Rosenberg builds his own notion of Christianity? They are numerous, but it is sufficient enough to identify five of them, as central to the belief system proposed to replace traditional doctrinal beliefs.

Positive Christianity's criticism of original sin is the best starting point. This Christian belief expresses the alienation of man and God and man's misery without God's grace. This concept of original sin, central to traditional Christian doctrine, is completely foreign in the Positive Christianity of Rosenberg. It is rejected by saying that original sin is a Near Eastern idea which is only used to weaken the purity and the force of Scandinavian blood. It is explained as follows:

> The doctrine of original sin would have appeared incomprehensible to a people whose racial identity was unadulterated. In such a people there dwells a secure confidence in itself and in its will, which it regards as Destiny. The concept of sin was as alien to the heroes of Homeros as it was to the ancient Indians, the Germans of Tacitus, or the epics and sagas of Dietrich von Bern. An oppressive sense of sin is a sure symptom of bastardy. . . . The sense of personal depravity leads to a yearning for grace, and this is the only hope for the products of miscegenation. It was natural, therefore, in whomsoever the old Roman character still lived, that a revulsion arose against the spread of Christianity.[38]

The second criticism of Rosenberg is more serious, because it denies any value of biblical divine providence. The entire base of traditional Christianity, recognizing the providence of God in preparation for the arrival of Jesus among the Jewish people, is rejected by Rosenberg. He sees there only the deification of the Israelite people and the obstacle presented by such homage to the Aryan claim to exclusivity of the chosen. He speaks about it in the following passage:

> In discussion with learned theologians, I was further able to establish the following: they conceded to me that the evaluation of ancient history from the racial soul aspect was correct. But when I drew the conclusion that the Jews must then necessarily also have their own completely determined character—their blood-linked idea of God—that consequently this Syrian life and spiritual form did not concern us in the least, then the Old Testament dogma arose like the Great Wall of China between us; suddenly the Jews appeared as an exception among folks. In all seriousness, the Cosmic God was said to be identical with the dubious spiritual assertions of the Old Testament![39]

It is obvious that a categorical rejection of biblical divine providence was meant to generate criticism of the identity of Jesus. Such suspicions introduce Rosenberg's third criticism, that of the traditional image of Christ. According to him, the character of Jesus was wrongfully represented in Christian history. It is necessary to clarify the truth of the founder of Christianity so that German youth would be released from the false ideas sown by the orthodox Christian dogmas and consequently enlightened by those of Nazism's Positive Christianity. This said, it only remains to include the understanding of what Rosenberg presents as "the great personality" of Jesus. He raises the influence of the "myth of Christos" in Asia Minor; he does not explain very well what it was, but he allocates to it a significant role in the misleading traditional image of Jesus:

> The great personality of Jesus Christ, whatever form it might have taken originally, was distorted and confused immediately after his death with all the rubbish of Jewish and African life. In the near east, Rome ruled with great firmness and exacted the taxes efficiently. Accordingly, among their subject populations there arose the desire for a liberator and leader of the slaves; hence the legend of Christos. Beginning in Asia Minor, this Christos myth spread to Palestine, where it became linked with Jewish messianic yearnings, and was finally attached to the personality of Jesus. Besides his own utterances, there were falsely attributed to him the words and doctrines of near eastern prophets.[40]

The Christian corruption of the true image of Jesus holds a central place in the development of Positive Christianity. All of these pernicious influences of Paul, of Augustine, and of Tertullian, without speaking about the religious history of Asia Minor, made for strenuous work for anyone seeking the historical origins of Jesus. However, Rosenberg does not become discouraged. He advances his theory of the racial origin of Jesus, which without any doubt will reject his Jewish origins and will give to Jesus Aryan blood. He affirms it in the first pages of his first chapter, which covers the subject of heart and race.

According to him, the Amorite people, founders of Jerusalem, bring the Aryan bloodline which extends back twenty-four centuries before Jesus Christ to the Libyan race, and it is from them that Jesus emerges. Therefore, Positive Christianity supports the assumption that Jesus was not Jewish, but that his bloodline extends back to that of the Amorites, who came from the Libyan race found in Egypt:

> Suddenly, around 2400 BC, there appear reliefs of men with fair skin, reddish blond hair and blue eyes, those blond Libyans of whom Pausanias later reports. In the tomb paintings of Thebes, we find four races of Egypt represented: Asiatics, negroids, Libyans and Egyptians. The last are depicted with reddish pigmentation; the Libyans, on the other hand, are always shown bearded, with

blue eyes, and white skin. . . . All these are racial memories of a prehistoric Nordic tradition in North Africa. The Amorites founded Jerusalem, and they formed the Nordic weft in later Galilee, that is, in the pagan region whence Jesus is said to have come.[41]

The fourth and fifth of Rosenberg's criticisms noted in this book concern the doctrines of the Trinity and the Holy Spirit. Their abstract character defines them as having no relationship with an organic existence, which is the basis of any interpretation of Positive Christianity. These criticisms propose multiple historical examples that deny natural forces from which these magic phenomena could have been borrowed:

Emergent Christianity, derived from a multiplicity of sources, demonstrated an astounding combination of abstract spirituality and demonic sorcery, as well as exceptional powers of infiltration irrespective of other currents which were assimilated in it. The idea of the trinity, for example, was familiar to many of the peoples of the Mediterranean basin in the form of the father, the mother and the son, and in the precept everything divides threefold.

The mother symbolized the fertile earth, the father, the creative principle of light. Now, in place of the mother there appears the holy ghost as a conscious retreat from the purely physical. Such was the hagion pneuma of the Greeks, the prana of the Indians. This spirituality and its emphasis were not rooted in a racial national ground conditioned by the polarity of organic life. Instead it became a force without direction.[42]

These five criticisms of traditional Christian beliefs constitute the basis of Rosenberg's critique of Negative Christianity, but the question still arises: What is Positive Christianity? It is noted that it has neither dogma nor theology, but it affirms that will and reason will direct the free spirit of the German elected race. It stresses the person of Christ, provided that he is defined according to his own criteria, because it is about a Jesus of flesh and Germanic blood. Rosenberg completely rejects the Pauline theology, which exalts the resurrected Christ, and advances the idea of universal salvation. In *The Myth*, Rosenberg provides us a short summary of his vision of Positive Christianity:

Thus, the world did not proceed from the life of the savior (soter) but from his death and its miraculous consequences. This is the single motif of the Pauline epistles. Goethe, on the contrary, held that it was the life of Christ which was important, not his death. In this he was attesting to the soul of the Germanic west expressed in Positive Christianity, as opposed to Negative Christianity, based on priesthood and witch mania and deriving from Etruscan Asiatic concepts. . . .

The Nordic Greek recognized no separate priestly caste. His priests came from the aristocratic families. His singers and poets related to him the deeds and acts of his heroes and his gods. The free Greek spirit was as alien to dogmatism as was the earlier Indian and the later Teuton. Gymnastics and music were the substance of his education, and these established the necessary prerequisites for the production of the hoplite, the citizen of the state. . . . Both reason and will, not always consciously, pursue the same goal. Both are true to nature, blood determined and organically conditioned. . . .

Negative and Positive Christianity were locked in conflict from the beginning, and that conflict is today being waged with ever more bitterness.[43]

With the publication of *The Myth*, it is interesting to note that Protestant churches as well as the Catholic Church claimed that Rosenberg had created a new religion. He denies this absolutely.

After having completed this brief study of Rosenberg's version of Christianity, one understands the basis of this categorical rejection. Rosenberg hardly creates a new religion, or, more precisely, a new Christianity. He reveals what to him is the essence of an original Christianity without obstruction. Moreover, he presents his version of a historical Christ without biblical interpretations, stressing an alternate biological origin to the figure of Christ based on Scandinavian blood. It is not at all a new religion, but, in Nazi terminology, it is an original Christianity, a "Positive Christianity" thwarted throughout history. The mission entrusted to Rosenberg by Hitler was to solidify the base of the Nazi Party in the tenets of the original faith of Positive Christianity. However, a textual analysis of Hitler's own work and its religious references is essential, and therefore brings us to the following section on Hitler and the religious elements within *Mein Kampf* itself.

NOTES

1. Presentation of the author in honor of his work, *Blood and Honor*, by Thilo von Trotha, quoted in the introduction of the French translation of *The Myth of the Twentieth Century* by Alfred Rosenberg (Paris, France: Déterna éditions, 1999), 12–13 (translation by the author).

2. Alfred Rosenberg, "Protestant Pilgrims to Rome: The Betrayal of Luther," foreword by Nathaniel Micklem, DD, Friends of Europe Publications, no. 66, Saint Stephen's House, Westminster, London (1938).

3. Ibid., 105–6, 214–15.

4. Jackson Spielvogel, *Hitler and Nazi Germany: A History*, 4th ed. (Upper Saddle River, NJ: Prentice Hall, 2001), 24.

5. Ibid., 22.

6. Ibid., 24.

7. Wilfried Daim, *Der Mann, der Hitler die Ideen Gab* (Munich, 1968), 180, cited by Spielvogel, *Hitler and Nazi Germany*, 24.

8. Spielvogel, *Hitler and Nazi Germany*, 27.
9. Adolf Hitler, *Mein Kampf* (*Mon Combat*), trans. J. Gaudefroy-Demombynes and A. Calmettes, (Paris, France: Nouvelles Éditions Latines, 1934 [1979]), 685.
10. Adolf Hitler, *Mein Kampf*, trans. Ralph Manheim (Boston, MA: Houghton Mifflin, 1943), 32.
11. Ibid.
12. Adler von Scholle, preface of the French translation of *The Myth of the Twentieth Century* by Alfred Rosenberg (Paris, France: Déterna éditions, 1999), 8 (author's translation).
13. Spielvogel, *Hitler and Nazi Germany*, 32.
14. Guenter Lewy, *The Catholic Church and Nazi Germany* (Boston, MA: Da Capo Press, 1965), 155.
15. Von Scholle, preface, *The Myth of the Twentieth Century*, 18.
16. Ian Kershaw, *The Nazi Dictatorship: Problems and Perspectives of Interpretation*, 3rd ed. (New York: Edward Arnold, Hodder Headline Group, 1993), 71.
17. Spielvogel, *Hitler and Nazi Germany*, 44.
18. Von Scholle, preface, *The Myth of the Twentieth Century*, 13.
19. Spielvogel, *Hitler and Nazi Germany*, 27.
20. Alfred Rosenberg, *Memoirs of Alfred Rosenberg*, with commentaries by Serge Lang and Ernst von Schenck, translated from the German by Eric Posselt (Chicago, New York: Ziff-Davis Publishing Company, 1949), 93.
21. Ibid., 30–31.
22. Rev. Richard Downey, in the foreword, "Rosenberg's Positive Christianity," Friends of Europe Publications, no. 27, London (July 1935), 5.
23. Ewa Kozerska, "Pius XI and German Anti-Semitism," in Marcin Wodzinski and Janosf Spyra, eds., *Jews in Silesia* (Krakow, Poland: University of Wroclaw Research Centre for the Culture and Languages of Polish Jews, 2001), 194. Quoted by Rabbi David G. Dalin, *The Myth of Hitler's Pope: How Pope Pius Rescued Jews from the Nazis* (Washington, DC: Regnery Publishing, 2005), 38.
24. Dalin, *The Myth of Hitler's Pope*, 38.
25. The Concordat of 1933 document is available in its entirety at the following website: http://www.concordatwatch.eu.
26. Ibid., 1.
27. Lewy, *The Catholic Church and Nazi Germany*, 151.
28. Ibid.
29. Rosenberg, *Memoirs of Alfred Rosenberg*, 92–93.
30. Von Scholle, preface, *The Myth of the Twentieth Century*, 9.
31. Spielvogel, *Hitler and Nazi Germany*, 236–37.
32. Spielvogel, *Hitler and Nazi Germany*, 15.
33. Dietrich Orlow, *The History of the Nazi Party: 1919–1933* (Pittsburgh: University of Pittsburgh Press, 1969), 70, cited by Spielvogel, *Hitler and Nazi Germany*, 45.
34. Rosenberg, *The Myth of the Twentieth Century*, 54–58.
35. Ibid., 51.
36. Ibid.
37. Ibid., 48–49.

38. Ibid., 49.
39. Ibid., 11.
40. Ibid., 51.
41. Ibid., 21.
42. Ibid., 52–53.
43. Ibid., 53–55.

Chapter 4

Religious References in *Mein Kampf*

The religious questions of point 24 are raised not only by the contents of *The Myth*. Hitler's religious reflections in his own writings are easily glossed over without the previous study of Rosenberg's volume. Make no mistake: *Mein Kampf* was written during Hitler's incarceration in 1923 as an elaboration and clarification of the NSDAP's 25-point platform of 1920, of which point 24 specifically addresses the faith of the Party.

With this in mind, we begin this chapter's examination of Hitler's own writings with the words of Sir Ian Kershaw, renowned authority on Nazism:

> The historicist tradition . . . rested on an idealistic—in the philosophical sense—concept of history as cultural development formed by men's "ideas" as revealed through their actions, from which their intentions, motives and "self-reflection" could be deduced. Historical writing concentrated on the task of trying to explain actions by "understanding" intuitively the intentions which lay behind them. In practice, this led to a heavy emphasis on the uniqueness of historical events and personages, on the overwhelming importance of will and intention in the historical process, and on the power of the State as an end in itself (and consequently the elevation of the Prussian-German national State).[1]

This philosophical method confirms the point of view of our analysis, which defends the following thesis: Hitler was the chancellor of a new German State which was meant to give rise to its "Germanic Ideal Reich," to reign for more than a thousand years.[2] *Mein Kampf* is here treated as a secondary source, as we will extract religious elements derived from Hitler's religious references expressed in the Germanic idealistic visionary style, explained above by Kershaw. The necessary place of a religious component within this "Nazi vision" is found in *Mein Kampf*. If one remembers that the purpose of his writing is to elaborate his 25-point political program, and Positive Christianity is an integral part of that program, in point 24, then, in studying his ideology from this vantage point, one discovers a policy well prepared and rigorously executed toward the Christian churches of Germany. Conversely, if this perspective is neglected, much appears as chaotic and haphazard. Bernard Reymond explains the tripartite goals of Hitler on this point:

> Germany was a country where it was impossible to make a political career without taking into account the faith of the very large majority of Germans in the traditional Christian Churches. . . . The absolute primacy that Hitler gave to political action . . . was to lead to his perfect Machiavellianism on the matter. This Machiavellianism consisted simultaneously of three objectives that were complementary from this point of view, but were completely contradictory and incomprehensible as soon as one came from a different point of view—for example, from that of rigorous Protestant honesty or ecclesiastical naivety:
>
> 1. To gain the confidence of the Christian communities in their collaboration in the "recovery" of Germany;
> 2. To gain control of the Churches and to gradually eliminate their influence while making use of vexations, intimidations, affronts, and police measures with regard to excessively opinionated religious leaders;
> 3. To replace the bimillenary influence of the Christian faith by that of Nazi ideology, supported by the rituals of the Germanic faith.[3]

These three objectives arise in the religious references of *Mein Kampf*. When one is clearly aware of them, their narrow complementarity expresses the Nazi Party's cultural and religious vision for Christianity, referring to both Kershaw's appraisal and more specifically to Reymond's analysis of these three objectives, through the Positive Christianity of point 24.

The goal of Hitler's religious policy is in the third objective: the replacement of the Christian faith by Nazi ideology and the Germanic faith. (The other two objectives involve practical implication and are the subject of the following sections.) Hitler considers the success of this goal as absolutely essential to the establishment of the Third Reich. Positive Christianity's dogma, with the belief in the Aryan people as the chosen people, is inculcated in a national faith. Two terms referenced below are important to clarify. The term *Weltanschauung*, used in the following excerpt, connotes a "view of a way of life," and Hitler explains the term *Völkisch* without ambiguity as well in this same citation, from the second volume of *Mein Kampf*:

> Without a clearly defined belief, religious feeling would not only be worthless for the purposes of human existence but even might contribute towards a general disorganization, on account of its vague and multifarious tendencies. What I have said about the word "religious" can also be applied to the term *völkisch*. This word also implies certain fundamental ideas. Though these ideas are very

important indeed, they assume such vague and indefinite forms that they cannot be estimated as having a greater value than mere opinions, until they become constituent elements in the structure of the political party. . . . From general ideas a political program must be constructed, and a general *Weltanschauung* must receive the stamp of a definite political faith. Since this faith must be directed towards ends that have to be attained in the world of practical reality, not only must it serve the general ideal as such, but it must also take into consideration the means that have to be employed for the triumph of the ideal. . . . To take abstract and general principles, derived from a *Weltanschauung* which is based on a solid foundation of truth, and transform them into a militant community whose members have the same political faith—a community which is precisely defined, rigidly organized, of one mind and one will—such a transformation is the most important task of all; for the possibility of successfully carrying out the idea is dependent on the successful fulfillment of that task. Out of the army of millions who feel the truth of these ideas, and even may understand them to some extent, one man must arise. This man must have the gift of being able to expound general ideas in a clear and definite form, and, from the world of vague ideas shimmering before the minds of the masses, he must formulate principles that will be as clear cut and firm as granite. He must fight for these principles as the only true ones, until a solid rock of common faith and common will emerges above the troubled waves of vagrant ideas.[4]

These quotations affirm the paramount importance given by Hitler to the field of faith and belief. He dedicated the second volume of *Mein Kampf* in 1926 to Dietrich Eckart, the "spiritual father" of National Socialism. Furthermore, he named Alfred Rosenberg in 1933 as the deputy of the Führer for the ideological and spiritual formation of the National Socialist Party. Why such gestures? After our study of Rosenberg's *The Myth*, it is clear that Hitler wanted Positive Christianity to serve as the base of faith for these million men. Two dimensions were needed: policy and spirituality. We continuously find these two elements in *The Myth* and *Mein Kampf*. The idea of the "Chosen Aryan People" is the thread which draws together all of the political policies. However, the religious aspect of Nazism has heretofore been neglected.

The following references from *Mein Kampf* show Hitler's view of the close connection between these two concepts and the two principal Nazi Party members responsible for their propagation: himself and Rosenberg.

Of course, the word "religious" implies some ideas and beliefs that are fundamental. Among these we may reckon the belief in the immortality of the soul, its future existence in eternity, the belief in the existence of a Higher Being, and so on. But all these ideas, no matter how firmly the individual believes in them, may be critically analyzed by any person and accepted or rejected accordingly, until the emotional concept or yearning has been transformed into an active service that is governed by a clearly defined doctrinal faith. Such a faith furnishes the practical outlet for religious feeling to express itself and thus opens the way through which it can be put into practice.[5]

Returning now to the objectives treated by Reymond—in particular, those of the practical application of policy—research on the political engagement of Hitler emphasizes with irony that his career was launched by an experience "described as spiritual" by some, "hallucinatory" by others. According to Spielvogel, it was in November 1918 that Hitler decided to engage in policy after experiencing a hallucinatory vision while temporarily blinded during the war.[6] Ian Kershaw refers to the book of Rudolf Binion, *Hitler among the Germans*, to describe the experience:

> Binion's "psycho-historical" study argues that Hitler's mission to remove Germany's Jewish cancer and to [remove] Germany's Jewish poison emanated from his hallucination while recovering from mustard-gas poisoning at Pasewalk, when he [was] allegedly traumatized [by] his mother's death while under treatment from a Jewish doctor, and brought this in hysterical association with his trauma at Germany's defeat in 1918. Hitler "emerged from his trance resolved on entering politics in order to kill the Jews by way of discharging his mission to undo, and reverse, Germany's defeat."[7]

From the point of view of such an experience, it is not surprising that Hitler himself refers to the 25 points of the Nazi Party as the "base of our religion and our ideology."[8] In a telling excerpt from Rosenberg's diary, a similar reference is made to the connection of Hitler to the religious basis in the Nazi program:

> In reply to the suggestion that posterity will not know the religious views of the Führer because he does not comment on them, he said: No, one can know them after all. Never has he allowed a cleric to be present at a Party gathering or the burial of Party members. The Christian-Jewish plague is surely approaching its end now.[9]

Hearing the clarity of thought directly from Rosenberg's personal diary, a short return to the religious dimension of this program proves to be useful here.

THE RELIGIOUS DIMENSION OF THE NAZI PROGRAM

We have just shown the osmosis that Hitler dreamed to achieve between religious life and political life. The influence of the Third Reich was to be total in the life of the Germans. Hitler imagines his "Ideal State" as follows:

> Then every activity and every need of every individual will be regulated by the collectivity represented by the party. There is no longer any arbitrary will, there are no longer any free realms in which the individual belongs to himself. . . . The time for personal happiness is over.[10]

However, to initiate this vision of a national community—*Volksgemeinschaft*—one needed specific policies. Starting from his release from prison until his rise to power in 1933, Hitler inculcated into the Nazi Party a Machiavellian mindset. Ian Kershaw describes it in these terms: "Before 1933, the one uniting aim of the dynamic but unstable and ramshackle Nazi movement was to gain power. The 'seizure of power,' however, could only be attained through the collaboration of the ruling elites."[11] A need for the collaboration of the elite, combined with the Church's cooperation, mentioned by Reymond's analysis in his three Nazi objectives, nurtured within the propaganda of the Nazi Party an ambiguity with respect to the interpretation of Positive Christianity cited in point 24 of the Nazi program.

Public clarity regarding the components of Hitler's religious policy would have caused a major alienation of the traditional churches and the elites which adhered to them. That the truth appeared only later, after the arrival of Hitler to power, is not by mere chance. On the contrary, the ambiguity of the Nazi religious term "Positive Christianity" was deliberate. All efforts were made to camouflage its true meaning. Vague references to Positive Christianity are made by members of the government, some defining it as simple humanitarian aid. The history of this Nazi conspiracy is recounted in a memorandum addressed to Hitler by the Confessing Church, a group of dissenting Protestant pastors, treated in more depth in later chapters of this book. This memorandum was written in 1936 and was published in Arthur C. Cochrane's book, *The Church's Confession Under Hitler*. Its clearness is exemplary, and shows irrefutably at which point the Nazi Party's religious terminology worked to block any premature comprehension of Positive Christianity by traditional churches.

HITLER'S PROPAGANDA GENIUS APPLIED TO THE CHURCHES

When the subject of Nazi propaganda is addressed, one usually limits oneself to mass tactics. It is indeed in this field of the psychology of the masses, by the use of repetitive slogans, demonstrations, and leaflets, that Hitler's propaganda obtained its many successes.[12] The Party's religious policy was an integral element in acts of propaganda which served the ends of the Third Reich in several manners. Here are three typical examples. In 1933, in his first speech shortly after his conquest of the chancellery, Hitler undertook an attempt at the propagandistic seduction of Christian communities by ensuring them they would receive the respect of his government, and by calling upon God and His grace.

> He [the government] will preserve and defend the bases on which the force of our nation rests. He will take under his firm protection the Christianity which is the base of our common morals. . . . May all-powerful God grant blessings to our work, direct our will, bless our thought and fill us with confidence for our people.[13]

The tenets of Nazism's Positive Christianity and those of traditional churches obviously differ considerably. In truth, the "firm protection" of the government would prove to be an exclusively Nazi definition of the content and of the form. One month later, Hitler refined his tactic and directed his propaganda according to the Christian audience, Protestant or Catholic. This flexibility of use became one of the largest assets of the success of Nazi propaganda and bore fruit in the religious field. Hitler saw this success as an essential element to his rise to power.

> Propaganda is a means and must, therefore, be judged in relation to the end it is intended to serve. It must be organized in such a way as to be capable of attaining its objective. And, as it is quite clear that the importance of the objective may vary from the standpoint of general necessity, the essential internal character of the propaganda must vary accordingly.[14]

A second example of the use of Nazi religious propaganda, this time addressed specifically to the Catholic Church, shows Hitler's practical application of the above citation. In September 1933, the Ministry of National Socialist Propaganda in Berlin organized a publicity ceremony without precedent in the Third Reich. A solemn mass in Berlin's St. Hedwig's Cathedral was amplified by loudspeakers to reach thousands of people amassed outside. Carrying swastika flags, there were groups of SA and Catholic SS bolstered by the presence of the papal nuncio, Archbishop Cesare Orsenigo, conferring legitimacy and reassurance to a world stage.[15]

The irony of the ceremony is evident, as many German priests categorically opposed the use of churches as places of open propaganda.[16] After the signing of the Concordat between the Catholic Church and the new Nazi regime in 1933, the Reich government dealt heavy blows to Catholic institutions. In 1936, the Reich engaged lawsuits against religious orders. Relating to charges of sexual perversion, these lawsuits received much attention in the press. The purpose of this propaganda was to discredit the religious orders and to start the progressive destruction of the denominational schools.[17] Another demonstration occurred in 1936, this time aiming at Protestant churches, at the time of the opening of the new Parliament on March 7, 1933. Bernard Reymond describes the event as follows:

> March 7th, after the Reichstag fire which had already allowed the arrest of many political opponents, Hitler succeeded in arranging the opening of the new parliamentary legislature in the Church of the Garrison in Potsdam, a place highly symbolic for German Protestants, and having himself photographed respectfully shaking the hand of president Hindenburg in front of the church altar—a scene that Nazi partisans among the Christians hastened to reproduce in postcard form.[18]

The support and confidence of the middle-class elite, from which Hitler would certainly profit considerably, could be measured in two manners: first, by the vote of the Reichstag, giving him absolute power two weeks later, thereby establishing a foundation where, in four months' time, the Reich decided to intervene directly in the business of the Protestant Churches. The second manner was Hitler's personal engagement in Nazi propaganda. On July 22, 1933, two days after the victorious signing of the Concordat with the Catholic Church, the new head of the government supported the candidacy of German Christians in the Protestant ecclesiastical elections. Under the pretext of national unity, Hitler spoke on public radio directly favoring the "German-Christian" candidates."[19] This Nazi tour de force produced the desired effect, since these candidates gained the majority in the elections.

It is not true, however, that their propaganda efforts always produced the desired effect. A significant case deserves our attention, because the repercussions of its failure considerably blocked the capacity of Ludwig Müller, the national Reich bishop.

The event, known as "The Sportpalast Scandal," occurred in Berlin in November 1933, at the time of the great propaganda ceremony organized by the German-Christian movement to celebrate the 450th anniversary of Martin Luther. Hubert Locke, in his book *The Church Confronts the Nazis: Barmen*

Then and Now, explains that the principal speaker at the ceremony, Dr. R. Krause, described the aims of the German-Christians in front of twenty thousand witnesses. Krause detailed the obliteration of any trace of Jewish traditions in Christianity, including the Old Testament, and all influence of Paul of Tarsus in the New Testament. Krause defended the idea that Christianity was, in the beginning, an Aryan religion, and that the stress should be laid on the Jesus of Aryan history and not on the Jesus of the crucifixion.[20] Reymond, who mentions the same ceremony of 1933, underscores the fact that among the twenty thousand witnesses, representatives of various Christian churches resigned in great number after this theological declaration.

> Faced with a contingent of churchmen who did not even dare to protest at the time, this certain Dr. Krause . . . did not hesitate to beseech in sharp and often excessive terms that German Protestantism remove all Jewish references in the Church as well as the Bible. . . . As soon as this conference was known, resignations flowed into Berlin, in particular those of theologians like Fezer or Weiser who were considered the guarantors or alibis of the movement. They led the defection of hundreds of colleagues, students and pastors.[21]

Locke also notes that a month and half after this scandal, the number of pastors engaged in the Pastors' Emergency League had exceeded seven thousand. This resultant growth in Nazi opposition did not seem to worry Rosenberg as much as the latent allegiance of the Reich bishop, Ludwig Müller. In his recently found diary, Rosenberg references this event in Berlin some nine months later during an encounter with Müller:

> When I was in Warnemünde a few days later, I meet the Reich bishop, too, there by chance. He comes up to me: . . . "I think we are not so far apart at all. Only since discarding all the dogmatism and returning to simple tenets have I really felt free." I don't believe my ears! Just a few months ago, Müller drummed Dr. Krause out of the *Deutsche Christen*, calling him a "false teacher," and he had only repeated what is in my *Myth*. . . . "The spirit of our times has set out in a direction from which it will not deviate. . . . It would be smart to recognize this and behave accordingly." He agrees vigorously. . . . The Nicene "Creed" is thus increasingly on the rocks. . . . The Reich bishop, at any rate, has reached his Hebraic wits' end; all the young people in the movement put their confidence in me.[22]

Furthermore, it is a pity, as will be evident in the next section, that Hitler could once again gain the upper hand in a counterattack against Martin Niemöller and his delegation from the Pastors' Emergency League. This would weaken these same faithful ranks fighting the continual progression of Positive Christianity. In short, Hitler had mastered the art of propaganda in

Mein Kampf, which he abundantly exploited in his religious policy. Thus will it be as well for his strategies of conquest.

STRATEGIES OF CONQUEST ROOTED IN THE MORALITY AND POLITICS OF *MEIN KAMPF*

Hitler disagreed with those who thought that national recovery would come from the economy. On the contrary, he supported the idea that Germany's future success was to begin in the moral and political fields. For this reason he aimed, without deviation, at the political and moral power and encouraged the publication of *The Myth of the Twentieth Century* even before his arrival to power.

> No improvement can be brought about until it be understood that economics plays only a second or third role, while the main part is played by political, moral and racial factors. Only when this is understood will it be possible to understand the causes of the present evils and consequently to find the ways and means of remedying them.[23]

Nazi religious policy was to be implemented in three stages: in the short term, by destroying Catholic influence; in the intermediary term, by dividing and gaining control over German Protestantism; and in the long term, by introducing Positive Christianity as a replacement for traditional Christian churches. Hitler would arrive at these goals by four principal Nazi strategies: divide and conquer; the carrot and the stick; backstabbing; and social Darwinism. In the short-term planning, Hitler wanted to quickly put an end to Catholic political power. According to him, Catholicism was one of the greatest contributors to Germany's decline because of the political parties under the Weimar Republic.[24]

Obviously, the most effective carrot was the legal settlement in the signing of the Concordat of 1933. More will be said about this agreement between the Nazi regime and the Catholic Church in part II. Suffice it to say here that once signed, the legal settlement was sealed and the stick replaced the carrot. Anti-monastic lawsuits, arrests of priests, and the destruction of the two Catholic Center political parties ensued;[25] there were even murders of eminent Catholic leaders,[26] but because of the legal settlement, the Church remained mute. Having succeeded in eliminating their centers of influence, Hitler's strategy was to let social Darwinism lead the German Catholic Church to its eventual demise through the aging population of the faithful and the expanding implementation of the Nazi omnipresence in German life, particularly in the Hitler Youth.

Following these initial moves of religious control, the strategy of "divide and conquer" was then applied to the Protestant Churches. German-Christians increased in number and influence, which conversely decreased the authority of the pastors of the evangelical churches to the point where these pastors were forced to find unity in organizing the confessing Church, refusing the centralization efforts of the Third Reich under one central bishop. Once this Church—also known as the Pastors' Emergency League—was established, the leaders who had formed it were targets of a "stab you in the back" tactic of Hitler. During a convocation of these recalcitrant pastors by Hitler on January 25, 1934, headed by the well-known pastor, Martin Niemöller, the latter wanted to require the resignation of the Reich bishop, Ludwig Müller. Hitler arrived at the discussion with a transcript of a telephone conversation between Niemöller and his colleague, Künneth, where Niemöller discussed the idea of bringing pressure on Hitler through the German president, Paul von Hindenburg. This act of Nazi espionage devastated the delegation and, after a discussion two days later with Müller, the Reich bishop, this same delegation was compromised. The Pastors' Emergency League was to be dispersed.[27] It is one of the reasons that Hans Asmussen's famous memorandum of 1936 appeared nearly two years later. Rosenberg does not neglect to comment on this event in his diary:

> The Führer then described the meeting with the church leaders, where the "confessionally faithful" and the "German Christians" almost came to blows before his eyes over benefits. He then imitated the unctuous expressions of Niemöller, a transcript of whose earlier telephone conversation [conducted] in sailor's slang the Führer immediately had someone read aloud. Result: humiliating collapse of the brethren.[28]

In the long run, Hitler sought to weaken all the traditional churches and to establish Positive Christianity to form his *Volksgemeinschaft*. Once again, Hitler supported the strategy of social Darwinism to achieve this goal. To expedite the process, the Nazi regime managed to reduce the number of active members in the churches by the arrests of pastors and anti-Catholic lawsuits.[29] These strategies contributed to promoting the goal of the Nazi religious policy. However, it was not without its obstacles. Pope Pius XI issued in 1937 the papal encyclical *Mit Brennender Sorge*, which condemned the government's unilateral dismissal of stipulations of the Concordat of 1933. Furthermore, in matters of faith, the encyclical emphasized the importance of the Old Testament and condemned the myth of race and blood, both obvious references to Rosenberg's Positive Christianity. The Vatican required that it be read from the pulpit in all German Catholic churches, surprising Hitler's new regime.[30]

Hans Asmussen's memorandum in 1936 instigated a series of reprisals by the government and an acceleration in the number of arrests of pastors. Unfortunately, these efforts, both overdue and inefficacious, proved futile in preventing Hitler from instigating his *Führerprinzip* when he became the new political and spiritual leader of the German State.

Hitler became chancellor on January 31, 1933, and received plenipotentiary powers voted by the Reichstag on March 23, 1933, which he kept until the end of the war.[31] As for his spiritual leadership, it is best to begin with his own comments on the issue in his speeches, and finally, in *Mein Kampf*. In his book *Hitler and Nazi Germany*, Spielvogel devotes a section of his chapter "The Dictator" to the religious authority of Hitler. He refers to Hitler's hospital stay, due to mustard gas, in 1919, where he reported receiving the "divine mandate to release the German people and to return glory to Germany."[32] In another reference to Robert Waite's *Psychopathic God*, Spielvogel highlights the parallel that Hitler draws between his mission and that of Jesus: "Like Jesus, I have a duty towards my people."[33] This quotation corroborates the thesis of the German people as the "elected people." It is also interesting to again note the painting where Hitler portrays himself before his disciples, under the biblical title *In the Beginning Was the Word*.[34]

In his writings, Hitler refers to his role as "providential." This assertion appears often when he speaks about race and its purity. His mission is to defend the German people, the purity of its blood, so as to bring God's kingdom through National Socialism:

> The nationalization of the broad masses can never be achieved by half measures . . . but national in the vehement and extreme sense. Poison can be overcome only by a counter-poison, and only the supine bourgeois mind could think that the Kingdom of Heaven can be attained by a compromise.[35]

Another quotation from *Mein Kampf*, already mentioned, deserves more attention. Hitler confirms here his position as a providential man entrusted with a divine mission.

> Out of the army of millions . . . one man must arise. This man must have the gift of being able to expound general ideas in a clear and definite form, and from the world of vague ideas shimmering before the minds of the masses, he must formulate principles that will be as clear cut and firm as granite. He must fight for these principles as the only true ones, until a solid rock of common faith and common will emerges.[36]

Two of these "firm as granite" principles will be treated in this last section: first is the extermination of the rival people, the Jews who usurped the rightful place of the Aryan race in the providential plan; the second is the disappearance of historical Negative Christianity, replaced by the emergence of the true moral guide of the Third Reich, Positive Christianity.

EXTERMINATION OF THE JEWS: THE FALSE CHOSEN PEOPLE

In his chapter, "Hitler and the Holocaust," Kershaw explains the "Hitlerist" approach of Third Reich historians, who confirm Hitler's systematic plan to exterminate the Jews. "The conventional and dominant, 'Hitlerist' approach proceeds from the assumption that Hitler himself, from a very early date, seriously contemplated, pursued as a main aim, and strived unshakably to accomplish the physical annihilation of the Jews."[37] If our thesis defends the same point of view as that of the Hitlerists, it diverges from it with the idea that the Final Solution was not its main goal. In fact, Hitler's prime objective was rather to establish the new German State by cultivating his vision of the chosen Aryan people. Such was its divine mandate for the world.

This point of view, joined with that of the "Hitlerists," is essential for a total comprehension of Nazism, because it integrates the religious components. According to Hitler, the Jewish race misled the world, since the dawn of history, by proclaiming themselves the chosen people. There can be only one. This Jewish lie destroyed, on several occasions in history, the establishment of a triumphant Aryan race and the realization of its providential destiny. Thus, Hitler's visceral hatred for the Jews, even if it found its origin in his social background and in his youth, really took form as he faced the obstacles of achieving the thousand-year Third Reich, establishing the Nazi Party platform, and at last, usurping the false chosen people with Germanic destiny. Such is the "great intention" to which Lucy Dawidowicz refers in her work, *The War against the Jews*, quoted here by Kershaw:

> By the time he wrote the second volume of *Mein Kampf* in 1925, he "openly espoused his program of annihilation" in words which "were to become the blueprint for his policies when he came to power." She writes of "the grand design" in Hitler's head, the "long-range plans to realize his ideological goals" with the destruction of the Jews at their center, and that the implementation of his plan was subject only to opportunism and expediency.[38]

In like fashion, Kershaw quotes the Hitlerist historian Gerald Fleming, who raises Hitler's Messianic tendency as a way to explain why "Hitler remains convinced that Providence elected him to achieve this imposing task," and at the beginning of the 1920s, the fact that "Hitler developed . . . a strategic plan for the realization of his political aim."[39] If the fate of the Jewish people in

Nazi ideology meant they faced physical extermination, then the traditional Christian churches had to undergo a spiritual extermination, transforming their dogmatic beliefs, called "Negative," into Positive Christianity.[40] This is what we will see next.

NEGATIVE CHRISTIANITY'S DISAPPEARANCE AND THE IMPLEMENTATION OF POSITIVE CHRISTIANITY

As mentioned before, Hitler's religious policy considered a gradual victory in the short, intermediary, and long term. As such, a short-term strategy by Hitler hardly wished to alienate traditional churches, knowing that such an alienation could only block the support necessary for the war to come.[41] In *Mein Kampf*, he says that it would be madness to eliminate the Christian bases previously established before putting into practice Nazism's Positive Christianity:

> The political leader should not estimate the worth of a religion by taking some of its shortcomings into account, but he should ask himself whether there be any practical substitute in a view which is demonstrably better. Until such a substitute be available only fools and criminals would think of abolishing the existing religion.[42]

An additional note here is not out of place concerning Rosenberg's "endgame" political view in the long term. He is clear as to the goal after the war:

> Because after the war we must win the peace. . . . I talked about that subject at the education conference in March of this year, and will now send this confidential speech to the entire Party leadership. The political and economic centralization must be somewhat mitigated in its effect by a cultural decentralization. . . . A large empire—and a people that is regressing in terms of mental initiative. And we need intellectual and spiritual strength for the last great conflict of our lives: for prevailing over the Christian denominations.[43]

In *Mein Kampf*, Hitler often criticizes the parliamentary system of the Weimar Republic, which made it possible for Catholicism to establish itself as a political force in the "Catholic party of the Center,"[44] leaving a foreign religious influence to remove. Here is a perfect example of the practical application of Nazi religious policy. This removal takes place in the Nazi regime's interpretation of the stipulations and their execution in the legal settlement with the Vatican in the Concordat of 1933. Hitler thus presents a text which requires as a condition the "political neutrality of the clergy, condition of a progressive obliteration of the Center."[45] Even the French Catholic press raised the significance of this requirement. *Le Temps* writes on July 10, 1933: "On the 10th, the Concordat is analyzed according to the perspective of the Church, but also presented as a political given: 'What is necessary to retain for the moment, is that Chancellor Hitler obtained the obliteration of German Catholicism as a political force.' "[46]

Why did Hitler want to so quickly convince the Vatican to accept his view of his government? It was to achieve his short-term religious policy. However, it should be said that it was not solely the political power of the Catholics to which Hitler wanted to put an end, but indeed, the whole mentality. If the legal settlement succeeded in preserving only mediocre Catholic influence without slowing down the enthusiasm of the thousands of German Catholics for the new regime, the opportunistic approach of non-alienation runs up against the long-term goal of affirming that the Catholic faith, its central seat in Rome and its universalist doctrines, must disappear.

At the end of World War I, the Catholics—in spite of their intensive participation in the patriotic cause and their feeling (equal to that of the German Protestants) of international injustice in the Treaty of Versailles—did not adopt the cause of National Socialism. Their fidelity emanated from Rome; Catholicism meant more to German Catholics than the German church meant to Protestants. As Reymond states concerning German Catholicism, "religion remained for them universal business, and not [sentimental] nationalism."[47] This explains the bishops' refusal to allow the use of their churches as political places of propaganda with the wearing of uniforms or deployment of symbols of the Nazi Party. Everything changed, one could see, as far as the Nazi propaganda machine at the time of the success of the legal settlement. The Nazis offered to Rome what the Vatican had pursued for fifteen years, and they received in exchange the total submission of the German Catholic Church. From now on, any protest by the German Catholics against measures taken by the Reich became illegitimate. Any actions taken concerning religion were deemed political in scope and not tolerated. They were all accused of political goals under the auspices of religion. Those who, at that time, wanted to disentangle the paradoxes of the Third Reich in this regard could find their reply in *Mein Kampf*, where the birth of Hitler's anti-Christian plan of attack had taken shape.

Was the Vatican unaware of it? For Protestant churches, the Nazi influence had started early because of the influence of the German-Christians. The clear implementation of Hitler's control was manifested in his desire to require a Church unified under a national bishop: Ludwig Müller. Faced with this accomplished fact, the progress of Positive Christianity had already begun to take root. In spite of the pressure Hitler exerted in his speech before the elections and the subsequent success of German-Christian candidates being elected to the Reichstag, Müller could not collectively rally all of the Protestants to the Nazi cause. Faced with an imminent war, Hitler had to give in the long run what he would have liked to achieve in the medium term with respect to the Protestant churches. If such was the situation between Hitler and the churches, we will have to see the reaction of the churches when faced with militant Nazism.

NOTES

1. Kershaw, *The Nazi Dictatorship*, 5–6.
2. Spielvogel, *Hitler and Nazi Germany*, ix.
3. Reymond, *Une Église à croix gammée? (A Swastika Church?)*, 81–82 (author's translation).
4. Adolf Hitler, *Mein Kampf* (London: Hurst and Blackett Ltd., 1942), 214–15.
5. Ibid., 214.
6. Spielvogel, *Hitler and Nazi Germany*, 26.
7. Rudolph Binion, *Hitler Among the Germans* (New York: Elsevier, 1976), quoted in Kershaw, *The Nazi Dictatorship*, 83–84.
8. Orlow, *The History of the Nazi Party*, 70, cited in Spielvogel, *Hitler and Nazi Germany*, 45.
9. Matthäus and Bajohr, eds., *The Political Diary of Alfred Rosenberg*, 183.
10. Joachim Fest, *Hitler*, trans. Richard and Clara Winston (New York: Houghton Mifflin Harcourt, 1974), quoted by Spielvogel, *Hitler and Nazi Germany*, 83.
11. Kershaw, *The Nazi Dictatorship*, 141.
12. Spielvogel, *Hitler and Nazi Germany*, 56.
13. Klaus Scholder, *Die Kirchen und das Dritte Reich (The Churches and the Third Reich)*, 281; cited by Reymond, *Une Église à croix gammée? (A Swastika Church?)*, 88 (author's translation).
14. Hitler, *Mein Kampf*, 106.
15. Lewy, *The Catholic Church and Nazi Germany*, 105.
16. Ibid., 23.
17. Ibid., 55–56.
18. Reymond, *Une Église à croix gammée? (A Swastika Church?)*, 88 (author's translation).
19. Scholder, cited by Reymond, *Une Église à croix gammée? (A Swastika Church?)*, 149 (author's translation).
20. Hubert Locke, *The Church Confronts the Nazis: Barmen Then and Now* (Toronto, Ontario: Edwin Mellen, 1984), 51–52.
21. Reymond, *Une Église à croix gammée? (A Swastika Church?)*, 121–22 (author's translation).
22. Matthäus and Bajohr, eds., *The Political Diary of Alfred Rosenberg*, 49–50.
23. Hitler, *Mein Kampf*, 131.
24. Ibid., 120–21.

25. Lewy, *The Catholic Church and Nazi Germany*, 103.
26. Ibid., 169.
27. Locke, *The Church Confronts the Nazis*, 52–53.
28. Martin Niemöller (1892–1984); German Protestant cleric; U-boat commander during World War I; 1931–1937, pastor in Berlin-Dahlem; 1937–1945, incarcerated in the Sachsenhausen and Dachau concentration camps, cited in Matthäus and Bajohr, eds., *The Political Diary of Alfred Rosenberg*, footnote 598, 183.
29. Spielvogel, *Hitler and Nazi Germany*, 115.
30. Lewy, *The Catholic Church and Nazi Germany*, 156–58.
31. Reymond, *Une Église à croix gammée?* (*A Swastika Church?*), 88 (author's translation).
32. Binion, *Hitler Among the Germans* (New York: Elsevier, 1976), cited by Spielvogel, *Hitler and Nazi Germany*, 131.
33. Robert G. Waite, *The Psychopathic God*, published in 1977 (republished by Da Capo Press, New York, 1993), cited by Spielvogel, *Hitler and Nazi Germany*, 131.
34. Spielvogel, *Hitler and Nazi Germany*, 159, from Army Art Collection, US Army Center of Military History.
35. Hitler, *Mein Kampf*, 191.
36. Ibid., 215.
37. Kershaw, *The Nazi Dictatorship*, 82.
38. Ibid., 83.
39. Gerald Fleming, *Hitler and the Final Solution* (Oxford, UK: Oxford University Press, 1986), cited by Kershaw, *The Nazi Dictatorship*, 84.
40. Hitler, *Mein Kampf*, 379.
41. Spielvogel, *Hitler and Nazi Germany*, 114.
42. Hitler, *Mein Kampf*, 152.
43. Matthäus and Bajohr, eds., *The Political Diary of Alfred Rosenberg*, 262–63.
44. Reymond, *Une Église à croix gammée?* (*A Swastika Church?*), 37 (author's translation).
45. Ibid., 26.
46. Christian Ponson, "L'information sur le nazisme dans la presse catholique française entre 1933–1938" ("Information on Nazism in the Catholic French Press between 1933–1938") dans *Eglises et chrétiens dans la seconde guerre mondiale* (*Churches and Christians in the Second World War*), printed in the papers from the national colloquium in Lyon, January 27–30 1978, Lyon, 1982, 3 (author's translation).
47. Reymond, *Une Église à croix gammée?* (*A Swastika Church?*), 37 (author's translation).

Chapter 5

Rosenberg's Early Writings and Friends of Europe Publications

Chapter 1's central purpose was to clearly expose the religion of Nazism. It was brief but essential, as we exposed what was hidden in plain sight: the self-declared "profession of faith" in point 24 of the Nazi Party platform of 1920, affirming Positive Christianity. We pursued the clarity of this creed in chapter 2 by examining Rosenberg's seminal work, *The Myth of the Twentieth Century*, which we have discovered is possibly interred with *Mein Kampf* in the cornerstone of the still-standing Nuremberg Congress Hall (reported directly by Rosenberg in his recently discovered diary,[1] and again mentioned, as we will see later, in the French underground newspaper, *The Christian Witness*). This indeed proves the importance of these two pillars, comparable to two stone tablets as a foundation for the Third Reich, well before the war. This study led to clarifications in chapter 3 as to Rosenberg's identity and the core of Positive Christianity's beliefs. The secondary sources in chapter 4, from Hitler's own writings in *Mein Kampf*, validate his foundational ideas of the need for Positive Christianity's role in the success of the thousand-year Reich. Part II will show the failure of Protestant unity in Germany at this pivotal time, and the fact that the Concordat of 1933 with Hitler tied the Catholic Church's hands. As we will see in part III, the Church will have to await the heroic efforts of a handful of Jesuits in France for a Catholic role in the Christian Resistance.

However, first, this final chapter of part I introduces a virtually unknown secondary source in London, which, throughout the 1930s, published clear critiques of Rosenberg's early writings, as well as critiques of other authors during the rise of Positive Christianity's influence in Hitler's Germany. Who was listening? Far too few—yet the Friends of Europe compiled an impressive seventy-five publications, a sampling of which we will analyze here.[2] Winston Churchill himself was published in volume numbers 19, 23, and 62 and Albert Einstein in volume number 4. Their work has remained unknown for far too long, and will serve an essential role in solving the puzzle of the Nazi religion.

Headquartered at Saint Stephen's House in Westminster, London, the Friends of Europe's first publication dates from 1933, the year Hitler became chancellor. Any of their seventy-five publications were obtainable upon request, and one-third of them concerned religion and Christianity. We have already cited references to Rosenberg's memoirs, written at the end of his life, as well as to his recently found diary. It is important not to neglect the Friends of Europe publications, which sought out early scholarly analyses of Rosenberg's own writings. These will be the first of three examples. The second, a politician's point of view, is written by a British member of Parliament in June 1936, titled "The Nazi Party, the State and Religion," and the third is a foreword by the president of Union Theological Seminary in New York City, Reverend Henry Sloane Coffin, published early in 1933 in a pamphlet with the title "The Creed of the Nordic Race."

The 1930s were a crucial time of exposure of the religious elements of Nazism. Hitler would consolidate and centralize his power in the elections of March 1936, which brought a result of 98.9 percent for the Nazi regime.[3] This obscure British publication's effort through the Friends of Europe was a lonely voice of alarm heard from across the English Channel during these crucial years before the war.

Rosenberg's own writings were commented on in a number of the Friends of Europe publications. I have chosen two commentaries on his early work by religious contributors, and a third by an academic who had close ties to influential religious leaders in Germany.

Volume 26 was published early on, in 1935. "Rosenberg's German 'Mythus': An Evangelical Answer" was written by Pastor Heinrich Hüffmeier, who was obliged to walk the treacherous road of being faithful to his flock as well as respectful to his government. Reverend Sydney M. Berry, the secretary of the Congregational Union of England and Scotland, writes in his foreword:

> But we can be grateful that among many German Protestants themselves, with all their natural sympathy with the Nationalist Movement, there is the courage to stand up to the essential challenge to Evangelical Christianity. That challenge is nothing less than the denial of revealed religion and the attempt to put in its place an emasculated alternative compounded of unhistorical fancies and racial fanaticism. The result is something as unlike Christianity as could well be imagined. Perhaps through the careful and measured language of this booklet that alternative is visualized more clearly.[4]

The uneasiness of Pastor Hüffmeier's treatise of Herr Rosenberg's "Mythus" is palpable as he tries to walk the gauntlet of criticism of such an esteemed Nazi Party official. To say that his conviction lacks authenticity would be unfair and inaccurate, yet the focus on the affronts against Christian faith brought on by "Rosenberg's German 'Mythus'" are obvious, and needed less solicitude. Concerning Rosenberg's ideas on Christianity, Hüffmeier uses a near placating tone:

> We make a clear and conscious distinction between the national socialist view of life and the Christian view of God. In the first category there is much in Rosenberg with which we can agree. . . . But we do not need a new teaching concerning God. What God is and what He wants, we know through Jesus Christ. . . . Our desire and prayer is that in the religious struggle of the present the light of the Divine revelation may shine the more clearly.[5]
> It is possible that Rosenberg's basis may have a certain historical foundation. What matters is the conclusions which are drawn. We find ourselves in conflict when this view of history becomes the instrument of a new world-outlook and religious teaching.[6]

When Hüffmeier cuts to the crux of the matter—Rosenberg's Positive Christianity—his lack of clarity is disappointing, being that Rev. Berry mentions that *The Myth* by 1933 was already in its ninth edition and ordered to be placed in all school libraries and high schools. Hüffmeier is rather equivocal, to say the least:

> What is the positive thing that Rosenberg offers to us? A new religion cannot live by mere attack on the Christian faith. Those who prepare the new German faith do not ask us to pray again to the old German gods. . . . Nor does Rosenberg. What concerns him is the truly great which resided in the olden time, behind the symbols in the spirit of the Germans—the unnamable Divine.[7]

The second of the three critiques of Rosenberg's own writings is volume 27 in the series and focuses directly on "Rosenberg's Positive Christianity." It was published in 1935 with a foreword written by the archbishop of Liverpool, Reverend Richard Downey, and contains a scathing critic by German Catholic scholars in Cologne. Reverend Downey ends his foreword with an ominous warning:

> The German scholars responsible for the present pamphlet must have found it an easy task to refute the biblical part of Rosenberg's Myth, for the whole section is nothing, if not shallow, naive, arbitrary, sometimes even nonsensical, as is clearly revealed in the many extracts printed in the pages that follow, and quite unworthy of the serious attention if not for the gravity of the issues involved. If this new Christianity represented by Rosenberg is to be forced on over twenty million Catholics and Evangelicals—and even as we write the signs of the times

are ominous—then our own generation may yet witness such a conflict of religious and political forces as the history of nations has never known.⁸

The consortium of Catholic scholars achieves a concise and well-documented critique of Positive Christianity. Here we cite two central topics. First, the reality of what is not new, i.e., the rejection of the Old Testament, in the idea of the Nordic faith:

> Rosenberg is not the first who, from the viewpoint of the Nordic man, has resented the Old Testament as a product of the Jewish mind. Paul de Lagarde and Rosenberg's direct teacher, Houston Stewart Chamberlain, held for decades similar views. In the postwar period, Friedrich Delitzsch, in his book, *The Great Illusion* (*Die grosse Täuschung*), published in Berlin in 1920, stated that the Christian Church and the Christian family could get along very well without the Old Testament.⁹

Second, the centrality and divine nature of Jesus:

> From what has been said it is clear that Jesus Christ is, for Rosenberg, only a *"great personality"* and nothing more. As Rosenberg rules out all recognition of the Divine Sonship of Jesus and His work as Savior, all references in the Gospels and other New Testament writings on these heads belong to the *"falsifying trimmings"*; they are *"Christian legends"* which provide no basis for belief.¹⁰

The third and final example of a Friends of Europe publication dealing directly with Rosenberg's work is an intriguing one. In August 1937, Alfred Rosenberg presented a small book at the World Church Conference in Oxford, England. His book's title, *Protestant Pilgrims to Rome: The Betrayal of Luther*, an obviously provocative one, has its main ideas presented in 1938 in volume 66, of the same title, with a foreword by Reverend Nathaniel Micklem, the principal of Mansfield College, Oxford. In his foreword, Reverend Micklem prepares the reader by stating in crystal-clear terms that the quid pro quos of Rosenberg's ideas serve as a mere smoke screen for a very definite duality of form and substance:

> It is one of the many insincerities in the Germany of today that Dr. Rosenberg prefaces his treatise by the observation that he is not for the moment writing in his capacity as an official of the National-Socialist party. In form this is true, for the Party is free to repudiate any of his theories. . . . But in substance it is false; for Dr. Rosenberg is the head of the ministry for the spiritual education of the nation.¹¹

The content of Rosenberg's book and his attendance at the conference is focused, of course, on the Protestant critics of Positive Christianity and the

Third Reich. Major doctrinal differences were already studied in chapter 3 (i.e., rejection of original sin, grace, the Old Testament, and the epistles of Paul). Reflecting the title of his book, which of course speaks of the betrayal of Luther, Rosenberg reprimands the Confessing Church, the group of defiant German pastors also known as the Pastors' Emergency League, for not recognizing the link between Luther the "revolutionary" and the current National Socialist "revolutionary" spirit. Rosenberg asserts:

> The Bible of Luther, which today is tradition, was once Revolution! The man who wrote it revolted against a thousand-year-old tradition in a struggle which shook the world. A struggle which the Church attacked, regarded as the end of the world and the end of all religions. And the ancestors of those who today honor Luther's Bible, stood of inner necessity in the ranks of the Protestant revolt, i.e., they regarded their attitude as a duty to their age and had the courage—to be themselves! ... And our age again demands—that we be ourselves. It demands that with all respect for the traditions of our fathers, the old teachings shall not be in conflict with the preservation of our life, or that alleged eternal dogmas and "revelations" be opposed to and condemn this life.[12]

Rosenberg also highlights Germany's Protestant leaders' negligence in attacking the Russian Marxist threat and instead focusing on the Reich government's policies. Rosenberg's frustration is evident in both his book's content and in his attitude at the conference, citing the appeal of the Bishop of Chichester in England to the Evangelical Church in Germany. Rosenberg's reaction is telling:

> This imprudent intervention into German affairs shows that many have not yet become aware of this out-of-place way of playing the Governor. As reference was made in the appeal, in the same breath, to Soviet Russia and Germany, it is plain that the gentlemen were concerned with political agitation.[13]

To end this first section of references in the Friends of Europe publications dealing directly with Rosenberg's writings, the intrigue of his attendance at this World Church Conference in August 1937 is all the more revelatory when we realize that the following month of September would be the largest Nazi Party annual rally, during which Rosenberg was to be honored as one of the inaugural recipients of the German National Prize for Art and Science, newly created by Hitler as a means to protest the Nobel Peace Prize of 1936 going to Carl von Ossietzky, a pacifist awarded the prize for his exposure of the Nazi secret rearmament. The conference was the final buildup for Rosenberg as he confronted his Protestant and Catholic adversaries just before the moment of his personal triumph and his recognition for *The Myth of the Twentieth Century*.

In the preface of this book, referring to recent publications, I mentioned *The Devil's Diary*, a book written by the founder of the FBI's National Art Crime Team, Robert K. Wittman, and Pulitzer Prize–winning reporter, David Kinney. It was written the year following the 2015 publication of Rosenberg's recently found journal. In *The Devil's Diary*, Wittman and Kinney describe Rosenberg's elation before hundreds of thousands of Party members, interestingly enough once again confirming the possible placement of *Mein Kampf* and *The Myth* side by side in the cornerstone of the new Congress Hall.

> By the hundreds of thousands, the party faithful convened for what promised to be the biggest rally to date, eight days of speeches and spectacle. . . . That week, Rosenberg was not just another speaker at the rallies. He was a guest of honor. Eighteen years after first turning up at a regular meeting of a tiny band of beer-hall anti-Semites in Munich, he was being hailed as the man who'd laid the ideological foundations of National Socialism. His master work, *The Myth of the Twentieth Century*, already rested beside *Mein Kampf* in the cornerstone of Nuremberg's Congress Hall.[14]

The second example drawn from the copious research and reporting of the Friends of Europe publications comes from a political vantage point. It is of utmost importance to mention here that Winston Churchill, not yet of course prime minister, which happened in 1940, published early in this collection in volume 19. Although his topic did not include a reference to the Nazi Religion—it dealt with his strong preoccupation at the time with German rearmament—it certainly affirms not only the importance of these publications, but also his knowledge of them. Once prime minister, his unwavering conviction is clearly inspiring in his famous speech of June 18, 1940, the same day as General de Gaulle's infamous radio broadcast to France, when Churchill declares:

> We have proclaimed our willingness at the darkest hour in French history to conclude a union of common citizenship in this struggle. . . . What General Weygand called the Battle of France is over. I expect that the Battle of Britain is about to begin. Upon this battle depends the survival of Christian civilization.[15]

It is certainly evident that more research beyond the scope of this present work is called for in the possibly great influential history of the Friends of Europe. Returning to the political nature of other submissions to this collection, Dr. Hugh Dalton, MP, ex-undersecretary of state for foreign affairs, in June of 1936, attempts to piece together what, at that time, they were receiving piecemeal in England on the beliefs of "The Nazi Party, the State and Religion." He lists the 25-point program, stating that it "was regarded as sacrosanct by the Leader and was only amended once, over the Leader's signature, through all the stormy years of the rise to power of the Party."[16] Commenting further on point 24, Dalton notes the association between Hitler's *Mein Kampf* and Rosenberg's *Myth of the Twentieth Century*:

> Point 24 in the Party Programme . . . indicates the involved and destructive way in which he is prepared to recognize and tolerate what he calls "Positive Christianity," an expression which receives further elucidation and definition through the book of his distinguished colleague, Reichskulturleiter Dr. Alfred Rosenberg in his *Myth of the 20th Century*, a book second only in importance in the education of German Youth to that of the Leader's autobiography.[17]

Regarding the religious question, one recognizes the influence of Hitler's views on the primacy of propaganda when he addresses the idea of separation between religion and politics. "One of the outstanding features in Herr Hitler's rise to power has been his attention to mass psychology and the arts of propaganda."[18] This was addressed previously in chapter 1, when discussing his propaganda genius, but here, in volume 41 of the Friends of Europe publications, Hitler's refined technique of dealing with the churches is elucidated.

> Herr Hitler's outstanding paragraph on the subject of religion lays down the principle of separation between religion and politics. The separation is, however, hedged round with qualification. . . . Herr Hitler takes the view that in any dispute between religion and politics, it is the political leader, the "State," which has the final and decisive word. . . . It is the exercise of this right of the "Political Party" to be the judge of these qualifications, which explains the religious struggle in Germany since 1933.[19]

One understands the reference here to the Concordat of 1933 with the Catholic Church, which fell victim to Hitler's philosophy, allowing him to interpret as he wished the "political engagement" of the church.

The third reference is an American one. The president of Union Theological Seminary, in New York City, Reverend Henry Sloane Coffin, wrote a powerful foreword to volume 31, which focuses on the brochure "The Creed of the Nordic Race" by Dr. Wilhelm Kusserow. Paul Tillich took refuge at Union Theological Seminary when he was exiled from Germany after the publication in 1932 of his work, *Ten Theses against the Nazis*, which will be presented in part II. A selection by an American theologian is significant, as it testifies to the expanse of the distribution of the Friends of Europe to include the United States, at least by January 1936. It is quite natural that Union Theological Seminary, one of the preeminent Protestant seminaries of America, would be a center for this distribution, and, when coupled with Tillich's presence, whose importance to German clarity on the beliefs of the

Nazi Party will be studied in part II, gives us a trail to follow as to American Christian knowledge of German churches in the 1930s.

Volume 31 treats the twenty-seven articles of the "Nordic Creed" that rose out of the German-Christian Movement. It was drafted and approved by the Leading Council of the Nordic Religious Association very early, in 1932, and was adopted the following September. Evident parallels exist with Positive Christianity, most obviously in the case of the Aryan Chosen People belief. There is in particular an interesting difference in the equality of women in the Creed (article 26) which is not supported in *The Myth*, and the shocking forthright acknowledgment of the necessity of eugenics for preserving the "healthy stock" of the Nordic people (article 17), which even Rosenberg dared not include, although the usage of it is well documented during the Nazi era. The commentary is well organized, with an analysis of each article coupled with a brief comparison with Christianity. The foreword by Reverend Coffin is a combination of breadth and brevity. This may be a result of information coming from Tillich, a German theologian, to Coffin, a theologian with an American perspective. He warns the Christian community at large to take heed of this Creed, even though its adherents were not large in number. "It would be a mistake to suppose this creed professed by a large number of Germans. . . . But the fervid devotion to German nationalism and the insistence on the maintenance of the purity of the German race are patently not of Christian origin."[20]

We have already seen that the German-Christians played their necessary role in bringing the Nazis to power, while Hitler had another strategy for the vast majority of Christians. Coffin alludes to this German-Christian influence:

> The cult whose creed and code and political programme are here set forth is the faith logically behind certain movements in Germany which have brought the present government into conflict with the churches. . . . We might dismiss such a cult as fantastic, were it not for the horrible fact that this faith is being shown in [the] works. . . . It is leavening minds.[21]

Unfortunately, his caution is belayed by his insistence on their small numbers. Coffin also clouds the centrality of the menace of this "Nordic Creed" by including references to the racial attitudes of the Jews—"It is significant that its immediate victims, the Jews, have also cherished a racialism"[22]—as well as white supremacy movements in America, which, while dangerous by definition, are not true in historical context or in parallel realities to the Germany of the 1930s. These unnecessary distractions in a condensed format detract from the importance of a foreword that tried to do too much in too little space, minimizing the purpose for which it was written: a warning to the Christian world that "Here is a religion to be reckoned with."[23]

To conclude, the archbishop of Liverpool in his foreword to volume 27, of July 1935, "Rosenberg's Positive Christianity: Rosenberg and the Bible," submits to his readers these ominous words:

> The German scholars responsible for the present pamphlet must have found it an easy task to refute the biblical part of Rosenberg's *Myth*, for the whole section is nothing if not shallow, naive, arbitrary . . . quite unworthy of serious attention, were it not for the gravity of the issues involved. If this new Christianity represented by Rosenberg is to be forced on over twenty million Catholics and Evangelicals—and even as we write, the signs of the times are ominous—then our own generation may yet witness such a conflict of religious and political forces as the history of nations has never known. Hitler, quo vadis?[24]

Where indeed was he going?

Following our study of several volumes of the publications of the Friends of Europe, we can conclude this final chapter of part I with a return to the warnings listed in the initial introduction.

Heed what is written, not what is said.

This cautioning phrase can understandably be repeated here because we have seen that the Friends of Europe, although to date still unrecognized for their in-depth publications, contrasted sharply with what was superficially and manipulatively being said.

Heed what is reported but not believed.

In the course of the research for part I, I encountered a book by Dan Stone, *Responses to Nazism in Britain, 1933–1939: Before War and Holocaust*. A promising title led initially to disappointment when I found no mention in the book of the extraordinary work of the Friends of Europe. Be that as it may, the book bears mentioning here for two important reasons. First, Stone lauds the efforts of two foreign-born intellectuals who fought hard in Britain to make known the reality of the mounting threat in Germany. The first author, Franz Borkenau, was a German intellectual who came to London at the outbreak of the war; and the second, Aurel Kolnai, was a Hungarian who taught philosophy at the University of London. In Britain, as we will see, many wrote about Nazi Germany yet few felt the same urgency as did Borkenau or Kolnai. Why is it that it took a handful of Continental writers to alert the British to the seriousness of Nazism?[25] An excellent question, to be sure.

Borkenau's indictment of the British government's failure to understand the situation from which so many of the exiles had fled was not due to a lack of effort on the part of those exiles to explain it.[26] His book *The New German Empire* (1939) is synopsized well by Stone, who shows Borkenau as a passionate writer reporting what he saw and experienced to an unbelieving British audience. Stone explains:

> Borkenau discussed the nature of the Nazi regime, arguing that it was genuinely revolutionary, but in a way that did not conform with "current ideas of revolutions." . . . Nazi Germany constituted a revolution because it satisfied the need for a new metaphysics: The Germans "reacted to the complete disintegration of all existing values with an outcry for a new faith and a new saviour" (p. 18) . . . the complete disintegration of the old economic structure and of the old spiritual values in Germany (p. 21). What the regime was, then, was not a one-party state so much as a new religion (p. 21). . . . The corollary of Borkenau's insistence on the regime's religious character was his claim that the notion of the Third Reich settling down to some kind of "normalcy" was "quite meaningless" (p. 22).[27]

Stone conveys Borkenau's desire to be believed by the British, at least by those who were willing to open their minds to his viewpoint, no matter how difficult the circumstances of the day. "The important message for British readers was that Nazism could not be understood using the conventional tools of diplomacy or methods of scholarship. . . . Nazism threatened the rest of the world with a zero-sum game."[28]

Beyond the earnestness of Borkenau, the most profound analysis of Nazism in Stone's opinion was that of Aurel Kolnai in his book, *The War Against the West* (1938). Here again is the voice crying out to be believed, especially since Kolnai's approach, much like that of this present work, was to quote the Nazis themselves and let their own words condemn their future plans. Stone comments that "the book is one of the few that insists on taking the phenomenon seriously, no matter how outlandish some of its claims may have sounded to the British ear."[29]

Kolnai takes on the Nazi view of community (*Volksgemeinschaft*), warfare, eugenics, and so forth, with a consistent method of "accepting the potential validity of the ideas on which Nazism was based, and then demonstrating that the Nazis themselves neither understood what it was they claimed . . . nor were [they] able to control the forces they had unleashed."[30] He especially focused on the racial anthropology of Nazism. Stone explains that Kolnai's method could effectively explain how it is that "competing and even contradictory strands of anthropological and racial theory could be incorporated into Nazi wisdom."[31] Unfortunately, for the subject matter here, this method was not applied to the religious sphere per se in his voluminous seven-hundred-page book. However, one can imagine that if this kind of extensive reporting and analysis had been coupled with the work coming from the religious studies of the Friends of Europe, more influential believers could have been found.

Stone himself expresses regret in his concluding remarks about Kolnai's lack of reception and appreciation due to his unconventional method. "Few thinkers have had the stomach to follow Kolnai for fear of lending too much credence to the thing they seek to destroy. But he paved the way for a philosophical understanding of Nazism that remains as yet unfulfilled."[32] We can certainly applaud Kolnai's efforts in the 1930s to report and to be believed. Parallels of method and presentation are certainly found here, as emphasis is placed on the actors themselves at the time before the war.

Heed what is not written.

Secondly, Stone's book is important to mention in this conclusion of part I because of his own efforts to bring to the fore the unheard voices of what should have been the "era of warning." He achieves to a great extent his goal, which he states clearly as follows:

> In this book I show, first, that the range of responses to Nazism was actually very wide; and secondly, that before the war and the Holocaust, the ethical dimension of responding to the Third Reich was rather different from what it would become just five years later. The sincere and even progressive democrats were embarrassed by what they had said in the 1930s, believing it now to be [the] result of naivety, blindness and the seductiveness of the Third Reich.[33]

This statement reads almost as a testament to the success of Hitler's propaganda goals we studied earlier, especially in what he wanted to accomplish in the ethical sector. Pride, arrogance, lack of knowledge, and lack of clarity were cultivated by Hitler, Rosenberg, and the tight entourage around the center of movers and shakers of the "Nazi Revolution." The statement "Heed what is not written" evokes the need to listen to those who wrote on what was happening on the ground. How regrettable for those applauded here who tried but failed to bring clarity in the 1930s to help avoid what would ensue in the 1940s. In part II we will explore the parallel efforts to sound the alarm of the Nazi threat, but within Germany, in the intellectual world of Protestant Christianity.

A quotation from the book *The Holy Reich: Nazi Conceptions of Christianity, 1919–1945* by Richard Steigmann-Gall will serve to create an effective bridge between parts I and II. The essential point of Steigmann-Gall's book is to show clearly the integral religious element to the Nazi vision of a thousand-year Reich. This is the same as the goal of part I, which showed both how this element was envisioned by the Nazi Party and how they conspired and propagandized very effectively to let others draw their own conclusions of what Positive Christianity was during the crucial years before the war, as they consolidated their control.

The idea that a political party would integrate a redefinition of the Christian faith was inconceivable to the existing Western world. Even with the efforts seen above in part I and the Christian expertise to follow in part II, the elements of "a perfect storm" in 1930s Germany were set in place and anchored in the cornerstone of Nuremberg's enormous Congress Hall. Steigmann-Gall gives us an appropriate thought-provoking passage to introduce Paul Tillich and Karl Barth as the preeminent Protestant thinkers of early Nazi Germany as we study the raising of Christianity's shield against the Nazi threat.

> To assert that leading Nazis conceived their movement to be in some sense a Christian one, or may even have been believing Christians themselves, may seem to some deliberately provocative if not outrageous. This is not to say that the relationship between Nazism and Christianity has not been a topic of scholarly inquiry; quite the opposite. There is a vast and still-growing literature on the churches in the Third Reich, which has explored the ways in which theologians and Christian clergy who were supportive of Nazism often drew connections between their traditions and Nazi ideology. . . . But the question of how the Nazis themselves possibly thought about such an ideological coupling has not led to a similar scholarship, largely because it is assumed that the response from the Nazis was overwhelmingly negative. . . . If we likened public pronouncements by Nazi leaders to the words of actors on a stage, and the German public to their audience, it is almost universally held that these actors completely rejected their Christian script after the curtain came down.[34]

NOTES

1. Matthäus and Bajohr, eds., *The Political Diary of Alfred Rosenberg*, 83.
2. The full list of Friends of Europe publications can be found in appendix C of this book.
3. Wittman and Kinney, *The Devil's Diary*, 191.
4. Rev. Sidney M. Berry, in the foreword to Pastor Heinrich Hüffmeier, "Rosenberg's German 'Mythus': An Evangelical Answer," Friends of Europe Publications, vol. 26, 4.
5. Ibid., 5.
6. Ibid., 9.
7. Ibid., 15–16.
8. Rev. Richard Downey, "Rosenberg's Positive Christianity: Rosenberg and the Bible," Friends of Europe Publications, vol. 27, 6.
9. Ibid., 9.
10. Ibid., 19.

11. Commentary on Alfred Rosenberg's "Protestant Pilgrims to Rome: The Betrayal of Luther," foreword by Rev. Nathaniel Micklem, Friends of Europe Publications, vol. 66, 4.

12. Ibid., 11–12.

13. Ibid., 20–21.

14. Wittman and Kinney, *The Devil's Diary*, 209–10.

15. Martin Hall, Carol Schaessens, and Martin Waters, Cambridge Editorial Partnership, *Speeches that Changed the World: The Stories and Transcripts of the Moments that Made History* (London: Smith-Davies Publishing Ltd., 2005), 94.

16. "The Nazi Party, the State and Religion" by Adolf Hitler, foreword by Dr. Hugh Dalton, Friends of Europe Publications, vol. 41, 7.

17. Ibid., 21.

18. Ibid., 15.

19. Ibid., 21.

20. "The Creed of the Nordic Race" by Dr. Wilhelm Kusserow, with a foreword by Rev. Henry Sloane Coffin, Friends of Europe Publications, vol. 31, 1.

21. Ibid., 5.

22. Ibid., 4.

23. Ibid.

24. Downey, "Rosenberg's Positive Christianity," 6.

25. Dan Stone, *Responses to Nazism in Britain, 1933–1939: Before War and Holocaust* (New York: Palgrave Macmillan, 2003, 9.

26. Ibid., 10.

27. Ibid., 25.

28. Ibid., 26.

29. Ibid., 29.

30. Ibid., 31.

31. Ibid., 32.

32. Ibid., 33.

33. Ibid., 8.

34. Richard Steigmann-Gall, *The Holy Reich: Nazi Conceptions of Christianity, 1919–1945* (Cambridge, UK: Cambridge University Press, 2003), 3.

PART II

Duped Christianity: Hitler's Propaganda Coup

THE CHURCHES CONFRONT THE POSITIVE CHRISTIANITY OF NAZISM

An analysis of the religious goals and content of *The Myth*, *Mein Kampf*, and the Nazi Party platform's point 24 necessitates a brief introduction to the reactions of the Christian churches facing Positive Christianity. Before studying the regrettable Protestant conflict of key theologians, Tillich and Barth, or the specificities of the disastrous Catholic path due to the agreement between Hitler and the Vatican, a brief introduction is necessary. We also find that the efforts of the Catholic and Protestant leaders would not be sufficiently expeditious, categorical, or confrontational, albeit for different reasons, to defeat the efficacious propaganda methods of the Nazis, or to have any lasting effect on the persecution that would follow.

THE CATHOLIC REACTION

While Catholics represent a significant minority of over twenty million—one-third of the German population[1]—the German Catholic Church finds, ironically, its strongest presence in Hitler's native province of Bavaria. Due to the minority situation of Catholicism, in addition to the unique *Länder* political system, the Vatican had to endure a prolonged absence of official status in Germany.[2] In order to arrive at a legal means capable of protecting and expanding this appreciable Catholic population, the Church signed agreements with each of the *Länder*: Bavaria (in 1924), Prussia (in 1929), and the country of Baden (in 1932).

Hitler knew that the Vatican had hoped for a concordat with the central government of the Reich since the end of the war in 1918. The term *concordat* is a specific reference to treaties negotiated by the Vatican. The terms of the one signed with the Third Reich in July of 1933 will be discussed later.

It did not take long before Hitler offered one to the Holy See. As early as April 1933, less than four months after coming to power, a draft was submitted by the Nazi regime. Suffice it for now to just briefly consider this fatal decision of the Church. It gives one pause to realize that the Church accepted this carrot dangled by Hitler when they knew of the content of *The Myth*—which expressed vehement disdain for the Roman Catholic Church and its beliefs—as well as the close links between Rosenberg and Hitler. As we will see, the extent of the Catholic Church's actions against *The Myth* was strongly influenced by the political negotiations for the Concordat of 1933, which took only six months from start to finish.

The Positive Christianity cited in the Nazi Party program was viewed by the Vatican as having its source in *The Myth*, and had been studied by the Catholic Church. Reference has already been made to the Vatican request in 1931 of a study of the book by church scholars in Bavaria. The political designs of the Vatican for further influence in Germany took primacy over any potential threat, and the German Catholic theologians wanted to reassure themselves by separating Rosenberg's thought from that of Hitler. The only in-depth criticism the Church as a whole undertook of *The Myth* appeared in an edition of the diocesan gazette of Münster in 1934. The study was called *Studien zum Mythus des XX Jahrhunderts*, with a publication of 100,000 copies, the majority of which reached the public before their confiscation by the Gestapo. It was followed by two epilogues, one in December and another in early 1935. Rosenberg responded with the publication of a small book, *An die Dunkelmänner unserer Zeit* (*To the Dark Men of Our Time*).[3] This study, in-depth as it may have been, was after the fact, as it appeared in 1934, after the treaty was already signed.

Catholic critics targeted the work of *The Myth* and its author without indicting Hitler himself. Yet we have seen that the program of the Nazi Party, to which Hitler was so attached, included this religious element, well-defined in *The Myth*. It is an irrefutable fact. The Catholic Church stealthily sought to separate Rosenberg's ideology from the leadership of Hitler, whose propaganda goals concerning the churches sought the same reaction in order to achieve the Concordat, and then, subsequently, apply it as they saw fit.

The symbiosis of Positive Christianity and the Third Reich manifested itself six months after the signing of the Concordat in July 1933, when Hitler appointed Rosenberg the spiritual and intellectual leader of the Nazi Party. While it was clear that a distinction did not exist between the religious ideology and Hitler's leadership, it was too late; Hitler's manipulation succeeded in defeating Catholic influence by an attack on two flanks. First, on the ideological plain, Positive Christianity as exhibited in *The Myth* was propagated by the official Nazi Party, incorporating a virulent anti-Catholicism. Then, politically, by means of the Concordat, Hitler succeeded in destroying all progress the Catholic Church had made during the Weimar Republic.

He forced the dissolution of the two Catholic Center political parties, and the Nazi Party began violently persecuting any and all Catholic institutions—monasteries, schools, institutions of higher learning—everything but the churches themselves. This focused persecution was interpreted by the Nazis as "political intervention," a pivotal point clearly denied to the Catholic Church, yet interpreted freely by the Nazis as they so pleased. All protests of the Catholic Church against what they saw as clear breaches of Concordat protocols were systematically rejected by the regime. A chronicle of the efforts of the Roman Catholic Church to combat these Nazi politics can be found in the book by Guenter Lewy, *The Catholic Church and Nazi Germany*. All of these reactions, sadly, came too late.

The criticisms of Eugenio Pacelli, who became Pope Pius XII in 1939, are many. The critique made here is clear and to the point. With his vast experience, knowledge of Germany, fluency in the language, and presence in Munich during the rise of Nazism, it is unmistakably clear: The papal diplomat Pacelli should have known better. In his book *The Myth of Hitler's Pope*, in the chapter entitled "The Future Pope," Rabbi David G. Dalin

The Signing of the Concordat between the Holy See and Nazi Germany, July 31, 1933 (Bundesarchiv, Bild 183-R24391)

traces the lifelong preparation of this exceptional diplomat for the Vatican. This distinction, in fact, came only two years after his ordination. Members of his family were Vatican lawyers; he was well-educated, and spoke many languages fluently, including German, French, English, Hebrew, Latin, and Greek.[4] After fifteen years codifying canon law, in 1914 he became the secretary for the Vatican in the Department of Extraordinary Ecclesiastical Affairs. Dalin explains Pacelli's growing experience in concordat drafting in this next passage:

> In his new position, Pacelli concluded a concordat with Serbia, the first of many such treaties that he would negotiate.... During the next three years, Pacelli was Gasparri's right-hand man, helping to formulate and draft all official documents prepared by the secretary of state for Pope Benedict XV's signature. Many important papal documents, including the Vatican's February 1916 condemnation of anti-Semitism, were first drafted and often proposed by Eugenio Pacelli.[5]

With a family linked in service to the Vatican, linguistic capabilities, and having drafted treaties throughout his career before the rise of Nazism, he was certainly the right person to send to Germany after the war. This is precisely what the Pope did. Quoting again Dalin's synopsis of Pacelli's career, now in Germany, he explains, "As Benedict XV's (and subsequently Pope Pius XI's) papal ambassador to Bavaria, Pacelli remained in Germany for twelve years, finally returning to Rome in 1929."[6]

These were pivotal years for the Weimar Republic, and the time of the birth of the Nazi Party, their attempt to overthrow the government in the Beer Hall Putsch of 1923, and the acts of the infamous "Brown Shirts" against the Jews. Once again, Pacelli should have known not to sign a concordat with a Nazi regime. One final note in the motivations of this treaty can be found in a reference to Pacelli's visit to the United States in 1936. As described by Dalin in the same chapter, Pacelli meets with President Roosevelt, and during the meeting Roosevelt asks the now cardinal if he could intervene with some trouble he was having with a very vocal Catholic radio broadcaster who was critical of the New Deal. Pacelli dealt with the situation, to Roosevelt's delight, but Pacelli also had a request of Roosevelt. He wanted to secure an official United States–appointed representative to the Holy See, which had not happened since the Pope had lost temporal power in 1870.[7] Dalin explains:

> Roosevelt assured Pacelli that he would appoint a personal envoy to the Holy See, a diplomat who would serve informally by presidential appointment and would not require Senate confirmation. Roosevelt made good on his promise in December 1939, when just before Christmas he appointed Myron C. Taylor as his personal representative to Pope Pius XII.[8]

This clarifies the importance of having representation in diplomatic circles, in terms of international relations. In this instance, Pacelli, becoming Pope himself, benefited from the presence of the US representative. Ironically—and tragically, for Europe, and France in particular—the same diplomatic strategy would be used against Pope Pius XI and subsequently, against Pacelli himself—that is, Pope Pius XII during the war—when Hitler used Vatican representatives to exploit his Nazi agenda across Europe. Pacelli should have known better back in 1933. After all, what was the rush?

It was obvious to Hitler that he was facing a formidably powerful international religious institution, and the Third Reich's budding political position had a religious agenda that did not show promise for prolonged protocols. The catastrophic results of the Vatican signature on this Concordat of 1933 cannot be overstated. It is important to be reminded that Pacelli was not the Pope. He was not elected to the papacy until the death of Pius XI in 1939, yet his influence and experience in concordat negotiations was considerable, as shown. He was personally involved in its drafting. After it was signed in 1933, the Vatican would have to face the reality of the situation that developed between 1933 and 1937, and how Rome would address the Jewish Nazi persecution that had become rampant.

The Holy See replied in 1937 with the encyclical, *Mit Brennender Sorge*. Written in German,[9] it denounced the aggravation of the persecutions against the Church in Germany. What does this encyclical say? We can answer in the negative by first indicating what it does not say. Nowhere is Nazism or National Socialism directly designated or condemned.[10] What a contrast with *Divini Redemptoris*, which, three times as long, attacks Bolshevik Communism as "intrinsically perverse."[11] With such gaps, one wonders what the purpose of *Mit Brennender Sorge* was.

Upon reflection, three objectives emerge.

First, the encyclical addresses the German bishops and condemns the religious persecution led by the Reich, which raged from 1933 to 1937. When the confiscations of convents and seminaries began, the same explanation would be given by the Reich. In his testimony, the bishop of Münster, Monsignor von Galen, confirms that:

> The Secret State Police [Gestapo] confiscated two convents of the Company of Jesus in our city. . . . Similarly to the Sisters of the Immaculate Conception in Wilkinghege in the Steinfuristrasse: their home was equally confiscated. . . . Why was that? I was told: "reasons of state policy." Other reasons were not given.[12]

Second, the encyclical served as a direct pontifical protest for all of these abuses. It also condemned certain doctrines of the Reich, such as those concerning race and blood, and the practices which resulted therefrom.[13] But it remained silent on Nazism and National Socialism.

This is explained by the third aim of the encyclical, which was to maintain the German policies in force since 1933, and the reasons why the Vatican did not break with the Reich. Étienne Fouilloux explains it in these terms:

> Thus, are justified, in addition to the signing of the Concordat, the multiple efforts to enforce the Pope's encyclical against constant unilateral violations. However, these did not push the Holy See to a rupture of relations: "The concern for the salvation of souls" requires, on the contrary, to "not neglect the still existing possibilities, however minimal, of a return to loyalty and an acceptable arrangement."[14]

Unfortunately, things went from bad to worse between the Vatican's insistence on the ways of God and Nazism. *Mit Brennender Sorge* condemned the ideological foundations of the Third Reich, but refrained from clearly denouncing Nazism. Always the same tightrope-walk: We must condemn Rosenberg's ideology, the actions of the Gestapo, and the persecutions of the Nazi Party, but we must not indict the Third Reich.

We will see the same fatal error in Karl Barth's viewpoint prior to 1939. There was not a word from the Vatican on the *Anschluss* (the invasion and occupation of Austria in 1937), about which our Jesuit hero of the French Resistance, Pierre Chaillet, wrote an entire book, *L'Autriche souffrante* (*Suffering Austria*), covered in chapter 9. Similarly, not a word on the murders of three Catholic leaders during the "Night of the Long Knives" in June 1934,[15] nor on the anti-Semitic violence of Kristallnacht in November 1938. Finally, the death of the Pope in February 1939, just before the start of the war, left the Vatican weakened in the worst possible circumstances. German Catholics would be the first victims. A sad letter from the German bishops reached the new Pope, former Vatican diplomat, Eugenio Pacelli, now Pius XII, in June 1941:

> The struggle has entered a new, perhaps final, phase. . . . There is strong pressure on the officials . . . so that they do not attend holy offices, or even that they abandon the Church. . . . The Catholic nursery schools have largely been closed. . . . The whole Catholic press . . . is silenced . . . many convents were abolished. . . . All these measures are a beginning. But much more important is the intention to found for the whole of Germany a Reich Church which will certainly not only have to be freed from Rome but also from Christ and a personal God. While not knowing its program, measures taken so far . . . already suggest what the Catholic Church should expect in Germany, when the *Reichskirche* is introduced. . . . Most Holy Father, the situation is tragic. The attack is tough. The

opponent's weapons are numerous. The Church seems to be almost helpless. And yet we should not and will not despair.[16]

The author of this letter—the future cardinal Clemens August Graf von Galen of Münster—was so engaged in his fight against the Nazi Party that he merited an entire page in the acerbic commentaries of Rosenberg in his memoirs.[17] Furthermore, it will be evident that the main negotiator of the Concordat, the future Pope Pius XII, Eugenio Pacelli, should have known the dangers, having spent so many recent years in Germany as the Vatican's representative.

The Vatican, not wanting to give the impression that they were calling into question the policy of Hitler's new government during the negotiations of the Concordat, instead relinquished its power, failing in its duty to protect the Catholic population from the Nazi religious threat, making it immensely difficult for the Catholic clergy to safeguard Jewish lives. This sad legacy of the German Catholic Church and the Holy See will have serious repercussions on the thoughts and theories of Gaston Fessard and Pierre Chaillet, the French Jesuits of the Christian Resistance in France, and their clandestine newspaper, *The Christian Witness* (*Témoignage Chrétien*), which we will discuss in part III.

THE PROTESTANT REACTION

In studying the Protestant reaction, of course, we do not include the German-Christians who supported the Positive Christianity of the Nazis, some of whom we studied in our discussion of the publications of the Friends of Europe, in chapter 5.

On the contrary, the pastors and theologians of the Lutheran, Reformed, and United churches in Germany were faced with the dire situation of a Christianity not prepared for what would become the most underestimated confrontation of their time. The complexity of the Protestant churches in Germany during the 1930s has been the subject of several books, the most famous being that of Swiss theologian Bernard Reymond, *Une Église à croix gammée?* (*A Swastika Church?*), already cited frequently in this work. Although Reymond does not organize his content in strict chronological order, the progression of his presentation indicates the importance of a sequential approach. Our study, of a considerably smaller scale, opts for a chronological presentation; it will focus on the actions of Protestants from the traditional churches, which will in reality be nothing but reactions against the dangerous convergence of German theology and Nazi power.

The German-Christian flag

The German-Christian influence and membership grew in the 1920s, parallel to the birth of Nazism.[18] This parallel is significant because traditional Protestant churches found themselves faced with these two phenomena without being prepared to respond. The threat carried by the principles of Positive Christianity wounded them in their faith, and the rise of Nazism confronted them on the level of political power.

Hitler preached national unity, and this was reflected in the Protestant churches, despite some historical failures. Kaiser Wilhelm had managed to make some progress in this regard, creating a loose Federation of Protestant Churches, and as early as April 1933, Hitler wanted to establish a Nazi hold on it by encouraging the successful election of German-Christian candidates for positions of power in the Federation. His intention to establish a national bishop at the head of this organization, with Ludwig Müller as the first one elected, prompted evangelical pastors to create the Pastors' Emergency League in September of the same year. These pastors filed complaints against the Nazification of the doctrines of the Church and Nazi racial principles. In less than a year there were over four thousand members, and soon after, "the Confessing Church" was born, to confront the Nazi religious threat.[19]

Three prominent theologians were featured in this creation: Karl Barth, Dietrich Bonhoeffer, and Martin Niemöller. In May 1934 they opposed the tenets of Positive Christianity in the famous "Theological Declaration of the Confessional Synod of Barmen." More than any other, this document represents the culmination of Protestant evangelical attempts to counter the proponents of Positive Christianity. It affirms the place of Sacred Scripture, the Gospel of Jesus Christ, and the confessions of faith of the Reformation. If this declaration is categorical on theology by clearly refuting Positive Christianity, it remains weak in terms of denouncing the association of the political with the religious in Nazism,[20] and, consequently and tragically, it comes back more or less to the same point as the Roman Catholic Church.

Hitler instituted three action plans against Protestant churches: administrative control to subject them to state authority; an ideological struggle to replace traditional Christianity with Positive Christianity; and a campaign of terrorism and intimidation.[21] The creation of the Confessing Church and the publication of the Barmen Declaration challenged the first two plans, which led to an intensification of the third. The persecutions having increased after Barmen, and the influence of Rosenberg having intensified, the leaders of the Confessing Church sent, in June 1936, a direct memorandum to the Führer. The content clearly expresses their ideas on these two points, although the format does not incite the same authority as the Barmen Declaration.

Published in the book by Arthur C. Cochrane, *The Church's Confessions Under Hitler*, this document is revealing in relation to the Nazi program and Positive Christianity. It traces the deception of the Nazi Party from the beginning in the program of 1920, mentioning the inclusion of Positive Christianity in point 24. It maintains that the Party deliberately chose not to define what it meant by this term. It denounces the "laissez-faire interpretation" strategy, which forced the traditional churches to catch up once the true meaning had been made clear. It was all too late. The tone of the document is that of a blind man who opens his eyes without wanting to believe what he sees. It begins with "our respectful greetings," but its content accuses the Reich of de-Christianizing Germany, spreading false doctrines, destroying the ecclesial system, and substituting National Socialist values for Christian mores. These accusations are true, but they come too late, since the three Hitlerian action plans described above were, by then, an integral part of the construction of the thousand-year reign of the Third Reich.

NOTES

1. Étienne Fouilloux, *French Christians between Crisis and Liberation, 1937–1947* (Paris, France: Seuil, 1997), 25 (author's translation).
2. Ibid., 24.
3. Lewy, *The Catholic Church and Nazi Germany*, 153.
4. Dalin, *The Myth of Hitler's Pope*, 45–47.
5. Ibid., 48.
6. Ibid., 50.

7. Thomas Maier, *The Kennedys: America's Emerald Kings* (New York: Basic Books, 2003), cited in Dalin, *The Myth of Hitler's Pope*, 58.

8. Appointment by President Roosevelt of Myron C. Taylor as the president's personal representative to Pope Pius XII, in *Foreign Relations of the United States*, Diplomatic Papers, 1939, vol. II (General, The British Commonwealth and Europe) (Washington, DC: US Government Printing Office, 1956), 869, cited in Dalin, *The Myth of Hitler's Pope*, 58–59.

9. The fact that it is written in German indicates that it was of limited scope. Encyclicals—Vatican policy statements—are usually written in Latin for the universal Church, like the *Divini Redemptoris* encyclical, which denounces Communism.

10. Fouilloux, *French Christians between Crisis and Liberation*, 28 (author's translation).

11. Renée Bédarida, *Catholics in War, 1939–1945* (Paris, France: Hachette, 1998), 13.

12. Monsignor von Galen, "*Notre Combat*" ("Our Fight"), *Cahiers et courriers du Témoignage Chrétien*, vol. 1 (December 1941 and January 1942), Paris, Editions du Témoignage Chrétien, 1979, 56–57 (author's translation).

13. Ponson, "L'information sur le nazisme dans la presse catholique française," 5.

14. Fouilloux, *French Christians between Crisis and Liberation*, 28 (author's translation).

15. Lewy, *The Catholic Church and Nazi Germany*, 169.

16. Monsignor von Galen, "Notre Combat" ("Our Fight"), 50–51 (author's translation).

17. Rosenberg, *Memoirs of Alfred Rosenberg*, 97–98.

18. Locke, *The Church Confronts the Nazis*, 43.

19. Spielvogel, *Hitler and Nazi Germany*, 113.

20. Ibid.

21. Ibid., 114.

Chapter 6

A Weak Christian Shield in Germany

The preface to this current work presents a list of questions to elucidate the Nazi Religion. Among them are: Who knew and understood this? Who fought against it? and Who failed in their attempts? Before the hope of an effective Christian shield against Positive Christianity was passed to France from Germany at the outset of the war, each of these three questions must be addressed, albeit summarily regarding the German situation. This is the focus in part II. It is necessary to understand basic answers to these questions regarding the seven years of the rise of Nazism. The focus will be on the two main Christian leaders of the time, Paul Tillich and Karl Barth. We will begin with Paul Tillich's writings, because he never considered Nazism as separate from the context of a spiritual struggle, and his was the most in-depth theological study of National Socialism. Karl Barth's influence will follow in chapter 7, with an explanation of their differences in dealing with Positive Christianity. These differences led to the rift between them, and the resultant weak shield that was unable to thwart Hitler's religious propaganda offensive.

Tillich's crucial work, "Ten Theses on National Socialism," was unfortunately, yet inevitably, the cause of his exile in 1933 to the United States. His was the clarity of mind that should have held high the Christian shield in Germany. He "knew and understood" the Nazi Religion. He applied his theory of "the demonic" to better comprehend it. He explained his view of what he termed the *prophetic voice* and the *kairos moment*. Both were needed to oppose it. Finally, he clearly defended traditional Christianity against it in his "Ten Theses." These three views of Tillich parallel the three questions from our preface and will organize our study of Tillich. In the end, an understanding between Tillich and Barth will fail, the repercussions from which thwarted a powerful German Christian shield. More is the pity.

It is evident that Tillich, as early as the 1920s, found himself engaged in a spiritual struggle within German Protestant society. The result of this struggle is found in his work of 1926 on "the demonic." A brief treatise of this theory is essential for an understanding of Tillich's "Ten Theses on National Socialism." It is present in many of his theological critiques of National Socialism. Having served as a chaplain in the trenches during the First World

Paul Tillich (INTERFOTO/Alamy Stock Photo)

War profoundly ignited in Tillich the desire to go to the root of man's inhumanity to man.

Tillich even said, according to Walter Braune, that if we burned all his works, he would like us to save at least the one on the demonic.[1] In his book, *My Search for Absolutes*, he indicates that this article represents one of the decisive steps on the path to knowledge.[2] An excerpt from this text will help us understand his theological concept:

> It is my belief that this concept is of not only historical but also dogmatic and above all ethical importance, and that it should not be listed as a "demon treaty" in an appendix to the treaty of sin, but that rather, it must be pursued, starting from the foundation of the philosophy of religion.[3]

If we harken back to the introduction to part I in the explanation of the Nazi Religion, we remember that Sir Ian Kershaw called for more than moral indignation to get to the essence of the Nazi enigma. Here Tillich attempts just that. The understanding of the demonic for Tillich represents the precedent necessary to grasp the true meaning of Germany's social reality in the 1930s. He explains:

> Less than anywhere else does one find [now] an awareness of the demonic in the social sphere. . . . It leads to the recognition of an opposite force which can be overcome, not by progress, not even by simple revolution, but by creation and grace. . . . The fight against the demonic forces of an era becomes an inevitable, religious and political duty. The politician receives the depth of a religious act. . . . It is however necessary to perceive demonic symbols in certain forms which carry a society, and with the mark of these symbols to engage the fight against the demonic force of an era. There is simply no other way. . . . It is thus and only thus that one will have to speak about the demonic forces of the present time.[4]

From this excerpt, it becomes obvious that Tillich is preparing for a spiritual struggle in society and in politics. The rise of the influence of the German-Christians (those who espouse the tenets of Positive Christianity) and the National Socialists parallels his writings. Tillich's view of their demonic character will take shape in the 1930s, when the Nazis come to power; hence, the importance of presenting his concept of the demonic.

The realization of the demonic depends upon the distrust of God. Original sin cannot, therefore, be understood without this essential element. It is expressed on a personal and social level, influencing our human conscience. Tillich explains:

> What was meant in the doctrine of original sin cannot be truly understood without the concept of the demonic. . . . Because the character of the demonic is due to the fact that it penetrates into the depth of what is natural and interpersonal on the one hand, and what is social and supra-personal on the other hand. . . . According to theological tradition, the root of sin is mistrust in the face of God. In this definition, its religious character is expressed most clearly. With this definition is also given the deepest vision of the essence of the demonic: for distrust in the face of God is the demonization of God in human consciousness.[5]

Tillich therefore introduces the demonic by an in-depth study of original sin. According to him, it is this sin that creates the paradox from which the dialectic of the demonic will be born. The demonic penetrates into the depths of what is natural because original sin also resides there. Both find themselves at the center of personal being and are born in the distrust of God. If original sin has its origin in the distrust of God, Tillich deduces a crucial and inevitable consequence of this distrust: a demonization of God in human knowledge. This human demonizing of God generates a negative force that Tillich calls "the satanic." It also creates a destructive form that Tillich calls "the demonic." Original sin is the basis of his conception of the demonic. It is certainly not a subject treated in the slightest by the theological tenets of Positive Christianity in Rosenberg's *The Myth*. As we have learned, original sin does not exist in Positive Christianity at all.

Contrarily for Tillich, in the following passage, a series of consequences following this original act of sin and mistrust leads us to the precise explanation of the demonic and the source of its power: the satanic. This force is the power source of the Nazi Religion of Positive Christianity.

> The demonic is based on a tension between the creation and the destruction of forms. . . . The satanic has no existence, unlike the demonic. Satanic is the active principle which in demonic acts in a negative, destructive, hostile sense. . . . Mythologically speaking, Satan is the first of the demons; ontologically speaking, it is the negative principle inherent in the demonic.[6]

According to Tillich, the satanic is a negative and destructive force of the spirit. It is born within the individual at the time of original sin and has remained present in the human conscience. Yet this force of destruction is only a force. *It needs an object for its effects to take shape. This satanic force needs the demonic to take shape.* This foundation of tension represents the confrontation of the divine creative force and the destructive satanic force.

Tillich's thesis supports its own hypothesis; that is, he recognized the dangers of National Socialism because of the spiritual struggle that it revealed. Tillich's response to Nazism can be traced in his writings on the demonic and the implementations of this concept found in Nazism.

Tillich affirms that "the depth of the demonic is due to its dialectic."[7] Therefore, the definition of this dialectic is essential. He first presents it as two forces which collide, the creative force and the satanic force, which create the base. The satanic force provides the strength for the demonic to take shape and dominate the process. The demonic dialectic is therefore manifest in the union of the force of creation of being and the satanic destructive force. This inner spiritual struggle of each person is rooted in the deep contradiction of the soul, where the unconditioned—whose essence lies in total confidence in the love of God[8] and which is expressed in the force of the creation of being—is thwarted by the abyss of distrust of this love, which gives birth to the negative satanic force.

Jean Richard, in the introduction to his book, *The Religious Dimension of Culture*, reveals an interesting edit in this regard by Tillich's American publishers. Richard explains that Tillich deals with this spiritual dichotomy in the introduction to his writings on the demonic, yet this introduction was judged by the American publishers to be so personal and controversial that they simply omitted it.[9] Here is Tillich's omitted text:

> True knowledge is always love, union of self with its object, which thereby ceases to be only an object. But the union with the demonic pays in self-destruction: either we highlight the creative aspect in the demonic, which alone allows us to speak of it, or we bring it back from the depths and strip it with the same blow of its substance. It is a strange experience: the discourse on the demonic succeeds savage violence or emptiness, or even both at the same time: the demon takes revenge for having been identified.[10]

Here in this quotation, Tillich laid the model for the base of his extraordinary analysis of the Nazi Religion. The crucial moment when each being takes shape, when the being manifests its creative force, seat of responsibility, and freedom, is also the moment when the demonic dialectic seeks its implementation. *The form which thwarts the form, born of the distrust of divine unconditional love, engages its demonic dialectic by the satanic force generated by this distrust in the soul. This demonic dialectic manages to dominate the creative force of being, and the original organic and preexisting forces capitulate to the destructive forces that transform them.*

By targeting the personality, the demonic dialectic maximizes its hold on being and facilitates the spreading of its influence at the social level, which will be evident later in Tillich's application of his theory to Nazism. The treatment of the three subjects—the satanic, the demonic, and the demonic dialectic, which implements the first two—is undertaken by Tillich to explain the society in which he found himself in Germany in the 1920s and early

1930s. Tillich's demonic leaves us unequivocal about his feelings toward National Socialism.

According to his theory, Nationalism is rooted in the original myth of being. But the creative forces can be dominated by the destructive force of the demonic, where the irrational and the foolish give birth to the idea of a nation's superiority over others. It is the presence of mistrust coming from the satanic force which reinforces a Nationalism which has become demonic. This leads to serious consequences both for the corrupt nation and for the national victims of its corruption. Tillich explains the gravity of such a dialectic:

> This also applies to the last great demonic force of the present time, Nationalism.... National things include sacred inviolability and cultural dignity—but that's where demonization begins. With the creative forces are linked the destructive forces: the lie, with which the proper justice of a nation distorts the true image of its own reality and that of others; violence, which makes the other people an object whose own being and independence are despised and crushed; the murder, which in the name of the protective God of the nation is raised to the dignity of sacred war.[11]

What matters here is the answer to the following question: How do you overcome the demonic? For Tillich, the victory over the social demonic does not vary from the solution to the individual level. He describes it unequivocally:

> There is no way that could be invented to overcome demonic, spiritual and social forces. The question of the means and the ways is the question of intellectualism.... The demonic force is broken only before the divinity, the state of possession before the state of grace, the destructive force before the redeeming destiny.[12]

In these quoted writings we find the importance of the *prophetic way* in comprehending National Socialism and the Nazi Religion. If original sin gave rise to mistrust of God, *it is only by God's unconditional love, recognized by the unconditional elements of our original creative force, that can overturn this mistrust and defeat the demonic.* This is the divine force and the redemptive destiny.

Recognizing Tillich's ontological base is completed with its counterpart, the *prophetic voice*. It is through this *prophetic voice* in history that the way is revealed. We will come back to this point when we talk about Karl Barth, because the two theologians, in agreement on certain points of the spiritual struggle during this period, definitely collide on this idea.

Tillich reluctantly undertook this analysis of the spiritual struggle of his time:[13] the onerous reality of Europe and the rise of Nazism. The role of the prophet is often discussed when studying prophetic history. Nevertheless, Tillich's writings on the demonic are essential to understand Nazism's religious elements, fighting the Nazi Religion on religious grounds.

The last term to grasp in Tillich's religious analysis in his writings relating to the Third Reich, one rejected categorically by Karl Barth, is the concept of the *kairos moment* of his era. The prophetic role that Protestantism should play against the demonic of Nazism goes beyond any dogma. According to Tillich, God reveals himself in a continual way in history while preparing for the coming of his kingdom. Tillich saw this interwar period as a defining moment in history and divine providence. Reymond quotes Tillich in the following excerpt, where he addresses his notion of *kairos*, or "decisive moment":

> Tillich clarified that for the Christian faith, there can be no *kairos* in the full sense of the term until the appearance of "Jesus Christ." But he immediately added that, in all *kairos* worthy of the name, the *kairos* of Christ is present in a veiled manner, because in it manifests something of the historical urgency linked to the approach of the Kingdom of God. He concludes: "We are convinced that a kairos, an epoch-making historic moment, is visible today.[14]

In the anthology *Writings against the Nazis*, Tillich's article "The Total State and the Claims of the Church" applies his theory of the demonic to the *kairos moment* of the battle against Nazism. In his view, such a *kairos moment* had not taken place since the time of the first Christian evangelization of the German peoples.

> Since the defeat of ancient paganism and the Christianization of the Germanic tribes, there had no longer been an autonomous non-Christian myth, to which a State could have conferred absolute validity and on which it would have founded the whole of its life. Now it is what happened on German soil.[15]

He denounces the new paganism, that satanic force which is present in the Nazi idea of Nationalism, and which, through the demonic dialectic, takes several forms to penetrate the German spirit.

> This new paganism is based on a different soil—on the sacredness of blood and soil, of power, of race and of the nation, all values that Christian ethics understates.... In itself, the nationalist idea is not pagan; but it becomes so as soon as it becomes absolute, when the idea of the nation takes precedence over all other ideas, even that of religion. By absolutizing itself, the nation claims divinity for

itself; therefore, it matters little whether or not it recognizes Christianity. Its very existence was enough to deny Christianity.[16]

Tillich summarizes in the passage which follows the idea that religious indifference will only serve to postpone and may be too late in a victory for the *kairos* of the moment over this demonic force of Nazism. The success of Protestantism will come by the state of divine grace:

> The recognition of the social demonic force makes utopia impossible, as well as a true faith in progress. . . . On the other hand, the recognition of the social demonic force makes impossible both religious indifference and the religious consecration of demonized social powers; and it compels an anti-demonic combat, in which undoubtedly takes place a powerful desire for transformation, but which can itself be victorious only if it is carried by the state of grace.[17]

A better quotation from Tillich could not be found than the one that follows to synopsize his *prophetic voice*, his *kairos moment*, and the application of his theory of the satanic force and the demonic dialectic to the Third Reich.

> The total claims of the State on man collide with the unconditional claims of God on man: . . . The myth of blood collides with the sacramental community, which transcends the community of blood; the absolute bond connecting the individual to the people comes up against the requirement to leave family and country, if necessary, to follow God; the devaluation of the individual comes up against the doctrine which recognizes an absolute value for the human soul. . . . The struggle between these opposites, their possible conciliation or their essential antagonism, decides both the fate of the total State and that of the German Churches.[18]

All the more so when Tillich alludes to *The Myth of the Twentieth Century* in the following two excerpts, which deal with the Churches. In the first he explains again the original fault, that of having sought to be the equal of God, and the way in which this original sin is projected on the social level in the character of the Führer and in Rosenberg's book. In the second he makes fun of the Baltic origins and the Russian studies of Rosenberg, who he calls "a former missionary." This remark is followed by a presentiment of the failure of the ideologue's attempts to indoctrinate the masses of the Third Reich. Tillich's exile will not allow him to see the real impact of this ideology. My book therefore questions his prediction and wants to show the importance of Rosenberg's book in the indoctrination of the masses:

> As a created thing, all reality is good; but this kindness does not come to itself from itself, it comes from the creative foundation from which it arises; it is finite and perishable, but also sacrilegious when it claims to be like God, infinite,

unconditioned.... For this reason, they are not only perishable, but also subject to judgment and in need of salvation. This is the case not only for every man, but also for all the powers and all the creatures of nature and history; it is also the case of races, peoples, states, [the] Führer and those who follow them.... In proclaiming the myth of the people and acting in accordance with it, one can perceive such tendencies to confer the unconditionality to a conditioned being. If we take the expression "the myth of the twentieth century" as seriously as it demands, then we grant its object, the people, a divine dignity; and followers of this myth cannot help but draw practical consequences.[19]

Paganism is openly propagated by a number of groups outside the Church; the most important of these is headed by a former missionary and tries to impose a kind of Aryan pantheism, composed of elements from Indian and Christian mystics. But as this movement is abstract in nature and has no concrete or living symbols, it will not be able to conquer the masses.[20]

As for inside the Churches, the last group that Tillich addresses is that of the German-Christians, who incorporate the beliefs of Positive Christianity yet still proclaim themselves Protestant Christians. However, Tillich overestimates the victory of the Protestant opposition. We have indeed seen that Asmussen's memorandum sent to Hitler denouncing Positive Christianity came too late:

Inside the Church, the radical wing of the group called "The German Christian movement" openly advocated the paganization of Christianity, striving to abolish the Old Testament and purify the New Testament. Several Protestants rebelled against this movement ... but in doing so we did not put an end to the pagan tendencies within the Church.[21]

Upon this foundation of Tillich's religious analysis of the Nazi Religion we can more readily understand his "Ten Theses on National Socialism." They are a clear testimony to this battle, its spiritual elements, and the central reason Hitler wanted him out of Germany.

TILLICH'S "TEN THESES ON NATIONAL SOCIALISM"

Tillich's Ten Theses juxtapose his religious socialism, based on a theological conception of history, with Hitler's National Socialism, based on the notion of the sanctity of the German race and blood. Tillich expresses his disdain for this Hitlerian ideology by a warning addressed to German Protestantism, which touches on each of the theses. We will examine some of these theses in the context of his theology of that time, emphasizing his theory of the demonic, treated in the previous section, and adding to it his conception of "the prophetic way."[22]

We once again turn to Swiss theologian Bernard Reymond, who gives his perspective on Tillich's Ten Theses:

> It was an in-depth analysis during which Tillich . . . attacked head-on, in Nazism, a system of "feudal and capitalist domination" in opposition to the preaching of the Kingdom. He recalled that the prophecy of the cross could not bow before the political and racial idolatry of which the swastika was the symbol.[23]

This quote shows Reymond's insight into Tillich's view in his references to "preaching of the Kingdom" and to "the prophecy of the cross." These two observations highlight the two essential points that we hope to raise from these theses. Is it possible to take Tillich's theses referring to the demonic and apply them to accentuate the religious perversion in Nazism? This leads to a second question: Can we adopt the same approach with regard to his theses which speak of the *prophetic voice*?

It should be mentioned here that in-depth analyses of the Ten Theses have already been undertaken by specialists in Tillich's thought,[24] the existence of which allows for a verifiable application of these theological concepts of Tillich—first, of the demonic, and then, of the prophetic voice. Additionally, Tillich's Ten Theses have been included in their entirety in appendix B at the end of this book.[25]

Only two theses speak directly of the demonic, the second and the ninth. We will deal with them separately. The second thesis accuses the victorious powers of National Socialism of demonism, and accuses Protestantism of falling under their domination by virtue of Lutheran dogma that declares the kingdom of God is not of this world. By apparently obeying the principle according to which the kingdom of God is not of this world, Protestantism shows itself, as it has often done already in its history, obeying the victorious powers and their demonism.[26]

What is this demonism to which Tillich refers in his second thesis? This demonic power emanates from the destructive force inherent in the demonic dialectic of Nazism. This power dominates the creative force and takes shape through the multiple anti-Jewish racial signs, symbols, and arguments of the NSDAP program, including Positive Christianity. Tillich warns German Protestantism not to delude itself into believing that they see possible progress and collaborate with the regime, thereby losing the spiritual perspective affirmed by Tillich.

In the following text, taken from the ninth thesis, Tillich expresses the hope of seeing National Socialism transform, as he indicates in the quotation above, by liberating this movement from its demonisms:

In this way, Protestantism can indicate to the political will of the groups united in National Socialism a true and just goal, responding to the expectation of their social distress, and free this movement from the demonisms to which it is subjected and which destroy the people and humanity.[27]

One quickly concludes that the naiveté of this thesis expresses too much hope for Tillich's religious socialism. Franz Feige maintained this view. He writes that Tillich "appeared more like a defender of socialism than of the church."[28] Feige's study of Tillich's writings on the demonic, and their application to this *kairos moment*, may well indicate a misinterpretation of Tillich's intention in these theses. For Tillich the survival of Christianity is at stake, and his desire is to see it overcome the demonic forces of National Socialism. Obviously, he believes this survival to be through Protestantism. But what he sees in the reality of the rise of Nazism goes much further than such a simple defense of socialism or the Church. For Tillich, the time has come for the *prophetic way*, with its own creative power, to overcome the destructive forces of National Socialism by the redemptive grace of Christ.

What is this *prophetic way* to which Tillich refers in theses three, five, seven, and eight? An answer to this question is needed before briefly touching on each of these four theses.

The *prophetic way* is essential to the *kairos* of the moment and to victory over Nazism. It prepares the way, and it comes from enlightened Protestantism as well as from the prophetic personalities chosen by God for these decisive moments. Tillich explains it in the context of a conference given at the Youth Club of Tübingen in July 1924:

> But the symbols of the Church have lost their force. The "Word" no longer sounds through its speech. Society no longer understands it. . . . But that we are aware of this desperate state and that we no longer believe that we can save culture through the Church or the Church through culture, this is the first and most important indication of salvation. . . . It is the prophetic personalities, not the priests of religion, nor the leaders of culture who create the decisive symbols. . . . What we can do is prepare the way. It was always like this and it must remain so in each era that is longing for revelation.[29]

If we reread the text of the ninth thesis, we note that Tillich speaks of the "just and true goal." He sees this goal as the *prophetic way* within Protestantism. This path serves as a spiritual compass for a Protestant movement without structure and without hierarchy. It requires the criticism necessary for a perspective capable of recognizing demonic forces. The third and the fifth theses introduce the importance of this *prophetic way*.

In the third, Tillich accuses Protestantism of having abandoned its prophetic foundation. He especially targets the German-Christian Movement, which accepted demonic nationalism and the demonic ideology of blood and race. "By justifying nationalism and the ideology of blood and race by the divine order of creation, [Protestantism] abandons its prophetic foundation for something new to paganism, patent or hidden, and betrays its mission to testify for the One God and for One humanity."[30]

Forms of self-criticism of the *prophetic way*, of judgment by the revelation of the Word and of repentance, are abandoned, and therefore the creative force of *prophetic preaching* cannot take shape and cannot be carried out in this environment invaded by the destructive force of Nazism's demonic dialectics.

If this is the status quo of Protestantism, the fifth thesis serves to explain the current state of affairs. First, Tillich regrets the absence of a clear and reliable compass for Protestantism; then, he questions the serious error of Protestantism to remain passive at the decisive moment when its own survival is at stake. It is here that he shows his bitterness toward this state of things. He mocks the irony present in the German-Christians, who see themselves alone in creating a real kingdom of God, even if this kingdom is one of a false god based on demonic forces.

> Protestantism is in very grave danger of embarking on this path which will lead it in all points to its ruin. Since its inception, it has lacked the support of an international independent body and has suffered national divisions. It lacks a prophetically founded and critical principle towards society. In the Lutheran context, it lacks the will to shape reality in the image of the kingdom of God. In Germany, it is no longer carried sociologically except by the group of those who rank behind National Socialism, and thus finds itself bound ideologically and politically.[31]

The seventh thesis is at the heart of the Ten Theses, if we follow the two main concepts of this study, which are the presence of the demonic in Nazism and the necessity of the *prophetic way* to overcome it. We present Tillich's seventh thesis in its entirety. "Protestantism must preserve its prophetic and Christian character by opposing the paganism of the swastika to the Christianity of the cross. It must bear witness to the fact that, on the cross, the sanctity of the nation, of race, of blood, of power is broken and subject to judgment."[32]

Convinced of his theological conception of spiritual struggle, Tillich virulently attacks National Socialism and its demonic symbol, the swastika. At the same time, he clearly explains to Protestantism its duty: to maintain the *prophetic way* and to submit to criticism so that it has a creative power strong enough to shape the Christianity of the vivified cross, which, alone, could defeat this ideology of National Socialism which divinizes the German nation, race, and blood, and in so doing, demonizes them. They constitute idolatry. The following passage from Jean Richard, taken from his introduction to the collection of Tillich's works, sums up the idea:

> All the elements of the national myth are given in this religious consecration and are thus deified: for example, the idea of the people as "the hidden sovereign," the "mystery of the covenant of blood," the Führer as the incarnation of the hidden sovereign, "the holy hour" of the German victory. Now all these pagan elements do not only insult God as idolatrous; they also have a destructive influence from the start for the human being and thus take on a demonic character. . . . We therefore require from them an absolute devotion to the national cause and an unconditional obedience to the Führer. And this is where it is most obvious how the myth of the people and the Führer is the most radical perversion of the first commandment, that of unconditional love of God.[33]

Finally, the eighth thesis deserves to be emphasized, because Tillich recalls that the creative force of all beings contains freedom and responsibility. For these to take shape according to this divine force, they must be submitted to the *prophetic way*. This is the case for all freedom and for all responsibility, whether in politics, in ecclesial reality, and in fact, in all human endeavor.

> According to its essence, Protestantism does not have the possibility of subscribing to a determined political orientation. It must preserve within itself the freedom which allows Protestants to join any political party, even the parties which fight Protestantism in its ecclesial reality, but it must submit any party, any human or any ecclesiastical enterprise, to the judgment and the hope of the kingdom of God announced by the prophetic preaching of primitive Christianity.[34]

For Tillich, those who lived in the centuries before the Middle Ages had an acute understanding of the presence of the demonic and the divine in life. The destructive forces did not manage to overcome the creative force as much because the Christian faith, at that time, revealed a soul open to criticism of *the prophetic way*, which guided it out of demonic force. Tillich sums up his idea of the merits of early Christianity in the following passage. "The Christological work of the old Church was devoted to this proof. All its formulas had no other meaning than to push back the demonic distortions, whatever their directions. The logical trinitarian Christological dogma is the powerful testimony to the antidemonic victory of the primitive Christianity. This is its meaning."[35]

For the main premise of this book, it is essential to understand the spiritual struggle against Nazism, its neglect academically, and Tillich's theological ideas on the demonic and the prophetic. They most certainly support this long-overlooked endeavor. Leaving their socio-religious implications here, these concepts go back to original sin and the myth of the origin. We affirm that Tillich prepared the way, in spite of considerable differences of dogma, for the possible success of a unified Protestant shield to stay the onslaught that was to come.

Tillich's theses were admittedly cloaked in his religious socialistic viewpoint born out of the horrors of World War I. It is important to note that in the interwar period, Tillich was part of the religious socialism movement which grew in strength in Germany. The question does arise: Is it possible to go beyond Tillich's religious socialism, which penetrates most of his theses, in order to arrive at an application of his ideas of the demonic and the prophetic, which also penetrate his Ten Theses? Franz Feige in his book, *The Varieties of Protestantism in Nazi Germany: Five Theological Positions*, maintains that Tillich's weak response to National Socialism and the Churches was precisely his religious socialism:

> There was only one weakness in Tillich's response, the blame of which rests less on the truthfulness of this response than on the general social situation in which he and religious socialism were caught. It appeared that in light of the politicization of the church and the growing polarization in society, his intimate identification with socialism in his religious critique limited the effectiveness of his stance. His critique of the nationalist and National Socialist elements in the church could not hide elements of socialist defensiveness. His socialist political interests loomed too large to warrant any effect on the nationalist forces who were pressing into the church under the opposite sign.[36]

Tillich himself renounced his beliefs in religious socialism after coming to America. However, as we will see in the following chapter, the efforts of his fellow theologian Karl Barth, whose Christocentrism will block his ability to be effective against the German-Christians, will couple with the ineffectiveness of Tillich's Ten Theses in contributing to a lack of a formidable Christian shield against the Nazi Religion.

NOTES

1. W. Schüßler, "Die Marburger und Dresdener Jahre (1924–1929)," op. cit., 71, quoted by Jean Richard in the introduction to the collection of Tillich's works, *La dimension religieuse de la culture* (*The Religious Dimension of Culture*) (Québec: Les Presses de l'Université Laval, 1990), 15.

2. Paul Tillich, *My Search for Absolutes*, quoted by Richard in the introduction to *La dimension religieuse de la culture*, 15 (author's translation).

3. Ibid., 155.

4. Paul Tillich, *Le démonique*, published in French in the collection of Tillich's works, *La dimension religieuse de la culture*, 147–48 (author's translation).

5. Tillich, *Le démonique*, 135 (author's translation).
6. Ibid., 127.
7. Ibid., 128.
8. Paul Tillich, *The Protestant Era*, abridged edition (Chicago: University of Chicago Press / Phoenix Books, 1957), xi–xii, cited by Richard in the introduction to *La dimension religieuse de la culture*, 26 (author's translation).
9. Richard, introduction, *La dimension religieuse de la culture*, 15 (author's translation).
10. Tillich, *Le démonique*, a contribution to the interpretation of history, published by Mohr in Tübingen in 1926, text by Gesammelte Werke, VI, 42–71, published in *La dimension religieuse de la culture*, 123 (author's translation).
11. Ibid.
12. Ibid., 151.
13. Ibid., 123.
14. Reymond, *Une Église à croix gammée? (A Swastika Church?)*, 71 (author's translation).
15. Paul Tillich, "The Total State and the Claims of the Church," published in the anthology of Tillich's works, *Écrits contre les nazis, 1932–1935* (*Writings against the Nazis, 1932–1935*) (Québec: Les Presses de l'Université Laval, 1990), 205 (author's translation).
16. Ibid., 181.
17. Tillich, *Le démonique*, 160 (author's translation).
18. Ibid., 205.
19. Ibid., 205–6.
20. Ibid. Text from the original American version, published in the review *Religion in Life*, vol. III, no. 2 (1934), 163–73.
21. Ibid., 182.
22. Paul Tillich's "Ten Theses on National Socialism" are included in appendix B.
23. Bernard Reymond, "Does the First Thesis of Barmen Also Apply to the Very Event of Barmen?," in *Theological and Religious Studies*, no. 4 (1984), Protestant Institute of Theology, Montpellier, Paris, Strasbourg, 463–68 (author's translation).
24. Notably by Jean Richard, author of the introduction to the collection of Paul Tillich's works dealing with the subject of Nazism, *Écrits contre les nazis*.
25. These theses first appeared in the collective work *Die Kirche und das Dritte Reich: Fragen und forderungen deutscher Theologen*, published under the supervision of Leopold Klotz, Gotha, Klotz, 1932. This reference can be found in Franz Feige's book, *The Varieties of Protestantism in Nazi Germany: Five Theological Positions* (New York: Edwin Mellon Press, 1990), 423.
26. Paul Tillich, "Ten Theses on National Socialism" (1932), found in the appendix in Bernard Reymond's book, *Une Église à croix gammée?*, 264–65 (author's translation), as well as in appendix B of this book.
27. Ibid.
28. Feige, *The Varieties of Protestantism in Nazi Germany*, 423.
29. Paul Tillich, "Church and Culture," published in the collection of Tillich's works, *La dimension religieuse de la culture*, 26, 113–14 (author's translation).

30. Tillich, "Ten Theses on National Socialism," found in the appendix in Bernard Reymond's book, *Une Église à croix gammée?*, 264 (author's translation).

31. Ibid.

32. Ibid.

33. Richard, introduction to collection of Tillich's works, *Écrits contre les nazis*, xiv.

34. Tillich, "Ten Theses on National Socialism," found in the appendix in Bernard Reymond's book, *Une Église à croix gammée?*, 265 (author's translation).

35. Tillich, *Le démonique*, 142.

36. Feige, *The Varieties of Protestantism in Nazi Germany*, 424.

Chapter 7

Disunity in Germany's Protestant Voice

Our discussion of the theologian Karl Barth will raise a new theological perspective of Nazism as well as explore the link between Paul Tillich and Barth. The first section will raise awareness of a connection between Tillich's theological theory of the demonic and the Christocentric response of Karl Barth, followed by a brief analysis of the implications of the link in the important Declaration of Barmen.

Finally, the disappointing resultant shortcomings of this declaration—mainly, the blatant lack of a stand on the Jewish question—will be presented.

The hypothesis proposed here seeks to bring together these two eminent theologians, not through the content of their thought, but rather in the missed opportunity of a dialectical relationship between the theory of the demonic of Tillich, applied to Nazism, and the Christocentric view essential to Barth's approach. Barth's Christocentric theology is indisputable. Reymond sums it up clearly. "God, and God alone, but in a vertical movement, coming from above, which can only be known in Jesus Christ: Barth resolutely parted company from all theologies. . . . Barth operated a 'Christological concentration' which undoubtedly made the originality of his position."[1] Barth was convinced of the need for a Christian faith well anchored in the centrality of Christ in order to be able to combat the force of National Socialism. If Barth was able to see clearly on these two essential points, which will lead us directly to the Barmen Declaration, it is all the more regrettable that he did not recognize until far too late the correlation between his Christological theology and the implementation of a Christian shield to combat the Positive Christianity of Nazism.

We will come back to this central point, but it is worth mentioning an interview between Barth and Tillich that sheds light on Barth's thought on Tillich's theological theories. Examined in Franz Feige's book, *The Varieties of Protestantism in Nazi Germany: Five Theological Positions*, the

Karl Barth (Everett Collection Historical/Alamy Stock Photo)

context of the discussion concerns Barth's membership in the German Social Democratic Party (SPD). This party proposed the resignation of all professors on pressure from the government. Barth asked Tillich for his opinion; Tillich agreed with the party's opinion, but Barth refused to resign. The party was dissolved anyway a few months later. But Barth wrote to Tillich that their socialist commitments had a different character, thus marking his opposition. He describes these commitments as exoteric and esoteric. In a letter to Tillich explaining his decision to remain in the Social Democratic Party, Barth characterized his own position as "exoteric" socialism as opposed to that of Tillich, which he described as "esoteric," carrying complex theoretical and theological dimensions.[2]

Feige concludes that Barth's remarks were crucial for Barth as a theologian, to be able to freely take a political position. However, the hypothesis that we make here would provide a more relational interpretation of Barth's commentary. His choice of words reflects a critique, the critique of Tillich's theological interpretation and theories of socialism. He accuses them of esotericism, insinuating their excessive complexity and their ambiguity vis-à-vis the public, while qualifying his exoteric socialism as simple, clear, and without complexity. If this perspective is not wrong, it is however regrettable that Barth lacked esteem for Tillich's theological depth. After all, the Nazi Party itself had its own definition of "socialism," and as evident by the present work, its own definition of other key terminology as well. Obviously, Barth had severely criticized Tillich's religious socialism, since Barth himself left their ranks in 1919.[3] It is affirmed here that this criticism was all the worse, fourteen years later, as Barth's comment, although more qualitative than categorical, blocked the opportunity to join forces with the strong points of the two theologians' views in order to combat their common formidable foe. This leads us to our relational hypothesis between Tillich's theology of the demonic embodied in the context of Nazism and the Christocentricity of Barth's theology.

If we return briefly to the demonic in Tillich's theology, we remember that according to his text of 1926, "the demonic force only breaks before the divinity, the state of possession before the state of grace, the destructive force before the redemptive fate."[4] Tillich takes up the same idea in 1932 in his Ten Theses against Nazism, when he claims in the seventh thesis the power of the Christian cross, which breaks and judges the swastika.[5]

If these theological premises of Tillich on the demonic are correct, his in-depth theological research reveals much of the theological nature of National Socialism. We deduce that Barth would have done better to explore more closely Tillich's theological theories on the demonic without dismissing them as too esoteric. As it stood, it was not until 1935, in exile in Switzerland, that Barth's own works of this period reveal a better understanding of Tillich's theories. We will examine excerpts from these writings of Barth in the following section, which deals with Barth's "turning point" (in the words of Tillich) regarding Nazism. However, it is important to note here that Barth, even at this late period, cannot help blaming Tillich for his forerunner's insight.

Everything has its own time. It was first of all fair and just to give even the political experiment of National Socialism as such its time and chance. What its aim was could certainly then be guessed, but could not be known in such a way that the Church, on the basis of this knowledge, must or even might take up her stand in relation to it with Yes or No. She had to keep herself to what she knew, and at first, she was kept quite sufficiently occupied with that. For this reason then I still remain convinced (and assume my share of responsibility for it) that the Church at that time in Germany did well to go into her starting-position for the discussion with National Socialism . . . to adopt that waiting (and that meant first of all neutral) attitude to the phenomenon. If she went wrong . . . then her fault was that she did not go into her starting-position with anything like the required resolution and consistency with which it had to be entered. . . . Now it is right and excellent when someone assures us to-day, that he had, already in that previous time, known and anticipated everything. I only ask myself and still to-day have no answer to the question, how anyone, even granting this presupposition, provided he was living in Germany himself and honourably sharing the life of the Church in Germany, with anxiety for the witnessing of Jesus Christ and not just for his own political principles—how he could have done and omitted to do anything other than what we at that time did and did not do.[6]

Written just before the outbreak of the war, these lines from Barth reveal resentment and a self-satisfied theologian. It is worth noting that Barth begins three paragraphs in a row with the same refrain, "everything has its time." From this reasoning, the following question arises: Can we miss our time, or miss the opportunity provided by God? These words of Barth suggest a positive response but return a completely different result. Even though Barth may be right, the theologically inspired thinking and choices of these two theologians could have benefited from dialogue and understanding. Barth always supported the idea that National Socialism should have had a chance in power, thanks to the initial neutrality of the Church. A parallel process is also supported by Tillich, with the purpose of exorcising the demonic from National Socialism.[7] In so doing, National Socialism could have possibly given birth to a socialism capable of confronting the social problems of Germany. With the passage of time, these two ideas seem excessively naive, but the absence of dialogue on these points at such a crucial moment forces us to think about it. Especially since, after a study of the writings of these two key theologians against Nazism, it becomes evident that the works of Tillich show an in-depth knowledge of the foundations of National Socialism, especially the content of the constituent program of the NSDAP of 1920, and leads to the poignant question in the next section: Had Barth seen their program? His late reading of *Mein Kampf* in 1933 raises doubts.[8] However, it is his book, *The Church and the Current Political Problem*, which further supports a new interpretation of the turning point in Barth's thought during this prewar period. We will consider it later. Furthermore, despite personality clashes and differences of ideas, the theological insight of Tillich in his theory of demonic dialectics needed a Christocentric component in order to thwart the attempts of the demonic Nazi grip on German Protestantism.

Tillich, exiled to the United States after his Ten Theses of 1932, established a solid foundation for spiritual struggle. However, the subject of this struggle required a form which could combat the demonic. He had that form in Barth's Christocentric theology, because in it, the divine (in Christ) would overcome this demonic force. With this in mind, a Protestant unity in the early 1930s in Germany, invoking such Christian power and such focus in the centrality of Christ, would have provided a powerful shield against the Positive Christianity of the Nazi Party platform and its elucidation in *The Myth of the Twentieth Century*. The window of opportunity in Germany for each of these prominent Protestant theologians was extremely limited. It seems that the answer to the aforementioned question—"Can we miss our time or miss the opportunity provided by God?"—would seem to be yes, as we will see in the weakened Christian shield manifested by the content (or lack thereof) in the Barmen Declaration. This leads then to a brief study of the struggle for the integrity of Christianity in Nazi Germany and the content of the Barmen Declaration.

THE HISTORY AND DEVELOPMENT OF THE CONFESSING CHURCH AND THE BARMEN DECLARATION[9]

The Confessing Church and the Barmen Declaration have been the objects of multiple studies. Not seeking to undertake what has already been accomplished, the present study is a new perspective in light of our elucidation of Tillich's demonic dialectic.

If Barth did not share Tillich's idea of a *kairos* moment in the 1930s in Germany, because of his theological conception of the otherness of God, he does in fact affirm the presence of divine grace. The following passage from Eberhard Busch's biography cites his thought.

> Despite all its limitations, the Confessing Church offered real resistance. In the end, it is difficult to explain how it happened. The inconceivable external pressure of the German Christians who sought to establish themselves everywhere, the lack of spiritual and intellectual training of almost all their leaders, the surprise caused by the pagan elements on this matter, all these elements played their role. But there must have been other elements at play when, at the beginning of 1934, something suddenly appeared in the Evangelical Church, we

noticed an independent knowledge, a force, and a vitality which I did not subject to any earthly power, but defined them in necessity.[10]

The firmness of this statement by Barth introduces the first point of this new perspective on the Christocentric character of the Barmen Declaration. If Tillich, in his writings on the demonic, saw clearly the need for a direct confrontation between the divinity of Christ and the Nazi demonic dialectic in order to vanquish the latter, it was also necessary to wait for the moment arising in the emergence of the Confessing Church under the influence of Barth. Defending the late nature of its emergence is futile. One can even question the need of its arrival by divine grace if these two theologians could have, between 1926 and 1933, dialogued more on the Christian shield against Positive Christianity and less on their confrontational ideas of early socialism post–World War I.

In Tillich's theology, the demonic cannot be fought without the direct intervention of Christ. The Christocentricity of the Barmen Declaration reveals this requirement. Comments on this centrality are indisputable. Georges Casalis, a Protestant French theologian of the time, states that "spiritual resistance was formed for the defense of the Church and the purity of its message."[11] When Bernard Reymond speaks of the Christocentric character of the Declaration, he quotes one of the great Lutheran voices of this period that we have already introduced, that of Hans Asmussen:

> It was a good Lutheran, Hans Asmussen, who explained to the confessional Synod the significance and the theological necessity of the text . . . that the six points of the declaration did not constitute a program, but rather are the expressions of a faith which is a gift from God and about which we cannot bargain, precisely because it is a gift from God. . . . Because we are not free to do or to let do that which we like. . . . But we are bound by the irrevocable fact that *Verbum Dei manet in aeternum*.[12]

Yet the definition of Barmen written by Barth himself is found in Busch's biography of Barth, and confirms the Christocentric will of the main editor of the text.

> At that time, we were preoccupied with fixing certain Christian truths in relation to deliberate and necessary action; at that time all the evangelical churches and the congregations in Germany had to resist and attack the assimilation and alienation with which the German Christians threatened them. The Church had to be strengthened by a reconsideration of its presuppositions and called to join the battle courageously and with confidence. With her back to the wall so that she could not fall, we had to confess by saying yes or no. The implementation of this confession was the significant action of Barmen. . . . Besides, This was

the only center around which we were gathered at that time, as shown in the sentences of the Barmen Declaration: the only Lord of the Church, Jesus Christ.[13]

Barth notes another element of Barmen in this quote: that of the ecumenical character of the participation of the synod. Briefly mentioning this subject will allow us to perceive the importance of the latter during our study of the spiritual struggle in France. Georges Casalis, in his article written for the fiftieth anniversary of Barmen, notes the importance of this new phenomenon.

> It should be underlined, the new character: bringing together resistance fighters from all parts of Germany, it is also interfaith; the need to confront national socialism, which presents itself more and more as a new aggressive pagan religion, shatters the traditional borders of the various Churches of the Reformation.[14]

Barth invokes this same attitude when he emphasizes the importance of bringing together all the evangelical voices in order to be able to establish a common front.

> What we wanted to do in Barmen was to bring together all the dispersed Christian minds (Lutheran, Reformed, United, positive, liberal, or pious). The goal was neither unification nor uniformity, but a consolidation for united attacks and therefore a united march. No historical difference or different tradition was exceeded, but we remained united by "the confession of one Lord in a single sacred, Catholic and apostolic Church," as the Declaration says.[15]

If the will of ecumenism seems obvious under the circumstances, this common front was not built without difficulty, and Barth alludes to it. However, Barth's dedication and that of the Barmen Declaration's editors on this cause cannot be underestimated. The ramifications were felt in France when this country confronted Nazism with the Pomeyrol Theses, mentioned in the next section. They will demonstrate a legacy received through the efforts of Barmen: The ecumenism which developed between Protestants and Catholics in France under the influence of Pierre Chaillet owes part of its success to the Declaration of Barmen.

To conclude this preliminary discussion on a new approach to the importance of Barmen, we note a point often dealt with by theologians and historians, which is the direct or indirect nature of Barmen. As Barth said (see quotes above), the direct target of the six points of the text was German-Christians and their beliefs. It would be more accurate to say that the Barmen Declaration affirmed the centrality of Christ as the only Lord and rejected the doctrinal confrontations of German-Christians. If the direct target was the German-Christian faith, one can assume that National Socialism was only targeted in the background. This is asserted by Feige:

> On the whole, Barth's response was indirect, the direct target being the "German Christians," and only National Socialism insofar as his critique of the "German Christians" entailed a critique of the influence of Nazi ideology on the church via "German Christians."[16]

Reymond is even more to the point in his article, which celebrates the fiftieth anniversary of the Barmen Declaration, when he refers to those responsible, who insisted only on the theological nature of their position and affirmed an indirect interpretation on the effect of the Declaration on the Hitler regime.

> Barmen officials, Karl Barth in mind, repeatedly emphasized that their position was strictly theological, not political. The Kirchenkampf was a debate between Christians, within the Churches, long before being a fight of the Churches against the inconveniences and abuses of the regime. The Barmen Synod did not therefore take a position against Nazism, considered as a political doctrine, but against the meaning that the "German Christians" believed they could and should give to the advent of this regime.[17]

However, if Tillich's demonic dialectic offered an appropriate strategy to overcome the Nazis' Positive Christianity from the Nazi program of 1920, and which was present in German Christian doctrines, a direct confrontation of the Christocentric power was required to overcome this force. Dialectic requires two forces in confrontation. According to Tillich's perspective, the creative force present in Christ would overcome that of the Nazi demonic and would take shape. This form appears in the Barmen Declaration's Christocentric text, which represents a consolidation of Christian voices united in their confession of faith. However, with the target being that of the German-Christians and not the Positive Christianity of Nazism itself, one would see that the united force of Christ was not in fact a direct confrontation. In this sense, it is possible to interpret the Barmen Declaration as an indirect attack on the demonic force present in the Positive Christianity of Nazism. While the purity of its message and the spirit of ecumenism contributed to the Christian shield, as we will see shortly, the creative force of Christ was not sufficiently wielded in the spiritual struggle against Nazism.

Before tackling the turning point in Barth's theology of this period, it is worth commenting on Barmen's shortcomings. The compromises with the government made by Barmen's signatories mitigated the effects of the Declaration. First, the small number of the most fervent signatories reduced its scope, but the biggest flaw in Barmen's statement is obviously its silence on the Jewish question. It bears mentioning that this would not have been the case if Positive Christianity itself had been the target, with the blatantly anti-Semitic nature of its tenets. Furthermore, the Christian rapprochement established in May 1934 at Barmen did not prove to be solid and long-lasting. In addition, the 139 representatives faced an increasingly heavy Hitlerian influence. That said, Barth knows that "unity is strength," and finds that the long-term effects of the Declaration will depend on a long-term commitment from the signatories when the Hitler regime challenges them.

The challenge comes in the form of a rumor about a possible recognition by the government of the Confessing Church. Nothing clear ever came from the rumor or the regime—everything remained at the level of rumor[18]—but the possibility of such recognition manages to divide the members and strike a mortal blow to the Church. Busch describes the situation in his biography of Barth:

> The big problem was whether the state could tolerate us in our present form? A group of extremely hardened members (especially Bishops Meiser, Wurm and Marahrens) answered "No" to this question. They hoped that a more conciliatory attitude towards the state would lead to wider contact and thus to the salvation of the "people's church." For this reason the group wanted to get rid of the people around Barth (for their theological, confessional, and political views).[19]

Where did these extreme members of the Confessing Church come from? This question becomes more serious when we note the selection which occurred among the participants in the Synod of the Church at the end of May 1934. According to Reymond, the Synod was strictly watched. In addition, the wording of the invitation presupposed a strict selection of the delegates according to their theological convictions.[20] Furthermore, Reymond adds that the restrictions as to attendees at Barmen drove the curtailment of any references to the Jewish question in Barmen's text.

> The composition of the Synod clearly shows moreover, that, at the time, Barmen's resolutions were not permitted to target anything in Hitler's regime: several well-known Nazis and sympathizers were among the delegates; one of them, Eduard Putz, was even a member of the small commission which, with Karl Barth, finalized the final wording of the famous declaration.[21]

The innate dichotomy between political and theological allegiances is evident here. Despite the strict nature of the selection of participants for the Synod of Barmen, this could not protect it from the infiltration of the Nazi demonic. The selection only aimed at the faith of the German-Christians without recognizing the fundamentally insidious religious element of Nazism.

The situation is actually a reflection of the dichotomy that existed in Barth himself, who, until his return to Switzerland in 1935, refused to mix theology and politics, despite the fact that Nazism, from its birth, had never stopped doing so. The fatal blow to the Confessing Church was only the result of this critical difference between the two theologians. The Confessing Church died of a parasite caused by the laxity of ideas on the very nature of Nazism. The pain caused by the demise of the Confessing Church was the coup de grace for any effectiveness of the Declaration of Barmen playing any substantial role as a shield against the onslaught of Nazism in Germany.[22]

Barmen's statement remains silent on the fierce anti-Semitism of Nazism and German-Christian doctrines. The presence of many Nazi sympathizers among the delegates sheds light on this silence, especially when Barth explains his regrets to this effect in Busch's biography—that is, of course, that he had not made the Jewish question a decisive element in the draft text.

> Of course, in 1934 no text where I would have done this would have been acceptable even for the Confessing Church, given the atmosphere of that period. But this does not exempt me from not having fought.[23]

Given this observation by Barth, some historians, including Casalis and Reymond, wonder if Barmen would have taken place if the Jewish question had been addressed, seeing as the famous Aryan paragraph of 1933 provided the impetus for the synods of the Confessing Church, which culminated in Barmen.[24]

Yet another regret emerges from the absence of a fruitful dialogue between Barth and Tillich. More informed on Nazi religious tenets, as is evident in the content of his Ten Theses, Tillich also had an idea of the importance of the Jewish question. This could have guided Barth in his synodal works prior to Barmen. An article by Jack Boozer[25] in this regard sheds light on this point. He notes that, according to Tillich, Judaism is at the heart of the constant struggle of Christianity against paganism. The context of Nazi neopaganism recalls Tillich's concept of Judaism and its monotheism, rooted in God's promise to Israel. Jewish history is crossed by the failures and successes of the Jewish people in remaining faithful to this monotheism and in fighting against paganism. Boozer explains:

> For Tillich, therefore, it is quite understandable that the Romans as well as the National Socialists regard Judaism as a threat to their Pantheon of the gods.[26]

The Concordat signed between Hitler's regime and the Vatican in July 1933 paralyzed any Catholic commitment against the anti-Semitic measures taken by Hitler. As for the Protestants, their belated knowledge of the true nature of Nazism delayed any significant impact on Germany and rendered the Barmen Declaration impotent when faced with the German-Christians and the advent of Positive Christianity. Tillich's perspective would have strengthened Barmen's foundation by an affirmation of the value of the Jewish tradition of historical promise to fight against all paganism. Without this dialogue, Barth missed the opportunity to renounce historical Christian anti-Judaism by adopting this perspective on the Jewish question. Hence, according to Tillich's theory of the demonic, the creative force generated by this attempt to include this central question could have brought considerable reinforcement to the creative force of the divine force of Barmen's Christocentricity, and the innate anti-Semitism in Nazism may not have gained the momentum it did in this crucial prewar era.

It is often noted by historians that a significant change in Barth's political theology took place at the time of his expulsion from Germany in 1935. The explanations for this change are diverse and inconclusive. We will first examine the theories of Franz Feige to this effect. Next, we will have to consult Barth's own writings during this period, and Tillich's judgment on one of these works, which he describes as Barth's "turning point." Finally, we will propose a hypothesis on this unexpected political reversal of Barthian theology. Feige sums up the enigmatic character of Barth's political about-face in his Swiss writings on National Socialism:

> By far the most obvious change which startled almost everyone in Barth's own time occurred in the first three years after his departure from Germany. It was then that Barth moved from his theological and church-political opposition against the "German Christians" to a forthright political opposition against the Nazis.... An enigma endures: why did Barth choose to concentrate on theology when a clear warning about the political dangers of Nazism was most necessary? Why did Barth discern a political *status confessionis* in 1938 and not in 1933?[27]

Feige offers two answers to this critical question. The first emerges from his own theories, and the second, which comes directly from Barth, introduces our analysis of Barth's writings in Switzerland. Feige attributes this turning point in Barth's theology to an intensive process of formation which characterized this period of his political and theological ideas. Through the war years of 1914 through 1918, the Revolution of 1919, the rise of the National Socialist movement, and the arrival of totalitarian regimes, Barth reflected on these new phenomena without having ready-made answers.[28] According to Feige, it is the very nature of his ambiguous and uncertain theology that reflects the overwhelming circumstances of this period.[29]

On this same question, Feige brings another answer which corresponds to the first, but which comes directly from the most important work Barth wrote in Switzerland on National Socialism, *The Church and the Political Problem of Our Day*. In his December 1938 conference, Barth affirmed the Church's decision to give the National Socialist regime a chance.³⁰ This laissez-faire attitude from the Church confirms Feige's preliminary explanation of the delay in Barth's political convictions on Nazism. The ambiguous nature of the progress of his theology from 1934 to 1938 defines the very nature of his writings prior to his exile. This is all the more so because, thanks to Feige's analysis of this conference, the Barthian perspective on National Socialism emerges more clearly. Barth's central concern, according to Feige, has always been the primacy of theology. A political stance has always come second. Barth did not oppose the socialists politically in 1921, even after leaving the party in 1919. It might be added that he did so in a very public manner, deciding to leave the religious socialist camp while giving a public speech that was meant to advocate their viewpoint. Furthermore, interestingly enough, he did not politically oppose the National Socialists in 1933 either. His interest concerned the process of clarification within the fields of theology and the Church, not politics.³¹

> His central concern was formal, that is, with the right theological understanding of the Church situation. It consisted in the theological clarification of ultimatums and was dominated by the exclusive principle of Christocentrism. . . . Theology and politics were only existentially related.³²

This analysis of Feige reveals to us Barth's tenacity as to the primacy of the theological in his thought, and the ambiguity in its evolution. These two elements, essential for an understanding of Barth when he was in Germany, prove ironic when we offer another hypothesis on the political-theological turning point of Barth in Switzerland. Indeed, what is the central idea of our hypothesis?

To define it, we must return to the constituent program of 1920 of the NSDAP. The 25 points are clear on anti-Semitism and on the Nazi commitment to Positive Christianity. We have seen that Tillich openly attacked these two religious elements of the Nazi program in his Ten Theses of 1932. He extended his theory of the demonic in 1926 to the beliefs declared by the Nazis in 1920, and applied it in the 1930s. In these Ten Theses, he appealed to the power of Christ alone to overcome the demonic within National Socialism.

To return to Barth, the question arises: Was Barth aware of the positions openly declared by the Nazi Party in 1920? Had he never seen the 25 points of this program, which included straightforward religious affirmations on Judaism as well as on Christianity? Could the shortcomings of this essential education in this fundamental program shed light on the ambiguity of Barth's theology in its relation to Nazi politics? The research undertaken for this section on Barth confirms the doubt in this regard. We will present three aspects of this research which seem to make a plausible hypothesis: first, in the excerpts from the biography of Busch; followed by the writings of Barth himself in Switzerland, including the central work of these writings, *The Church and the Current Political Problem*; and finally, a commentary by Tillich himself on this particular work of Barth's.

The Nazi program of 1920 is unequivocal on its anti-Semitic position, touched on in points 4, 17, and 24. Obviously, Nazi policy reflects the execution of these beliefs. In his biography, Busch cites a circumstance where Barth was invited to preach in December 1933. The topic touched on the Jewishness of Jesus. Busch therefore explains his treatment of the Jewish question by the following quote from Barth: "not because I wanted to, but because I was forced to by my comments on the text."[33] Busch explains that Barth wrote a letter to a member of the congregation confirming that "anyone who believes in Christ . . . simply cannot take part in the contempt of the Jews and in their evil treatment, which is now the order of the day."[34] This personal opinion of 1933 contrasts sharply with what he said in Zurich in 1938, during his conference, "The Church and the Current Political Question." There, he evokes the Jewish question in these terms: "Anyone who is in principle hostile to the Jews must also be perceived in principle as an enemy of Jesus Christ. Anti-Semitism is a sin against the Holy Spirit."[35]

In five years, he passed from the personal level to the level of principles, and from the infamy of government-sanctioned anti-Semitism to the Third Reich's actions as globally sinful to the Godhead. However, nothing had changed in the Nazi program, and one wonders if this gradual strengthening of Barth does not come from the discovery of the basis of the commitments of the NSDAP. A clue in this regard is found in Busch's work highlighting the complacency that Barth recognized. "I failed to warn enough about the trends I saw in the Church and in the world around me; as threatening as they were, I should have warned people explicitly as much as implicitly, in public as well as in private."[36]

The fact that Barth waited for Hitler's takeover in 1933 before reading *Mein Kampf*[37] confirms for us a certain neglect of the political scene. Did he do the same with the 1920 program? Busch notes Barth's reaction when he hears that Hitler has become chancellor on January 30, 1933. He defines Nazism as nihilism, with the aim of eradicating Christianity.[38] Tillich saw, with more lucidity, the true paganism of Nazism, which sought the transformation—or rather, the "distortion," according to the demonic—of Christianity in a Nazi version of Positive Christianity.

Barth's knowledge of the details of the NSDAP program becomes clearer in Busch's biography, when he speaks of the relations between Hans Asmussen and Barth. We have already met this passionate Lutheran pastor of the Confessing Church in the first part of this book, when Bernard Reymond spoke of Asmussen's memorandum to Hitler on June 6, 1936.

Asmussen was among the visitors who brought news to Barth in Switzerland.[39] The content of Asmussen's memorandum supports our hypothesis. Indeed, it is only in this memorandum, dating from 1936, that reference is made specifically to the NSDAP party program. In the second part of this document,[40] Asmussen reveals the true nature of Positive Christianity and denounces the sham of the Hitler regime. These eleven pages, containing six poignant arguments, would not have been overlooked during the conversation between these two friends. Barth, already in exile since the previous summer of 1935, outlines the "turning point" of his political commitments and their relationship with Nazism at a time parallel to the writing of this document from Asmussen. The question arises: Does the clarity of Asmussen's memorandum of 1936 also bring clarity to Barth as to the true nature and definition of Positive Christianity and that of the 1920 Nazi program? When we examine Barth's works after 1936 and their vehemence in this regard, our hypothesis can only gain validity.

Moving from Busch's biography to Barth himself, in this brief section we deal with two texts which provide surprising support for our hypothesis. We focus on a conference that Barth gave in 1938 that was published in 1939, "The Church and the Current Political Problem," of which Tillich published an account in 1940. However, before addressing that veritable turning point for Barth, his article in February 1937 for the newspaper *Neue Zürcher Zeitung*, subsequently published with the title "The German Church Conflict," should be mentioned, as an introduction. The following excerpts from Busch's biography are revealing, as Barth talks about the Nazi imposture and the "muddled elements" of this ideology, where he is among the victims.

> This is a good opportunity to say a few more words about this case, which, hidden from most of us behind a seeming amateurish and even misleading report, is continuing its journey tirelessly. I will do so in the form of a comment on the most recent communications received by the press.[41]

After having warned against the danger of the Nazi imposture, he undertook in his article to explain the National Socialist method in three points. His first point clearly exposes the NSDAP program and accuses it of imposture by its use of Positive Christianity:

> First of all, they [he means by that the inseparable whole of the State, the Party, and the Secret Police, which in Germany held public power] claim to preserve an official tolerance, even grateful, and attentive, of the organization of the Church as it stands. Does this not mean in the NSDAP program, after as before, gaining the confidence of all innocent people, that the party is committed to the line of "positive Christianity"?[42]

These two excerpts, from an article written shortly after Asmussen's famous memorandum, confronted the Hitler regime and accused it directly of imposture vis-à-vis the Church. Barth questions the terminology of the Nazi Party program by directly and clearly citing point 24 and Positive Christianity. It shows its intentionally ambiguous nature. According to our hypothesis, it is here that Barth perceives the religious elements inherent in Nazism since 1920. Hitler aligned, from the start, his conception of Positive Christianity with his political ambitions. Religion and politics had been intentionally mixed for him since the Party was conceived, while Barth spent years keeping them separate in his struggle for the Confessing Church. Seventeen years later he talks about it. From this awareness comes the impetus and zeal for what Tillich calls "the turning point" in Barthian theology, and which we will find summarized in the excerpts from a poignant lecture by Barth in 1938, and published in 1939 with the title "The Church and the Current Political Problem."

A preliminary analysis of the lecture is made by Feige. Given in Zurich, Barth organized his talk into eight theses, of which the fourth will be studied here. It begins with the following statement by Barth:

> The dual character of National Socialism as a political experience and as a saving religious approach eliminates any possibility of answering the question that it poses "only" in political terms and not, indirectly and directly, in terms of faith as well. Consequently, under no circumstances can there be a neutral attitude towards current political problems.[43]

Barth clearly recognizes in this fourth thesis the inherent religious nature of Nazism.

Tillich, in his report published in the review *Christendom* in 1940, seizes the moment and declares it a "turning point" in Barth's theology:

> No one can make an adequate judgment on a man and his thinking who does not know these eight paragraphs in which he [Barth] deals with the theological problem of National Socialism as he perceived it in 1939.... This year—there, first, National Socialism became for Barth a directly theological problem; not just indirectly, as in all previous years. Now, he has taken the decisive step to attack National Socialism as a political reality by name and with the authority of the Christian Church. The political neutrality of the Church is impossible because National Socialism claims a religious element.[44]

"Karl Barth's Turning Point" is the title Tillich chose for his article in the journal *Christendom*, on Barth's book, *The Church and the Current Political Problem*. Barth became involved in politics when the Hitler regime forced him to return to Switzerland. There he reflected and, we maintain, discovered the true source of the Nazism religion found in the program of 1920 and the religious commitment of the Party in point 24. The clarity of his analysis is irrefutable, and thus vigorously supports our hypothesis.

Yet the same contempt expressed in the other passages of this text, where Barth charges Tillich, is felt in the *Christendom* article Tillich wrote about Barth's book. He criticizes the transcendentalism of Barth's theology, which had blinded many theologians to the religious elements of the postwar political situation. Its separation from history and supra-history had devastating effects on religious-socialism, to which Tillich belonged. However, at the end of this review, Tillich respects Barth's honesty, addresses the consequences of Barth's turning point, which he calls "dynamic power," and the "realistic honesty of his intellectual character."[45]

What would have happened if these two theologians' theories had not been so radically alienated by their theological differences? If each had been able to see the merit of the other without rejecting everything? In the end it can be said that Barth's orthodoxy brought to Tillich's theory of the demonic the Christocentrism necessary to overcome this force, and that Tillich's foreknowledge of the religious nature inherent in Nazism would have been able to make Barth understand the dual character of Nazism. Without a dialogue between these two central theological voices of this critical era in Germany, the victory of Christianity remained partial. The Barmen Declaration, Christocentric in nature, but without understanding the demonic of Nazism, did not contribute all of its vital potential to create and maintain a viable Christian shield. Barth's realization of the religious nature of Nazism came too late in 1938 to catalyze Christian unity in Germany, Switzerland, or elsewhere.

This failure was obviously not total, and we will see the considerable influence of Barth in France among French Protestants, whose history is recounted by Bernard Reymond in his book *Theologian or Prophet: The French Speakers and Karl Barth before 1945*. Barth's influence was not limited only to Protestants. He would also contribute letters to the ecumenical and clandestine French publication by Pierre Chaillet, *Témoignage Chrétien*. But to finish this study of Barth and Nazism and to introduce the following part concerning France, it is fitting to cite Reymond's book, just mentioned. In the section where Reymond discusses the debate of Barth's political attitude and concerning the author's theological about-face on Nazism's religious goals, his conclusion sheds light on the situation of French Christianity in 1939, to which we will now turn our focus:

> From the summer of 1939, the problem was no longer whether or not Barth had flip-flopped, or whether or not he was right to advocate the armed struggle against Nazism: weapons now had the floor, and the only problem was to hold

on. Barth then became one of the voices listened to, not because of his theology, but because, in France and Switzerland, we knew that he spoke from experience. From the beginning of Kirchenkampf, he had resisted the hold that the regime wanted to have on the Church; he knew what it was to resist Nazism and why it had to be done.[46]

NOTES

1. Reymond, *Une Église à croix gammée?*, 55.
2. Feige, *The Varieties of Protestantism in Nazi Germany*, 222.
3. Reymond, *Une Église à croix gammée?*, 53–54.
4. Tillich, *Le démonique*, 151.
5. The "Ten Theses on National Socialism" by Paul Tillich are in appendix B.
6. Karl Barth, *The Church and the Political Problem of Our Day* (New York: Charles Scribner's Sons, 1939), 35–36.
7. Tillich's "Ten Theses on National Socialism" (number nine of which is cited here) can be found in appendix B.
8. Eberhard Busch, *Karl Barth: His Life from Letters and Autobiographical Texts*, trans. John Bowden (Philadelphia: Fortress Press, 1975), 223.
9. "The Theological Declaration of the Confessional Synod of Barmen" ("The Barmen Declaration") can be found in its entirety in French in Bernard Reymond's *Une Église à croix gammée?*, 290–96, and in English in Feige's *The Varieties of Protestantism in Nazi Germany* and in Arthur C. Cochrane's *The Church's Confession Under Hitler.*
10. Busch, *Karl Barth: His Life*, 235–36.
11. Georges Casalis, "Documents et témoignages sur le synode de l'église confessante allemande (29–31 mai 1934 et ses suites)," dans *Etudes théologiques et religieuses*, no. 4 (1984), Montpellier, 471 (author's translation).
12. Reymond, *Une Église à croix gammée?*, 176.
13. Busch, *Karl Barth: His Life from Letters and Autobiographical Texts*, 247.
14. Casalis, "Documents et témoignages," 471.
15. Ibid.
16. Feige, *The Varieties of Protestantism in Nazi Germany*, 233.
17. Reymond, *Une Église à croix gammée?*, 466.
18. Busch, *Karl Barth: His Life from Letters and Autobiographical Texts*, 254.
19. Ibid.
20. Reymond, *Une Église à croix gammée?*, 164–65.
21. Ibid., 466 (author's translation).
22. Busch, *Karl Barth: His Life*, 254.
23. Karl Barth, *Äù Brief an Eberhard Bethge, Äù, Evangelische Theologie* (Dankesworte: Evangelische Theologie,1966), 618, cited by Busch in *Karl Barth: His Life from Letters and Autobiographical Texts*, 248.
24. Reymond, *Une Église à croix gammée?*, 464.

25. Jack Boozer, "Paul Tillich's Interpretation of Judaism as an Indication of His Understanding of Religion and Culture," in *La Religion et la culture* (Quebec: Laval University Press, Editions du Cerf, 1987), 549–78 (author's translation).

26. Ibid., 553.

27. Feige, *The Varieties of Protestantism in Nazi Germany*, 214–15.

28. Ibid., 220–21.

29. Ibid., 221.

30. Ibid., 241.

31. Ibid., 22.

32. Ibid., 233.

33. In a letter from Karl Barth to E. Imoberst, March 15, 1946, cited by Busch op. cit., 234.

34. In a letter from Karl Barth to E. Steffens on January 10, 1934, cited by Busch op. cit., 235.

35. Karl Barth, Collection of Conferences IV, Eine Schweizer Stimme, 1938–1945, cited by Busch op. cit., 290.

36. Karl Barth, *Zum Kirchenkampf*, Beteiligung-Mahnung-Zuspruch 1956, 1965, cited by Busch op. cit., 274.

37. Busch, *Karl Barth: His Life*, 223.

38. Barth, Collection of Conferences IV, Eine Schweizer Stimme, 1938–1945, cited by Busch op. cit., 223.

39. Ibid., 273.

40. "The Program of the National Socialist German Workers' Party" can be found in appendix A.

41. Karl Barth, *The War Against the Evangelical Church in Germany*, published in Karl Barth's *The German Church Conflict* (Richmond, VA: John Knox Press, 1965), 53–60.

42. Ibid., 53.

43. Karl Barth, *The Church and the Political Problem of Our Day* (New York: Charles Scribner's Sons, 1939), 29.

44. Paul Tillich, "Karl Barth's Turning Point," *Christendom* vol. I, no. 5 (1940), 129–31.

45. Ibid., 131.

46. Bernard Reymond, *Théologien ou prophète: les francophones et Karl Barth avant 1945* (Lausanne, Switzerland: Symbolon, Editions l'Age d'Homme, 1985), 98 (author's translation).

PART III

The Rise of the Christian Resistance in France

France, at the time of the war, was a Catholic country with a Protestant minority; therefore, its Christian population was the reverse of the faith base of Germany. For a better understanding of this difference, it is essential to clarify the unstable situation of Catholicism in France during the war. Furthermore, it will be useful to present some clarifications of the French Protestant position vis-à-vis the German occupation. First, the nature of the collaboration of the Church of France will be studied. Why did the Church not heed the warnings of the Protestant churches or those of their own Catholic brethren among the Jesuits?

Chapter 8

The French Churches Confront Nazism

THE SITUATION OF THE CATHOLIC CHURCH IN FRANCE

In our exploration of the Nazi Religion, we have already encountered the Catholic Church in regard to Positive Christianity and Rosenberg in part I; in regard to the Vatican and Germany in part II; and now, in part III, in regard to the repercussions of the Catholic Church's signing of the Concordat of 1933 upon Catholics and Jews alike in occupied France.

Before engaging in this study of the Catholic Church in France during the war, however, in terms of our perspective of this period, it would behoove us to be aware of contemporary steps taken by the Church to repent of this regrettable legacy. In 1997, the episcopate of the French Catholic Church began to take responsibility for the silence of the Church and the subsequent consequences that that silence had on Christians and Jews alike who were fighting to survive. In the French magazine, *L'Express*, the article "The Repentance of the Church" addresses these episcopal efforts:

> The time has come for the Church to submit to its own history during this particular period, to a critical reading without hesitation to recognize the sins committed by her sons and to ask forgiveness of God and of men. . . . Before the scope and the drama and the character of the unprecedented crime, too many pastors of the Church offended the Church itself and its mission by their silence. Today, we confess that this silence was a mistake. We recognize also that the Church of France in so doing failed its mission of educating the conscience and by this fact carries with the Christian people the responsibility to not have lent aid from the very first instant when the protest and the protection were possible and necessary, even if afterwards there had in fact been innumerable acts

of courage. This is a fact that we recognize today, because this failure of the Church of France and its responsibility toward the Jewish people are part of its history. We confess this fault. We implore the forgiveness of God and ask the Jewish people to hear these words of repentance.[1]

Within the repentance document itself those cited by name, Jacques Maritain and Archbishop Jules-Géraud Saliège, were noteworthy in their personal efforts; Maritain even wrote for *The Christian Witness*, and Archbishop Saliège, after encouragement from Pierre Chaillet, would speak out in his archdiocese. Despite these contributions, neither founded an underground ecumenical network, as did Chaillet.

The second question that the document contemplates is:

What protests and acts of courage saved the honor of the Church? Here there is more encouraging content. Although not mentioned by name as the founder, *The Christian Witness* is cited as [a publication that] . . . without hesitating to choose the clandestine method, religious persons, priests, and laypersons saved the honor of the Church, often in a discreet and anonymous manner. They accomplished this as well in the editions of *The Christian Witness*, denouncing with force the Nazi poison.[2]

Without mentioning Pierre Chaillet, there was at least—with emphasis on *at least*—written recognition of the extraordinary role that *The Christian Witness* played against the Nazi Religion in France, the information disseminated to the bishops throughout France, and the work that was done to rescue the Jews.

Of note as well are the dates of the two repentance statements of the Church of France and the Vatican. The former preceded the latter by one year, and France has the honor of showing the need for and the importance of this repentance to the Holy See.

Once again it is vitally important to understand the Christian reality in France, a Catholic country. The Church of France was a powerful influence on the French people in the 1940s. The only greater influence, of course, would have been the pontiff himself and the Vatican. So in this introduction of the Catholic situation in France, we must take another look at the Concordat of 1933, signed by Pope Pius the XI, and the subsequent devastating results to the Catholic Church throughout Europe in the 1930s and under Pope Pius XII, when the former died in 1939.

France, in particular, was affected like no other country, being Catholic, bordering Germany on many fronts, and subsequently enduring the Nazi occupation and the severing of the nation into various zones. In part II, when discussing the time of the actual signing of the Concordat, mention was made of Rabbi Dalin's book, *The Myth of Hitler's Pope*. Dalin makes a scholarly and laudable defense of Pius XII as not being an anti-Semite, and furthermore, having used the means at his disposal to help save Jewish lives. His main topic was to irrevocably refute the attacks on the Pope in this context. He does that well.

Other literary works have questioned the silence of the papacy during the war years and have found fault with Pope Pius XII for not engaging the Vatican more publicly. The concern here, however, is neither one of these viewpoints of the papacy of Pius XII, but rather the fact that the points repented for in the above declaration are directly linked to the fait accompli by the signature of Pope Pius XI on the Concordat treaty with Nazi Germany in 1933. The Catholic Church in Germany began its subjugation to Nazi interpretations of the treaty immediately, and persecution ensued. We cited this when Rosenberg became the spiritual and philosophical leader of the Nazi Party only weeks after the signing. Austria, a Catholic country like France, suffered severely before and after the annexation to the Third Reich in 1938. Then, in 1939, Pope Pius XI died. He uttered his most famous quote just before his death when visited by Belgian church representatives in 1938: "Anti-Semitism is inadmissible; spiritually, we are all Semites."[3] This is clearly a man of principle, yet the hubris of the Holy See and its underestimation of the ability of Hitler's Positive Christianity to affect the Christians of Europe calls for a statement of repentance not unlike that of the Church of France, quoted above.

In the introduction of part II, we spoke about Pope Pius XII, then Eugenio Pacelli, who was the papal nuncio to Germany and one of the main drafters of the Concordat with Hitler. This is the crux of the matter. The ramifications of this Concordat of 1933 will place a representative of the Church of France next to Philippe Pétain and representatives of his collaborationist government throughout the war. This government will be responsible for the immense confusion among French Catholics. It will divide priests and drive the most devoted to the Resistance efforts underground. Catholics, looking to the Church of France to guide them, will not get direction as did the Protestants, who began their relief efforts much earlier, as will be seen in part III.

Philippe Pétain, the elderly hero of World War I, was chosen by the occupying forces as the "Chief of State." Pétain's regime made an appeal to the Church of France to toe the line on the stipulations of Rome's Concordat, and his order gained momentum in the French episcopate. A prominent personality in this collaboration was Cardinal Alfred Baudrillart. Despite a clearly anti-Nazi viewpoint in the 1930s, a dizzying about-face by the same cardinal occurred during the Vichy regime. This was addressed in *Témoignage Chrétien* (*The Christian Witness*)[4] in a volume with the title "Racists: A Self-Portrait" ("*Les racistes peints par eux-mêmes*"). This elderly cardinal, who died in 1942, proved to be one of the greatest supporters of Marshal

Pétain, of the "National Revolution," and of Nazi collaboration. Such a great contradiction in convictions is not easily found, but it is true that the seduction of "Grand Marshal Pétain" succeeded in convincing many Catholics.

What are the main elements of Pétain's seduction of the Church of France? First, we notice its precipitous nature. Pétain needed the support of the Church to legitimize his regime, but without knowing how far she would follow him, he needed attractive incentives. He took advantage of the anticlericalism of the Third Republic and the government's general disdain for Catholics who had been ostracized for the last forty years. From October 1940, unlike the previous regime, the Vichy government offered Catholics economic measures in favor of religious congregations and private education. Laws like that of October 15, 1940, authorizing subsidies for poor Catholic children,[5] were an effective means to seduce the hierarchy.

Second, Pétain's regime equally convinced Catholics that their moral values and those of the Church were in fact the same. Vichy benefited from the fact that almost all the bishops were veterans, and part of the spirit of solidarity that dominated the period between the two world wars. This loyalty to past glory became a boundless veneration, where Pétain's coming to power was interpreted as the object of divine intervention and Providence, which at this dark hour in French history led their leader of the Great War to once again save the nation. Jean Chélini, in his book, *L'Église sous Pie XII* (*The Church under Pius XII*), describes this loyalty:

> Now, providentially, the national revolution arrives and the man proposed to them is their leader of the Great War, the hero of Verdun, the Maréchal Pétain whom they revere—the word is strong, but, for clerics, it retains all its meaning and in which they have total confidence.[6]

If this convincing loyalty had been established so quickly, it must be recognized that accepting ex officio a head of state, venerated or not, meant accepting him in the totality of his policies and his programs. But did the Church know anything about his policies and programs? Pétain began with clear denunciations of those responsible for the defeat, and among them, it should be noted, was the military. The culprits, listed by Chélini in the following passage, are clearly accused. The Church, by close association with Vichy, can hardly deny those denounced.

> To denounce the evils, was also to designate the guilty, which the Marshal will do very quickly: politicians and demagogues like the anticlerical Blum, authors of literary pleasures like Gide, unpatriotic Communists like the deserter, Thorez, and in block, ministers of The Popular Front, leftist deputies, Freemasons, anarchist trade unionists, "stateless and rotting" Jews. Now, it so happens that all

these men or all these categories are, rightly or wrongly, regarded as enemies of the Church by the hierarchy and by the great mass of Catholics.[7]

It is all the more regrettable that the hierarchy was not more careful with regard to the Marshal's program, or more precisely, the lack of a program. Chélini notes that this was a gap common with the majority of French Catholics.

> Having taken so comforting a stance, Catholics are not thinking to take an inventory of Pétain's program not yet presented, an inventory that they would not be capable of taking at any rate due to the state of moral prostration into which they find themselves plunged by defeat.[8]

Once established, the "National Revolution" program, with its conservative policies and its motto, "Work, Family, Fatherland," pleased French Catholics, who, in June 1940, were massively Pétain supporters.[9] However, these naive illusions diminished considerably after the famous meeting of Pétain and Hitler in Montoire in October of the same year. Renée Bédarida noticed a change in the Catholic population, which was more suspicious after Montoire.[10] Étienne Fouilloux also refers in his book, *The French Christians Between Crisis and Liberation*, to this equivocal adhesion of the majority of French Pétain supporters, using a timely metaphor:

> Thus, French believers are distributed well, like the enormous majority of their compatriots, in the vast space which separates the two minority poles that are Collaboration and Resistance. Initially fervent for Pétain, they deviate from him more or less discreetly at the phagocyting of the French State by the Nazi octopus.[11]

This conclusion is reinforced by the opinion of the American historian, Robert Paxton, in his book, *Vichy France: Old Guard, New Order*. In his discussion of the National Revolution, he deduces that the Vichy regime simply resolved certain questions that remained without reply since the separation of the Church and the State in 1905. The weakening of this separation after 1940 and, finally, the massive deportation of Jews during the summer of 1942, provoked the opposition of a number of the members of the religious hierarchy. Paxton concludes that "Vichy divided the Church of France as much as it divided France itself."[12]

Before turning our attention to the Church of France, Paxton's analysis of the laws passed by Vichy against the Jews bears mentioning. Pétain worried, according to Paxton's research, about the opinion of Rome concerning the anti-Semitic laws of 1941. In another of Paxton's books, *Vichy and the Jews*, he successfully provides a glimpse of the mentality of Pétain's regime.

Through contact with his representative at the Vatican, Léon Bérard, Pétain sought the approbation of the Holy See concerning his anti-Jewish legislation. Bérard replied in a detailed report that the Vatican was only concerned for the Jews converted to Christianity. These Jews were no longer considered Jewish, but were part of the Body of Christ. Therefore, the Vatican accorded tacit freedom to act on those who did not fall into that category. His conscience appeased, Pétain began a political persecution of the Jews which pleased the Nazis, with the implicit approval of Rome. Vichy looked to please the Third Reich, aided by the strictly religious position of the Holy See in regard to cases of converted Jews.[13]

If the Church of France was collaborationist from the start of the Vichy regime, it is astonishing that the official document which recognized Pétain only appeared a year later. Despite its late appearance, it is important to analyze its content and its influence on the second document to be presented, that of the implementation of official church directives. The official text of the Assembly of Cardinals and Archbishops (*l'Assemblée des cardinaux et archevêques*) (ACA) was finally released on July 24, 1941. From this episcopal text, author Renée Bédarida draws out three lines of conduct required by the ACA from both the clergy and the faithful.

First, the obligation to loyally submit to the established power had been part of the doctrine of the Church since St. Paul, but, as the next section will indicate, when we examine the debate on the interpretation of "legitimate power," we can see that the Vichy regime was not considered legitimate by everyone, and even if its power had been "established," the debate focused essentially on the degree of loyalty.

The second expected conduct of the occupied French population was the insistence on veneration for the head of state—namely, Pétain—as well as the call to rally the nation to his work of recovery. The idea of France even existing as a nation was drawn into question, as the Nazi division of the country into various zones certainly had never been seen before. J. Duquesne in his book, *Les Catholiques français sous l'occupation* (*French Catholics under the Occupation*), explains, like the majority of French historians, "that, by the text of July 24, 1941, the episcopate went beyond what was required in the traditional doctrine of the Church on loyalty due to established power."[14] We can note here the irony of the situation of the Catholic Church, where, in Germany and Austria, she was repeatedly accused and reprimanded for playing politics; in France, on the other hand, she was encouraged to do so as long as it supported those who supported the heavy grip of the Reich. This Nazi utilitarian strategy would not be ignored, either by the French Christian resistance or by their underground publication, *The Christian Witness*.

The third element cited as expected behavior for the episcopate and the population at large was the expression of desired unity by the ACA. Renée Bédarida explains it as follows:

> These instructions the episcopate will maintain until the Liberation, and will persist in its will to make the Church and the Christians speak "with one voice," so much does it fear divisions (which, moreover, it is in no way ignorant of, including among the clergy).[15]

This leads to the execution of these required behaviors in action, which, for the Jesuits, was not long in coming. Written on the same day as the ACA document, this implementation for the Society of Jesus (The Jesuits) was written by Father Norbert de Boynes, assistant of the Jesuit order of France. The text was accompanied by a recommendation to make it a public reading.[16] In Renée Bédarida's biography of Pierre Chaillet, a long extract from this document is cited, which leaves no margin for error in its interpretation. It is evident in its content that it targets certain priests, with the intention of warning them of the risks of engaging in Christian spiritual resistance.

> Here are the guidelines that I believe I must give you in conscience to face today's difficulties. In defeated France there exists a legitimate government, the chief of which, universally esteemed by honest people for his patriotism, his devotion and his disinterestedness, is Marshal Pétain. Apart from this government there is no other French government. . . . Besides this established government there is the fact of dissidence which tends to destroy the unity of France. . . . We must first accept the established government and obey it in all that is not contrary to the law of God, whatever our political preferences. In any case, we must not oppose it either inside our communities or outside. We must even use our influence where it is exercised, to induce souls, if necessary, to practice the obedience that all, especially Catholics, owe to the Head of State. . . . Having said this, it is clear that, for the same supernatural reasons, we must in no way encourage dissent. . . . Too much has been said in certain circles, even in the entourage of the government and in high ecclesiastical spheres, that the Jesuits were opposed to the government of Marshal Pétain. . . . Without wishing to exaggerate, you can easily imagine what influence these rumors can have on the government.[17]

After reading this document, it must be remembered that it came out in July 1941, more than a year after the defeat. Acts of resistance had already been happening for months, and the first volume of *The Christian Witness* was in fact released less than four months after the defeat. Nevertheless, this text forces each Jesuit priest to decide, in the face of his own conscience, on resistance, whether within the Jesuit order or on acts of dissent in general. As Renée Bédarida wonders in her biography of Father Chaillet, what internal debates might have been stirred up among a number of Jesuits, caught between the imperatives of obedience and the dictates of conscience?[18] We obviously think of Fathers Chaillet and Fessard, who by their training fully understood the Nazi threat and could not accept any compromise. For them, the sentence of the document, "everything that is not contrary to the law of God," would dictate their actions against the Catholic Church hierarchy and in the Christian resistance movement.

But the question still arises: Why did the ACA not consider the warnings of Christians from across the Rhine, either Protestant or Catholic? Two main explanations can be advanced: first, the presence of a Vatican nuncio (representative) to the new regime, who served as the supreme validation for the ACA. Renée Bédarida explains:

> Legally invested with full powers, Marshal Pétain hastened the next day to assassinate the French State. . . . His government is recognized by many States which accredit their ambassadors in Vichy, including the United States, the USSR and the Vatican. The apostolic nuncio, Monsignor Valerio Valeri, will remain in this post during the four years of Vichy, which will not be without consequence for the Church of France, since the Vatican seems to legitimize the regime of the Marshal.[19]

However, Catholic intellectuals who were opposed to the regime remembered the encyclical of Pope Pius XI, *Mit Brennender Sorge*. After his death, Pius XII encouraged the French by referring to the certain salvation of France. What salvation, one wonders, with occupation, Nazism, Pétain's collaboration, and the treatment of the Jews, both French and foreign? It is not surprising that this lack of continuity between the word of the Pope and his actions vis-à-vis the regime caused general confusion and deep frustration on the part of certain members of the French episcopate who already did not sympathize with the new collaborationist government.

Apart from the apparent legitimacy granted to Vichy by the Vatican nuncio, a second explanation of the indifference of the ACA is proposed by Chélini in his book, *L'Église sous Pie XII* (*The Church under Pius XII*). Chélini analyzes the organization of the French episcopate in the ACA, which, because of its unbalanced organization and infrequent meetings, was not able to disseminate information about events to archbishops and cardinals, let alone to simple priests. Those who knew the most about Nazism's religious elements and the realities of the persecution against the Church across the Rhine, i.e., the Jesuits who had studied in Germany, had little contact with the leaders of the French episcopate. It is important to note that this was not the case for German Catholicism, and equally clarifies the importance of the underground newspaper, *The Christian Witness*, in France. Chélini elaborates further:

To understand the dangers, the bishops should have displayed a political lucidity, a culture and a sense of history for which nothing had prepared them. To do otherwise, they would have had to meet, discuss the attitude to adopt towards Vichy, and would have had to take into account the opinions, reserved from the outset, of some of them, like Monsignor Théas de Montauban, and Monsignor Saliège, from Toulouse. In fact, they were very isolated, badly informed. Unlike Germany, there was not in France at that time an assembly of the episcopate, but only an assembly of cardinals and archbishop, [the] A.C.A., from then onward obligated to assemble in two sections, one in the free zone and the other in the occupied zone. In 1940, France had bishops but no episcopate.[20]

Badly informed and isolated as they may have been, Renée Bédarida takes to task such a paltry excuse because of the prioritizing of deliveries to the French church hierarchy by the efficacious network of the thoroughly informative underground newspaper, *The Christian Witness*.

Even if the Church of France had been pleading ignorance of the Nazi anti-Christian persecution, this defensive attitude could not have continued after the appearance of the first volume of *The Christian Witness*, entitled, "*France, prends garde de perdre ton âme*" ("France, Beware Not to Lose Your Soul"). It was hand-delivered (a dangerous task, to say the least) to the bishoprics and was guaranteed before any other.[21]

THE POSITION OF FRENCH PROTESTANTISM

If French Catholics largely supported the collaboration of their episcopate after the defeat, French Protestants looked across the Rhine before the war to judge with disapproval the increase in adherents to "German Christianity" and the close relationship between the racist ideas of the new regime and the doctrine of these German-Christians. French Protestants benefited from the spread of Barth's doctrinal writings and their translations into French by Pierre Maury, director of *Faith and Life*, a major cultural journal of French-speaking Protestantism. Barth's warning to and influence on the French Protestant population before and after the defeat helped to express skepticism toward the Vichy regime.

Different from the division among Catholics, and on a much smaller scale, there were nevertheless divergent opinions on this subject. There was the intransigence against Vichy expressed by those like Pastor Roland de Pury, who would publish in the underground *Christian Witness*. Furthermore, there were also outspoken pastors like Marc Boegner, who would keep a certain distance toward the principles of Vichy, but at the same time have an active presence near the regime. Whether Marc Boegner was a collaborator or not has been debated. It was not the central question. The issue is more that Boegner's prominence, so central to French Protestantism, had an equivocal political position, and thereby contributed to confusion within Protestant congregations. As with Catholics and the ambiguous position of their leaders, the difference is in the effect. The Catholic confusion will push French Catholics toward Pétain and the National Revolution, while that of the Protestants will leave them, on the whole, skeptical toward the regime.

The theological influence of Barth began among French Protestants with the translation of his book, *Le cult raisonnable*, by Pastor Pierre Maury in 1934, and was the subject of discussions and studies the following year in parishes and working groups. The director of *Faith and Life*, Pierre Maury served as an initiator of Barth's views in France. The same year, he spent a day in Die with the Protestant youth, a day mentioned in an article in the *Nouvel Echo* (*New Echo*) in November 1935.[22] This regional periodical published a large number of articles on the "brown plague" of Nazism, and also on the itinerary of the Basel theologian. The readers of the periodical "could not ignore his attitude towards Nazi paganism and the battles of the German Confessing Church."[23]

As we learned in our discussion of Barth in chapter 7, he is responsible for the creation of the Confessing Church. His six theses form the basis of the Theological Declaration of the Confessional Synod of Barmen of 1934, and serve as its constitutive charter. This declaration confirms the refusal of any other source of revelation, other than the "Word of God" in Jesus Christ, and affirms a categorical rejection of the totalitarian demands of the State. Protestant youth were nourished by Barth's theology. Barth himself participated in a retreat in the Ardèche, in Saint Jean-Chambre, during the summer of 1938.[24]

Following the inspiration of the Barmen Declaration's six theses, and that of Jacques Monod, president of the French Federation of Christian Student Associations (FFACE), who will be killed later in the Resistance in Cantal, a group of young French Protestants formulated what was called the "Pomeyrol Theses" in 1941–1942. Well anchored in Barth's theses, they affirm their roots in the "Word of God," in their current faith, in human freedom from all servitudes, the rejection of any racist and anti-religious regime, and solidarity between Christians and Jews.[25]

> We were convinced that, without a deep theological and spiritual renewal, there would be no real resistance. This is also why we could not be satisfied with living by the interposition of Barth and Niemöller: to the Nazi challenge on French soil, a French response was needed.[26]

Karl Barth's influence on French Protestants could also be found in his letters, the contents of which often showed a less theological perspective and policy. The first letter, written in December 1939, directly asked the French faithful "to wage war against National Socialism and the barbaric chaos which it threatened to spread to the whole of Europe."[27] Barth even warned them that defeat was possible, and urged them to stand firm no matter what. His second letter to the French congregations was published in October 1940, after the defeat and the establishment of Pétain's new regime. Barth is adamant in his denunciation of Pétain and his collaboration with the Reich. As Casalis describes it, "With extreme perspicacity, he denounced the vicious propaganda of Vichy . . . which left the present time filled with remorse and penance."[28] After these initial letters, the information began to pass in two directions, where Barth was kept informed in Switzerland of what was happening in France as much as he kept French Protestants informed of what was going on beyond the Rhine.

What was the position of the Protestants vis-à-vis the Vichy regime? Certainly, the role that Pastor Roland de Pury played in the face of the French defeat and Marshal Pétain cannot be underestimated. His intransigence greatly inspired the Protestant communities in Lyon, especially the youth movements.[29] However, not all of them appreciated his frankness. Renée Bédarida comments on the reactions of members of her congregation after the protests of Pastor de Pury during his preaching against newspapers, which had questioned the correctness of the Allied struggle:

> Judging from the reactions to the fate of the temple, it appears that these strong words were unequally appreciated by the audience. . . . Warmly thanked by André Philip and a minority of parishioners, the pastor found others very reserved, and soon a group of the faithful left the rue Lanterne.[30]

Indeed, it was during an interview between Renée Bédarida and Pastor de Pury that he clarified the real religious division, which did not occur between Catholics and Protestants, but within each Church between resistance forces and collaborators.[31]

In the same vein, Emile Léonard, in his book, *Le protestant français* (*The French Protestant*), deepens the argument by indicating that among Protestants there had always been two tendencies within their communities. The first was social selection, which, in the case of defeat and Vichy, prepared the intellectuals for resistance, but neglected the others; and the second, which was that of "retirement," where the faithful hid behind pity.[32]

However, there were those who thought it prudent not to automatically dismiss the importance of an official Protestant presence in Vichy, and these voices were certainly not the least influential. This was the case with the famous Pastor Marc Boegner. President of the Reformed Church of France and also president of the Protestant Federation of France, Pastor Boegner took up residence in Vichy with the new regime for the same reasons as the delegate of ACA, Monsignor Henri Chappoulie—that is to say, "to follow the files and maintain a consistent link with the government and its services."[33] The motive of Pastor Boegner was twofold. On the one hand he worried about the Catholic presence around the marshal. So, according to Chélini, he wanted to "counterbalance to a certain extent the Catholic influence which he considered predominantly in keeping with the entourage of the Head of State."[34] On the other hand, to enhance this presence, the French State appointed Pastor Boegner as a member of the Vichy National Council.[35] The confusion of many Protestants vis-à-vis Boegner did not come from this fact, but rather from the degree of his adhesion to Pétain's program. In this regard, Renée Bédarida refers to an excerpt from the book by Henry du Moulin de Labarthète, *Le temps des illusions* (*The Time of Illusions*), which in 1940 indicated an enthusiastic support from Boegner for Marshal Pétain when he echoed the unswerving support of Cardinal Gerlier, who said, "Pétain is France and France is Pétain."[36]

Even more serious was the effect that Pastor Boegner's speech had in Pomeyrol. This Congress represented the critical moment for the resistance to take shape in Protestant groups. The "Pomeyrol Theses," mentioned above, were written with the purpose of resisting any influence that restricted the free exercise of faith, especially concerning the Nazis. Pastor Boegner made a zealous speech supporting Marshal Pétain and against division by hatred. The report of this Congress is published in the collection, *Fédération Correspondence of February 1941*:

> Mr. Boegner, in a very documented speech . . . shows us the imperative need to support even more strongly Marshal Pétain and those who work with him. We owe them our trust, our dedication and our prayers. Our President concludes by calling on us to fight with all our might against division and hatred.[37]

The irony of this statement is evident when we witness Jacques Monod's efforts to rally young Protestants to the Resistance, and then, during the same rally, we see Pastor Boegner arise with a message of unity with Pétain. Boegner only succeeds in dividing the Congress participants by his words of support for the marshal. These quotes would not mean, however, that Pastor Boegner did nothing for Resistance efforts. On the contrary, in 1946 he published the collection of his letters of protest to unjust official measures. These letters were sent to Marshal Pétain, Admiral Darlan, and Pierre Laval, in a report to the General Assembly of French Protestantism, in a collection titled *The Protestant Churches during the War and the Occupation*.[38]

The question still arises: Did the reality of war and the occupation exceed the effectiveness of even well-founded letters written in his capacity as "national adviser" to the Pétain regime? In any case, what is clear is that there were inconsistencies among the Protestants which made it difficult to organize a solid resistance against the Vichy regime. Casalis unequivocally notes, "However, the ambiguities and oscillations of the leaders frequently contributed to disorientate the base, especially in the case of resistance."[39]

To conclude, we note that the Protestants engaged more quickly in the Resistance, for several reasons. Since the Barmen Declaration of 1934, they had heard of the persecutions in Germany and had been aware of the anti-Christian measures taken by the Nazi regime. Most of this information came thanks to Barth and his Confessing Church. Despite this, the efforts of the Protestant resistance could not avoid the same ambiguity traps as those of the Catholics, because whether it was dissidence within the Catholic hierarchy or the oscillations of the Protestant leaders, the division of obedience to Vichy existed in all French Christian communities. The victory of Hitler's "divide and conquer" method exported efficiently, at least in part, at the beginning of the French Christian Resistance.

NOTES

1. "La repentance de l'église," *L'Express*, September 30, 1997 (author's translation), http://www.dialogue-jca.org/Repentance_des_eveques_de_France.htm.
2. Ibid. (author's translation).
3. Dalin, *The Myth of Hitler's Pope*, 40.
4. *Le Témoignage Chrétien* will be referred to in the rest of the book as *The Christian Witness* for ease of reading. Furthermore, since part III is predominantly treating the French situation during the war, most of the references were originally in French; therefore, unless specifically stated otherwise, the translations are those of the author.
5. Renée Bédarida, *Les catholiques dans la guerre (1939–1945)* (Paris, France: Hachette, 1998), 48–50.
6. Jean Chélini, *L'Église sous Pie XII, la tourmente, 1939–1945* (Paris, France: Feyard, 1983), 184.
7. Ibid., 186.
8. Ibid., 187.
9. Ibid., 182.
10. Bédarida, *Les catholiques dans la guerre (1939–1945)*, 101
11. Fouilloux, *French Christians between Crisis and Liberation*, 103.
12. Robert Paxton and Michael Marrus, *Vichy et les Juifs* (Paris, France: Calmann-Lévy, 1981), 200–202 (originally published in French).
13. Ibid.

14. Jacques Duquesne, *Les catholiques français sous l'occupation* (Paris, France: Éditions Grasset, 1968), 55.
15. Bédarida, *Les catholiques dans la guerre (1939–1945)*, 52.
16. Renée Bédarida, *Pierre Chaillet: Témoin de la résistance spirituelle* (Paris, France: Fayard, 1988), 107.
17. Cited from Norbert Boynes, "My Reverend Fathers and My Dear Brothers," July 12, 1941 (private archives), quoted by Bédarida in her book, *Pierre Chaillet*, 107–8.
18. Bédarida, *Pierre Chaillet*, 108.
19. Bédarida, *Les catholiques dans la guerre (1939–1945)*, 41.
20. Chélini, *L'Église sous Pie XII, la tourmente, 1939–1945*, 184.
21. Bédarida, *Pierre Chaillet*, 155.
22. Pierre Bolle, *"Les chrétiens et la résistance,"* published in "Les églises et chrétiens dans la seconde guerre mondiale, la region Rhônes-Alpes," Proceedings of the Grenoble Conference, 1976, Presses Universitaires de Lyon, 225.
23. Ibid.
24. Ibid.
25. Georges Casalis, *"La jeunesse protestante en zone non occupée,"* in *Les églises et chrétiens dans la seconde guerre mondiale: La France*, Proceedings from the national colloquium held in Lyon, January 27–30, 1978, Presses Universitaires de Lyon, 1982, 106.
26. Ibid.
27. Ibid., 105.
28. Ibid.
29. Bolle, *"Les chrétiens et la résistance,"* 223.
30. Renée Bédarida, *"Les armes de l'esprit," Témoignage Chrétien, 1941–1944* (Paris, France: Editions Ouvrières, 1977), 36.
31. Ibid.
32. Emile Léonard, *Le protestant français* (Paris, France: Presses Universitaires de France, 1953), 235–36.
33. Chélini, *L'Église sous Pie XII, la tourmente, 1939–1945*, 192.
34. Ibid., 192–93.
35. Ibid., 193.
36. Henry du Moulin de Labarthète, *Le Temps des illusions*; cited by Bédarida in *"Les armes de l'esprit,"* 16.
37. Casalis, *"La jeunesse protestante en zone non occupée,"* in *Les églises et chrétiens dans la seconde guerre mondiale: La France*, Proceedings from the national colloquium held in Lyon, France, January 27–30, 1978, Presses Universitaires de Lyon, 1982, 103.
38. Ibid., 102.
39. Ibid., 103.

Chapter 9

The French Christian Resistance

INTRODUCTION

During the war, Renée Bédarida was a colleague of Pierre Chaillet's in the work for *Le Témoignage Chrétien* (*The Christian Witness*). In her foreword to his biography, she cites a passage in a book by Michel Debré, Resistance fighter and prime minister under de Gaulle. His book, *Trois républiques pour une France: Mémoires* (*Three Republics for One France: Memoirs*), presents a description of Father Chaillet that is both dense and concise, and to which we will refer in the presentation of this hero of the Christian spiritual resistance.

> During the dark years when France lived [with] the presence of Vichy and Berlin, there began to circulate, clandestinely, under the very nose of the police, tens of thousands of pamphlets proudly titled, in the name of the spiritual resistance to Nazism, *Les Cahiers du Témoignage Chrétien* [*The Volumes of the Christian Witness*]. At the origin of this audacious adventure, called to make an immense impact, [was] a Jesuit from Franche-Comté, professor of theology at the scholasticate of Fourvière in Lyon—an unknown whose reputation until then did not exceed the small circle of his colleagues and of his students. On the other hand, this specialist in German theology had already attracted the attention of the Nazi authorities by his travels across the Rhine and by his writings, in particular a book published in 1939 on the tragic destiny of Austria since its annexation. From 1941 to 1944, the relentless fight led by Pierre Chaillet against the corrupting mystique of the victor, his indomitable will to wrest France from the grip of Nazism on the nation's conscience, his multi-form efforts to save the victims of Hitler's barbarism, made this intrepid and passionate religious man, an exemplary witness to evangelical demands, and a hero of the Resistance.[1]

Pierre Chaillet

We begin this introduction to the chapter on Pierre Chaillet with this quote because it serves a double objective. First, the last sentence of the text recognizes Pierre Chaillet as a hero of the Resistance, as this chapter will make clear. Second, the quotation is divided into three parts, facilitating the presentation of this chapter which will follow these three ideas, since each is deserving of further development.

Michel Debré describes the Nazi religious element as "the corrupting mystique of the winner," and the fight led by Pierre Chaillet as "tireless." The first part of this chapter is devoted to the theological preparation for Chaillet's fight against Nazism. The influence of the nineteenth-century German theologian Johann Adam Möhler[2] will create the base from which will emerge three central ideas in Chaillet's own thought. First is his quest for true Christian unity, which served as the impetus of the ecumenism of *The Christian Witness*. Second are Möhler's writings on the unity of the early Church. These two points will inspire the spiritual lucidity of Chaillet's work during the Nazi period. The third relates to Möhler's emphasis on the power of religious devotion, which will fuel Chaillet's single-minded drive in the Christian struggle against Nazism. To conclude this first part about the importance of the early Church example in Chaillet's preparation, we will review a connection to Paul Tillich's "Ten Theses on National Socialism," previously studied. This will show the common spiritual orientation of both key figures in the German and French Christian resistance.

In the second part, we will present, as Michel Debré described, "the indomitable will [of Pierre Chaillet] to wrest France's conscience from the grip of Nazism."[3] The emergence of his mission in France, after the publication of his testimonial book about the suffering caused by the Austrian annexation in 1938, will be studied, coupled with his prophetic message to the French people through the spiritual battle exemplified by the clandestine publications of *The Christian Witness*.

The master work of Pierre Chaillet, *The Christian Witness*, will be the subject of chapter 10. Its unrelenting goal in influencing the Catholic hierarchy in France, collaborating with French Protestantism and working tirelessly to help save the Jews in France, is a story whose recognition is long overdue.

CHAILLET'S FIGHT AGAINST NAZISM

Pierre Chaillet was a professor of theology at the scholasticate (a college-level school for men preparing for the priesthood) of Fourvière in Lyon. Little known because of his frequent trips and stays abroad, notably in Jersey, Algiers, Rome, and especially in Austria and Germany, this Jesuit was a reserved, discreet man, but one of passionate convictions. He knew how to dominate this passion with remarkable delicacy and showed a warm kindness.[4] These qualities would serve him well later in the Resistance. It should also be added that living in Lyon, the center of Resistance activity and a place close to the French Protestant communities, would be a blessing once the occupation was established and the work of the Resistance had begun.

Pierre Chaillet was part of a very small group of Catholic intellectuals who were interested in ecumenism and the unity of Christians. According to Bédarida, "Already for some time Pierre Chaillet [had] frequented the small academic group in Lyon enamored of ecumenism around Abbot Couturier."[5] Because of his specialty in German theology, Chaillet focused his work on the Catholic School of Tübingen, about which he would write a thesis during his stay in Rome.[6] Tübingen had undertaken, at the end of the nineteenth century, to breathe new life into the German Catholic Church, which had gone through a period of decline and had a minority status in a two-thirds Lutheran country. The work of Johann Adam Möhler, a theologian of the school, would inspire Father Chaillet, who would become an expert in his theology.[7] There were two central ideas in Möhler's theology: first, that of Christian unity; and second, the example of such unity in the early church. Chaillet's ideas concerning this period of Christian history revealed its parallel with the 1940s. Another interesting parallel shows that Tillich and Chaillet both recognized that forces of evil were present during the early Christian church and the Nazi occupation.

Chaillet wrote the introduction to a new translation of a book by Möhler, *Unity in the Church*. The central idea so strongly supported by Chaillet is described by Renée Bédarida in these terms:

> For Father Chaillet, *Unity in the Church* exposes, in line with the fathers of the first three centuries, the "principle of Catholicism," namely that Christ, by the Holy Spirit, is at work through the faithful, and brings them together in unity. For Möhler—and Father Chaillet fully adheres to this conception—the Church, instead of standing in front of the Christian people as a hierarchical institution whose function would be to build the faithful, is itself the community of believers quickened by the Spirit.[8]

This emphasis on the mystical element and the role of the Holy Spirit in the Church deeply interested Chaillet, and was evident in his esteem for Möhler, who faced an absence of mysticism in the religious imperatives of his time in the nineteenth century. Möhler's writings on this subject inspired the ecumenical efforts of Pierre Chaillet, asserting that Christian humility can be the tie that binds and ensures the continuity of the Church of Christ. This approach by Möhler toward the unity of Christianity influenced Chaillet's writings on the current situation of European Christianity in the face of Hitler's National

Socialism. Chaillet, convinced of the need for Christian unity, believed that "Love alone attracts, unites and shapes."[9]

In her biography of Pierre Chaillet, Renée Bédarida comments on an article written for *La Revue apologétique*. She reminds the reader that he wrote this text in 1938 just before the war's dawning, a moment to favor hope for the unity of Christianity.

Father Chaillet immediately composed a beautiful lesson, steeped in history and ardently ecumenical. In these pages, before the crumbling of Christianity, a sorrow and sadness [was] made more poignant by the rise of Nazi power. For even where Father Chaillet, thanks to Möhler, had discovered "the attraction so strong and so penetrating of unity," now reigns the swastika. "Tubingue [Tübingen]," he writes, "has become National Socialist. . . . Alongside the young neo-pagan movements of the German Faith . . . the official denominations are threatened more than ever in their fundamental faith. They have at least come together in nostalgia for unity, . . . but true Unity cannot be the work of fear."[10]

If the concept of unity in Möhler's thought had a profound influence on Chaillet during the war, Chaillet deepens his respect for this perspective when he describes the source of Möhler's inspiration in the texts of the early fathers of the Church. Chaillet explains this perspective on history in his introduction to *L'Unité de l'église* and in a few brief lines from his article for *La Revue apologétique*.

> It is, in fact, the essence of the Church that the theologian proposes to determine. . . . It is not a question of dreaming of a chimerical return to the primitive "purity" of the first three centuries . . .[11]
>
> . . . if the Idea were already fully realized in time, the Body of Christ would have reached its fullness and the story would end. The submission of the Church to the passage of time, to the rhythm of duration, therefore leaves a gap between the Christian idea and historical Christianity.[12]

When we return to the tumultuous situation between the Catholic Church and Hitler's regime—first in the Vatican Concordat of 1933, and later, with the collaboration of the Church of France—we note an interesting coexistence between the drama of the Church and the coming of war. It is an interesting subject to be sure. It suffices here to ask these questions and to deduce from Möhler's theology that Chaillet sees the Church develop and progress in spite of itself. This primacy of the presence of the Spirit of Christ in the unfolding of Christian history attracts Pierre Chaillet and convinces him of the veracity of his theological convictions. It also establishes a close link to the *kairos moments* of Tillich's theology.

This conviction leads us, therefore, to the last element of Möhler's influence on Chaillet's thought—that is, the relationship between Church and State during the time of the early Church. Here, Chaillet finds surprising parallels between spiritual requirements from that distant time and the difficult times of the Third Reich. In his in-depth study of Möhler's thought on the relations of Church and State, Chaillet was particularly interested in "the confrontation between the early Church and the Roman Empire which could serve to clarify the confrontations of the twentieth century."[13] In what context do we find parallels between two eras that are so far apart? In May 1938, Chaillet published an article in *La Vie intellectuelle*, "The Freedom of the Church," where he explained that one of the problems of Christian unity lay in the relationship between Church and State. Renée Bédarida cites his observation:

> This conflict risks, in fact, becoming more acute than ever between the Church and secular power. . . . The most skillful accommodations of concordatory formulas would prove ineffective to safeguard the freedom of the Church, without a deepening and a purification of the Christian attitude to the new behavior of states and nations.[14]

This article helps to understand the deep motivations of Pierre Chaillet because it reinforces his intransigent position among Christians in the face of a repressive and abusive State. In her biography of Chaillet, Renée Bédarida insists on its importance because it contains, in its content, the key to the mystery of Chaillet's writings and actions in spiritual resistance:

> This document, centered on the double necessity of fidelity and witnessing for Christians, is therefore essential to understand the future choices of its author, while confirming the close link existing between Chaillet's adherence to Möhler's theology and his future commitment to spiritual resistance.[15]

To conclude this first part, treating the spiritual foundations of Chaillet's mission against Nazism, it is very interesting to briefly discuss the parallel that exists between Paul Tillich and Pierre Chaillet regarding the example of the early Church. Indeed, the eighth of Tillich's "Ten Theses on National Socialism" speaks directly of the early Church in the context of the duty of Protestantism: "[Protestantism] must subdue any party as well as any human or ecclesiastical enterprise to the judgment and the hope of the kingdom of God announced by the prophetic preaching of primitive Christianity."[16]

Tillich even defines the meaning of the Church in these terms in his writings on *"Le démonique"* in *La dimension religieuse de la culture* (*The Religious Dimension of Culture*). Taken from our previous chapter on Tillich, the three ways to triumph over the demonic in the Church are through ascetic mysticism, Jewish prophecy, and the sacrifice of Christ.[17] This fierce struggle of the primitive Church against the demonic, raised here by Tillich, does not escape the lucid and penetrating spirit of Pierre Chaillet, because it is part of his deep interest for this era of Christianity and for the parallel that it presents with the dark years of the Third Reich.

To conclude this analysis of Möhler's influence on the thought of Pierre Chaillet, there is a description given by Renée Bédarida supporting a certain reciprocity between the two theologians. She wrote it during the conference in Biviers in 1984, which honored Father Yves de Montcheuil, who died as chaplain of the Christian resistance fighters.

> The discovery of Möhler's theology seems to us to have been the great intellectual and spiritual adventure of Fr. Chaillet.... His mission was to make known the work of Möhler.... In return, Möhler will have helped Father Chaillet to meet the demands of his time.... Father Chaillet has been able to decipher the Möhler message when he wrote in early 1939[18]: "It will take Christians heroic patience to wait for the hour that Providence reserves to thwart this new form of oppression. The line of spiritual resistance can at least be unequivocally marked and Christian courage, for a moment disoriented, will resume on blind strength its certainty of victory."[19]

PIERRE CHAILLET'S BOOK *L'AUTRICHE SOUFFRANTE* (*SUFFERING AUSTRIA*)

Chaillet's first warning to the French people about the spiritual struggle to come appears in his book, *L'Autriche souffrante* (*Suffering Austria*). This will be our subject of study here. If we concluded the first part with a quote from Pierre Chaillet's biographer Renée Bédarida, so we will defer to her firsthand experience again to introduce Chaillet's book, *Suffering Austria*. His private archives reveal his absolute lucidity concerning the forces of evil that resided at the heart of Nazism. They also indicate to us the will of the theologian to engage in the fight against it.

> I knew Nazism from its beginnings and its monstrous challenge. I had witnessed its surge in Germany and Austria; I had tried before the war with articles and lectures to disturb the peace of mind of the blind and the ignorant.[20]

Indeed, Chaillet witnessed the fear produced by this surge during his stays in Austria before and after the March 1938 annexation, when the Third Reich extended its power over the Austrian State. A moving book, to which Michel Debré at the beginning of this chapter made reference, resulted from his testimony: *Suffering Austria*, written to warn the public.[21] This book begins in the 1930s and deals mainly with religious persecution in Austria after annexation.

Chaillet describes the heavy atmosphere of the country: "A deaf dissatisfaction pervades the country . . . a feeling of insecurity which does not facilitate the task of the new masters. . . . The absolute power of the Gestapo prevails with such refinement that one is not surprised by the paralyzing epidemic of fear."[22]

Chaillet tackles a delicate chapter in which he expresses his disappointment with the disconcerting attitude of the Austrian hierarchy. He found there the same mindset he had found with the German Church during the preceding five years. Did the Austrian Church ignore this, or did it think that it would not risk the same fate by being larger and more powerful? Chaillet asked himself if perhaps these "good dispositions" were due in part to ignorance, because, he writes:

> The Austrian episcopate may, at the beginning, [have] been mistaken in tactics, by not taking opportunistically enough advantage of the lessons of the experience of German Catholicism for five years in the face of the gigantic enterprise of de-Christianization methodically pursued by National Socialism in its struggle against the Churches.[23]

Chaillet paid the price for his convictions because he became a victim of the ambiguous relationship between the Church and State during these dark years. First, his book, *Suffering Austria*, "did not escape the vigilance of the Nazi censors, and from 1940 [on] he [would] be registered on the famous Otto list of banned publications."[24] Chaillet was hunted abroad because of this book, and he found it difficult to return to France. "In June 1940, he was on a mission in Budapest, at the French embassy. . . . Already noticed by the German agents who abounded in the Balkans, he managed to return to France, via Turkey and Syria."[25]

The fate of Christianity in Germany and Austria would precipitate the deep analysis of Pierre Chaillet and his definitive engagement in his mission to warn French Christians against the dangers of Nazism. Bédarida evokes his determination that emerged from his incredulity. "The spectacle given to him by annexed Austria . . . the unbearable spectacle of a Church facing harassment from the occupier and that of an anti-Semitic policy at work, completely revolted his conscience."[26]

In the last chapters of his study of the Austrian situation, he makes a lucid warning to France. Denouncing the atrocity of Nazi acts and appealing to the French conscience, they would serve as an important precursor to the masterpiece of Resistance by Gaston Fessard, *France, Beware of Losing Your Soul*, which we will study briefly at the end of part III. Pierre Chaillet's text resonates with his courageous character—that of a French Christian who is preparing for battle. Bédarida recognizes the prescient nature of his work, which tragically predicts what is awaiting France.

> In this sadly prophetic little book, everything is planned in advance: submission to Hitler's ultimatums which leads to definitive capitulation, terror which provokes paralyzing fear, passionate anti-Semitism ... brutal measures against the Churches.[27]

Our brief analysis of *Suffering Austria* will be in three parts, following the order given by the author: the Nazi method in politics, racial politics, and theology. Chaillet wrote the foreword to *Suffering Austria* in June 1939, three months before France declared war on Germany. The book was published in Paris and registered on the famous Otto list. In his introduction to his last chapter, Chaillet addresses the French people directly, accentuating the prophetic nature of the work by sounding the alarm against the laissez-faire attitude of the "Munich" mentality of the late 1930s. He explains to the French that they are deluding themselves by embracing such an attitude.

> In a very short time, where it was almost compromising to speak of Germany without passion, we tried loyally to bring to the study of Franco-German relations and the problems which divide our two peoples, a sympathy which gives rise to mutual trust and esteem. . . . The situations are now tragically reversed. . . . In this resolute desire for peace, we cannot, however, acquiesce to a confidence that will leave us blind.[28]

It is here that Chaillet begins his message to the French. It introduces the reality of the fraudulent Nazi order with an incentive to lead both as a Christian and as a Frenchman against this order. "The Hitlerian Order is powerful. . . . This Order, in fact, is established on an overly disturbing betrayal of moral and spiritual values, for us to resign ourselves, even by our silence, to becoming the accomplice of a pacifist hypnosis which threatens to paralyze the salutary reaction of consciences determined not to sacrifice to fear the honor of freedom."[29]

It is obvious that Möhler's concept of unity manifests itself in this collective call to Christian moral and spiritual values. Chaillet's reference to freedom reminds his compatriots of their French heritage, and his reference to sacrifice and fear harkens back to the early Church, in the need for courage in the face of oppression. But this harkening back to the early Church and Chaillet's prophetic spirit are found in the following words, which resonate with the spirit of the Church in the first centuries. He will deal with the three essential points in this message that reveals its intimate form and its unequivocal conviction.

My French compatriots, we do not have to meddle with the internal policy of the Third Reich. . . . But being human and Christian, we cannot give up questioning anxiously the principle of this Force and the means implemented to carry out this Order, which because of this very Force, pretends to impose on the world a new Order; we cannot be indifferent to the spiritual drama menacing to damage the human and Christian ideal. In the face of this drama. . . . It is enough to present here the requirements of a witness's sincerity who is content to let the facts speak, of which Hitler's regime in Austria makes no mystery, but glorifies. In this time of contempt, for those who know how to keep, resolute and lucid, the courage to hope, the growing shadow of the swastika on Europe is a serious warning; it imposes the urgency of a fundamental option, which gives the life of peoples as well as individuals control over their destiny.[30]

The First Lesson of *Suffering Austria*: The Systematic Glorification of Political Murder

Violence against dissent is part of any totalitarian regime, but the difference with the Nazi Party, explains Chaillet, "is that they organize terror as an ordinary means of government."[31] The author cites the murders, the disappearances, the arrests, but according to him, "what perhaps exceeds most any measure, is the systematic glorification of political murder."[32] The great men of contemporary Austrian history, such as Chancellor Dollfuss (assassinated in 1934 by a member of the Austrian Nazi Party) and Chancellor Schuschnigg (held prisoner at the Hotel Métropole), became traitors in the Nazi revisionism of "Greater Germany." Even children learn about these deviations from history at school, and their parents are afraid to contradict them.[33]

Yet this is not the worst. Anti-Semitism and its basis in "Nazi theology" will be the subject of the next section.

The Second Lesson of *Suffering Austria*: The Relentless Racism of the Third Reich

A more poignant study of Chaillet's writings on anti-Jewish racism will be presented in the volume of *The Christian Witness* with the title "The Racists' Self-Portraits." The impressive aspect of this text is the lucidity of its spiritual perspective and the way in which the author interprets the origin of Nazi anti-Semitism in a similar way as Tillich does in his writings, when considering the Nazi interpretation of original sin (presented in part II). Chaillet clearly indicates, in the following excerpt, the origin of Hitler's fierce and unequivocal anti-Semitism. He quotes Hitler's *Mein Kampf*, tracing the origin of this anti-Semitism before commenting on its spread. To reiterate, for emphasis: These are Hitler's words quoted by Chaillet—therefore, quite obviously, the exact opposite of Chaillet's personal views:

> It was the time when the most profound revolution that I had ever brought to fruition took place in me. The lethargic cosmopolitan I had been until then became a fanatical anti-Semite. This is why I believe I act according to the spirit of the Almighty: by defending myself against the Jew, I fight to defend the work of the Lord. The original sin is for the Aryan predestined as the sin against the purity of the blood, source of the virtues of the race. The Third Reich therefore intends to solve the problem of the purity of the race by the ruthless termination of those whom the laws of Nuremberg deliver defenseless to the unleashing of the worst instincts of passionate anti-Semitism.[34]

These two lucid theologians, Tillich and Chaillet, on the spiritual level, go to the source of this perverse ideology of Nazism. They strive to decipher and unmask what Hitler's propaganda is trying to confuse, divide, and therefore defeat.

Chaillet continues his message to the French after having explained in detail the atrocious situation of the Jews of Austria. He asks the French people to remember that France, a land of freedom and Christianity, has always served as a refuge for the oppressed. The case of foreign Jews could not be an exception. In the end, according to him, it is their Christian obligation to welcome and give refuge to the Jews despite the risks and sacrifices incurred. Here again he is inspired by the early Church.

> France remains a country of refuge; it is not without merit and without sacrifice. . . . It is our strength to believe that the virtue of spirit and love is more active and more fruitful than the virtue of blood alone. . . . But it is also the duty of every well-born man and the most imperative requirement of the Gospel of Christ to open our souls to all miseries and to remedy them to the extent of our abilities.[35]

The Third Lesson from *Suffering Austria*: The Anti-Christian Persecution

The last subject raised in Father Chaillet's prophetic message to the French deals with the devastation brought by the persecution of the Church in Austria, a Catholic country, after Nazi annexation. The central message is divided into two overarching questions: What should France expect in the event of war? And if this Nazi ideology sweeps over the country, what could it learn from the waves of persecution that preceded it? Certainly, at the time of their writing, these words seemed revolutionary. But, from a historical point of view, they are rather prophetic, since France was going to indeed face such questions shortly after the publication of *Suffering Austria* in June 1939, as France would declare war on Germany the following September.

Pierre Chaillet finds little guilt in the Austrian episcopate despite the five years of the Third Reich's bad faith concerning the provisions of the Concordat and the papal encyclical *Mit Brennender Sorge*, released in July 1937. Although these years are exemplary of Nazi fraud, Chaillet notes the good faith interventions of the bishops of the Austrian hierarchy toward the regime. "The Führer himself had given this assurance to Cardinal Innitzer and the Gauleiter Bürckel, who had renewed the commitment that this promise would inspire. . . . The bishops believed they should trust, despite everything."[36]

However, Chaillet cannot help reacting when the official letter of the episcopal conference held in Vienna in August 1938 only pronounces on Christian marriage and on the charity to give to the faithful who had lost their jobs due to school closings![37] This lukewarm intervention by the hierarchy was undertaken following the exasperated declaration of Austria's Cardinal Innitzer: "We have been miserably deceived. Germany came to us like a mother to her children; we know now what it means. . . . They want to make Austria a field experiment to see just how far they can go toward the annihilation of Christianity."[38] This official letter follows Nazi initiatives against any continuity in the present or future existence of the Catholic Church. Father Chaillet only makes a partial list. The closure of the Jesuit theological faculty of Innsbrück, the ban on the recruitment of students for Catholic colleges, the dissolution of all Catholic associations, and the suppression of the Catholic press, clearly and bluntly indicate the desire of the regime for a slow but sure death of the Church.[39]

Father Chaillet does not limit himself to eloquent explanations. He goes straight to the point when he says: "The Concordat has become a dead letter. . . . Hatred against the Holy Father overflows everywhere in odious posters."[40] So, what should France learn from these lessons of the anti-Christian persecution in Austria? Father Chaillet ends his book with a warning to which all Christians and especially French Christians should pay attention. However, it is not aimed at threatened France, nor defeated Germany, nor annexed Austria, but to the Hitler regime. This warning contains the fundamental weakness of Nazism according to Chaillet: an underestimation of invisible powers. Pierre Chaillet's faith in the principles of unity, in the strength of the Holy Spirit, and in the example of the perseverance of Christians in the primitive Church, which appear in Möhler's theology and influenced Chaillet's thought, are clearly expressed when he chooses a phrase from Novalis on the foundations of the victory of any spiritual State. He affirms the ultimate victory of Christianity, which will also be the basis of the ultimate death of the Third Reich: the invisible and invincible power of Christ.

"The basis of the great spiritual states," said Novalis, "has so far been their complete assurance vis-à-vis the invisible powers. The Great German Reich, which was built on the death of Austria, can find this assurance vis-à-vis itself only in the pride of its dominating force; this pride presupposes the negation of invisible powers. The power of the Third Reich thus makes its irremediable weakness."[41]

It is upon the certitude of this conviction that Pierre Chaillet warns France and begins his work in building the spiritual resistance in his native country after the defeat in 1940.

We turn now to Chaillet's masterpiece of ecumenical clandestine Christian work, *The Christian Witness*.

NOTES

1. Michel Debré, *Trois républiques pour une France: Mémoire*, with the collaboration of Odile Rudelle (Paris, France: Albin Michel, 1984), 272, cited by Renée Bédarida in foreword to *Pierre Chaillet* (Paris, France: Fayard, 1988), 107.

2. It is important to note that the spelling of Johann Adam Mœhler varies according to the reference: French, English, or German. This thesis will opt for Renée Bédarida's choice of "Johann Adam Möhler," as will be evident in the quotes.

3. Debré, *Trois républiques pour une France*, 107.

4. Bédarida, *Pierre Chaillet*, 25–26.

5. Ibid., 66.

6. Henri de Lubac, *Résistance chrétienne à l'antisémitisme, souvenirs 1940–1944* (Paris, France: Fayard, 1988), 38.

7. Bédarida, *Pierre Chaillet*, 48–49.

8. Ibid., 58.

9. Pierre Chaillet, "Centenaire de Möhler: L'amour et l'unité—Le mystère de l'Eglise," *Revue apologétique*, LXVI, no. 631 (May 1938), 513–40, cited by Bédarida in *Pierre Chaillet*, 67.

10. Ibid.

11. Pierre Chaillet, Introduction to *L'Unité dans l'Eglise, ou le Principe du catholocisme d'après l'esprit des Pères des trois premiers siècle de l'Eglise*, by J. A. Möhler (Paris, France: Éditions du Cerf, 1938), xxvi–vii.

12. Chaillet, "Centenaire," 538.

13. Pierre Chaillet, "La Liberté de l'église," *La Vie intellectuelle*, vol. lxvii (June 10, 1938), 166–67, cited by Bédarida in *Pierre Chaillet*, 63.

14. Ibid.

15. Ibid., 64.

16. Tillich, *Écrits contre les nazis*, 4.

17. Tillich, *Le démonique*, 142.

18. Renée Bédarida, *Père Chaillet: de la théologie de Möhler à la résistance*, Colloque de Biviers Yves de Montcheuil under the direction of Pierre Bolle and Jean Godel, Grenoble, Presses Universitaires de Grenoble, 1987, 59–60.

19. Pierre Chaillet, *L'Autriche souffrante* (Paris: Bloud et Gay, 1939), 124–25, quoted by Bédarida, *Père Chaillet: de la théologie de Möhler à la résistance*, 59–60.

20. Bédarida, *Père Chaillet: de la théologie de Möhler à la résistance*, 49.

21. Duquesne, *Les catholiques français sous l'occupation*, 148.

22. Chaillet, *L'Autriche souffrante*, 124–25.

23. Ibid., p. 78.

24. Henri de Lubac, *Résistance chrétienne à l'antisémitisme, souvenirs, 1940–1944* (Paris, France: Fayard, 1988), 39.

25. Ibid., 148.

26. Bédarida, *Père Chaillet: de la théologie de Möhler à la résistance*, 55.

27. Ibid., p. 57.

28. Chaillet, *L'Autriche Souffrante*, 106–7.

29. Ibid., 107.

30. Ibid., 107–8.

31. Ibid., 108.

32. Ibid.

33. Ibid.

34. Ibid., 109.

35. Ibid., 111.

36. Ibid., 113.

37. Ibid., 121.

38. Ibid., 114.

39. Ibid., 115–18.

40. Ibid., 115–16.

41. Ibid., 127.

Chapter 10

Témoignage Chrétien (The Christian Witness)

INTRODUCTION

To begin our study of the volumes of *The Christian Witness*, let us return to the quoted introductory text by Michel Debré. He describes Chaillet's determination to preserve France from the fate of Austria and Germany, citing "his indomitable will to wrest France from the grip of Nazism." Indeed, once back in France, Chaillet is surprised by the complacency of his people and their resignation.[1] Faced with his disappointment, he embarked on a dual strategy of spiritual and temporal: "the defense of Christian values [and] the help to be given to the victims of National Socialism."[2] The details of Father Chaillet's articles and writings, his success in bringing Christians together, and his own commitment to the victims of the Reich will be the focus of this chapter.

A brief history of this ecumenical, courageous, and clandestine newspaper is essential to understanding its content and its scope. A worthy introduction to Pierre Chaillet's work and to *The Christian Witness* can be found in the collection called *The Twilight of Civilization*, written by Jacques Maritain and published in the United States in 1943. Maritain wrote in his foreword:

> By their doctrinal solidity, *Les Cahiers du Témoignage Chrétien* occupy a special place in clandestine literature. Among the other publications in which the devotion to the fatherland of so many heroic companions of the French resistance were registered, they will remain as a monument to Christian fidelity. They mark an important and significant moment in the religious history of our country. Catholics and Protestants cooperated fraternally in it, to defend together the eternal values of Christian civilization, to prevent France from losing its soul, and to testify to the freedom of the Christian in the face of the deceptions

and sham imitation of a regime in order to maximize the betrayal of the vocation of France and its people, and to exploit for its ends the Church and religion.[3]

THE CHRISTIAN WITNESS: ITS BIRTH AMONG CLANDESTINE PUBLICATIONS

The clandestine publications of the Christian resistance in France began sporadically from its defeat in June 1940. Paul Petit, a spokesman for a small group of Resistance fighters in the occupied zone, was the publisher of one of the first clandestine newspapers, *La France Continue*. One of the first to perish for his convictions, he was captured and guillotined. To this first effort was added the work of groups of Parisian Catholics who cooperated under the name of "Valmy." They made thousands of posters on children's printing presses which they stuck on the walls of the capital. Later they founded a clandestine newspaper, also titled *Valmy*. These two newspapers, although of Christian inspiration, were mainly concerned with anti-Vichy policy.[4] The honor of being the first clandestine Catholic newspaper is granted to *La Voix du Vatican* (*The Voice of the Vatican*), which distributed the text of Vatican Radio broadcasts after the general jamming of the airwaves by the Germans.[5]

More on the level of philosophical thought, Robert d'Harcourt, a German aristocrat, decided to warn French Catholics against Hitler. In an individual effort, and despite his precarious status with the German authorities because of his anti-Nazi writings of the 1930s, d'Harcourt had clandestine texts printed at his own expense to wake up Christians who were too partial to laissez-faire. From these kinds of courageous but isolated commitments were added the activities of Christian newspapers: *Temps nouveau* (*New Time*), *L'Aube* (*Dawn*), *Sept* (*Seven*), *Le nouvelle echo* (*The New Echo*), and *Foi et vie* (*Faith and Life*). Here was born a nursery of resistant Christian spirits from which Pierre Chaillet would draw the best for his noble but perilous work of the Christian resistance.

In fact, Robert d'Harcourt, after a meeting with Chaillet, decided to collaborate in *Les Cahiers du Témoignage Chrétien* (*The Volumes of The Christian Witness*).[6] They wrote together the thirteenth volume, titled *Power of Darkness*.[7] On the Protestant side, the same phenomenon of amalgamation with *The Christian Witness* transpired with a small underground publication, *La Feuille* (*The Leaf*). When the publishers of *La Feuille* were informed of the work of *The Christian Witness*, they decided to join squarely with them.[8] The more the research deepens, the more it becomes obvious that *The Volumes of The Christian Witness* were what Renée Bédarida called "the spearhead" of the Christian resistance.[9] It is interesting to note that the title was almost *The Volumes of the Catholic Witness* (*Les Cahiers du Témoignage*

Catholique). At the last moment, however, Father Chaillet decided that in order to represent the ecumenical work and the collaborative efforts of both Catholics and Protestants, the title had to reflect this unity.[10]

As for the method used by Father Chaillet to find loyal and qualified members for the publication and distribution of the newspaper, there was a systematic approach in Christian circles in Lyon. Contacts, besides obviously those already established in the Jesuit milieu of Fourvière and in the milieu of the courageous pastor, Roland de Pury, were being sought out even before *The Christian Witness* was founded. The recruitment began when Chaillet undertook writing articles for small clandestine resistance newspapers under the direction of Henri Frenay, a Lyon native. Frenay served as a captain in the French army, was captured, escaped, and later returned to Lyon to become an editor of *Vérités* (*Truths*). Jacques Duquesne explains that:

> At the request of Henri Frenay, Father Chaillet immediately agreed to write religious chronicles in *Les Petites Ailes* (*Little Wings*), then in *Vérité* (*Truths*), using the pseudonym "Testis." He endeavored to demonstrate that Nazism is a fundamentally anti-Christian and anti-human doctrine.[11]

Thanks to these meetings and this association with Frenay, Chaillet was able to find numerous distributors for *The Christian Witness*. One of the most devoted, Louis Cruvillier, accomplished effective propaganda for the newspaper, *The New Times* (*Temps nouveau*), before its banning. Many friends of *The New Times* would be the first activists for *The Christian Witness*. Others would come from among the readers of the newspapers already cited. After a meeting between Frenay and Jean Moulin—the envoy of General de Gaulle and the future president of the National Council of the Resistance, and a famous martyr of the French Resistance—the clandestine publications of the Resistance fused. During a meeting between Frenay and Pierre Chaillet, the separation took place between political resistance and Christian spiritual resistance. The birth of *The Volumes of The Christian Witness* would soon follow.[12]

THE MAIN PURPOSE OF *THE CHRISTIAN WITNESS*: THE SPIRITUAL STRUGGLE AGAINST NAZISM

During his exploration of Christian circles, Chaillet had to decide on the idea of "presence policy"—that is, adherence to the Vichy government and Pétain, held by some of these circles. The most convinced of this group was the founder of *Esprit* (*Spirit*), Emmanuel Mounier. Duquesne describes the tense atmosphere which warned Chaillet against the politics of these circles.

Emmanuel Mounier still thinks that the "presence policy" is possible. Father Chaillet repeated to him in vain that there would be no resistance if there was not first a total break with Vichy. During the summer, another meeting with a Lyon engineer with several representatives of the Catholic bourgeoisie had no more effect: the participants were very numerous; hating Hitlerism, but still trusting the Marshal, and were therefore reluctant to get involved. Father Chaillet was so disappointed with this meeting that he was afraid of leaks. He drew the conclusion that he would have to act from now on in the greatest secrecy.[13]

Renée Bédarida comments on this dispute between Chaillet and Mounier, clarifying Chaillet's adamancy as to Vichy and the resulting reaction by Mounier. "For Father Chaillet, whose intransigence contrasted with the accommodation and hesitation of most, any participation in Vichy's creations was in principle dangerous, because, on the one hand, it inevitably added to the confusion of minds and, on the other hand, it led inexorably to chained compromises. Hence the disagreement with Mounier, who, himself, was very critical of what he called all-or-nothing politics."[14]

Chaillet's intransigence enters into the objectives of *The Christian Witness*. From Gaston Fessard's first volume, the objectives are clear. This text, *France, prends garde de perdre ton âme* (*France, Beware of Losing Your Soul*), will be studied later in this chapter. Its place as the introductory edition of *The Christian Witness* indicates that France's soul was in serious peril, the essential goal of the Nazis. It is reproduced in Marcel Ruby's book, *La Résistance à Lyon*.

> The French who present you these editions do not express politics for or against this or that. They have no other concern than to prevent the slow suffocation of consciousness. They bring you controlled facts and authentic truths. They remind you of doctrinal directives. . . . In Hitler's Germany, it is no longer enough to enslave the body of nations. He must also domesticate their soul, make them deny their soul. . . . For a year . . . a whole underground movement, properly spiritual, has been deployed. . . . The last goal is enslavement of the very soul of France. These pages are intended to be strictly limited to this spiritual aspect of the present situation; but they desire an opening of the eyes of all French people still concerned with human and Christian values.[15]

Attacking and repelling Hitler's National Socialism and anti-Semitism were two spiritual objectives that saw invaluable success, but staying safe from the political quarrel of the time, despite a sincere desire to avoid it, was an objective that could not be maintained, especially after November 11, 1942, the date of the German invasion of the southern zone. This subject is the central argument of *The Christian Witness* volume *Collaboration and Fidelity*, written by Fathers Chaillet and Fessard in the autumn of 1942.

The average number of pages in the volumes of *The Christian Witness* was fairly high; in fact, most of them exceeded thirty pages per copy. Despite this unusual length, aggravated by problems with printing, distribution, and costs, their printing began with five thousand copies, thanks to the funds and printing of Henri Frenay's *Combat*. This would grow to more than fifty thousand copies for the volume written in 1943 and distributed in May 1944. It was written by Georges Bernanos from his exile in Brazil, with the title, *Où allons-nous? (Where Are We Going?)*.

However, the need was felt to also issue leaflets which were less voluminous and easier to circulate. To fill that need, they created *Les courriers du Témoignage Chrétien (Letters of The Christian Witness)*. André Mandouze would be responsible for this new clandestine offshoot, which released its first issue in the spring of 1943.[16] *The Letters* would acquire their own personality while keeping the same Christian foundations, and would reach a very high circulation of 200,000 with their twelfth leaflet.

The Christian Witness was an extraordinary publication in its depth and breadth of ecumenical authorship, readership, and influence. Father Chaillet, its founder, was well prepared, as we have seen, for the moment of its birth. The very first volume was a seminal text by Father Fessard and will be covered below, following Chaillet's personal contributions to the publication. Ruby sums up his extensive research of *The Christian Witness* with these words from his book: "Passionate defender of the human person, of Christian spiritual and moral values, *The Christian Witness* occupied a striking and original place in the press of the French Resistance."[17]

In the last part of this chapter we will analyze the specific texts written by Pierre Chaillet for *The Christian Witness*, pay homage to Father Gaston Fessard for his substantial contribution in volume one, and finally, examine Chaillet's irreplaceable and unprecedented influence on the Catholic hierarchy in France and in the French Protestant community.

PIERRE CHAILLET'S MAIN TEXTS IN *THE CHRISTIAN WITNESS*

Among the fifteen volumes of *The Christian Witness*, the texts of Pierre Chaillet appear mainly in five of them: *Notre Combat (Our Fight)*, *Les racistes peints par eux-mêmes (Racists: A Self-Portrait)*, *Antisémites, Droits de l'homme et du chrétien (Human Rights and the Christian)*, and *Les voiles se déchirent (The Veils Rip Apart)*. In each of these, Chaillet is recognized as the main editor.[18] The three themes we treated earlier in our study of Chaillet's thought will again be our guide through his contributions to *The*

Christian Witness. His prophetic voice and his warning to the French against the imminent threat of the Nazi Religion are poignantly presented, followed by Möhler's influence in the second and third themes. References to the early Church are compared to France's heartrending reality of war, concluding with a highlight of his devotion to the unity of Christianity and its central place in the phenomenon that was *The Christian Witness*.

Chaillet's Prophetic Voice in *The Christian Witness*

In the third volume of *The Christian Witness*, *Les racistes peints par eux-mêmes* (*Racists: A Self-Portrait*), Chaillet briefly describes the purpose of *The Christian Witness* and assures French readers of the Christian and prophetic character of his action.

> We would like to repeat, although the reading of our first editions should have been enough to convince any reader in good faith: our action concerns Christian defense, it is human and religious. It aims above all to provide honest, solid, authentic documentation; it wants to inform the conscience and alert souls to one of the greatest dangers that faith in Christ has ever had to undergo. It will not be said that the satanic enterprise with all the weapons of force and of lies could have taken place on our soil without encountering organized resistance. In doing so, we have the assurance that our Christian defense is a significant contribution to the fight waged by all those who are not resigned on a purely temporal and national level, to the enslavement of France.[19]

This summary by Father Chaillet captures the tone of his writings, which target the French people, evoke their Christian heritage, and exhort courage and duty. These are the essential components of his prophetic message against the Nazi Religion of Positive Christianity which was invading his country. In the same volume, he brings together extracts from *Mein Kampf*, which reveal the true nature of Hitler's hatred for France. This hatred stems from Hitler's contempt for France for soiling its racial heritage by miscegenation, by its glorification of universal human rights, which, according to Hitler, the Jews exploited, and finally, by loyalty to Catholicism. Chaillet's comments on Hitler's views of the French people are brief and clear:

> We can confine ourselves to a few texts, chosen almost at random from the last three chapters of *Mein Kampf*. We will not find a line from the Führer which corrects or weakens the judgment on France taught as a definitive dogma to all young Germans.[20]

Here it is important to emphasize a brief extract from Hitler's quotes chosen by Father Chaillet, because it is certain that most French people of the time had no access to *Mein Kampf*, even in its original German version. In the following two passages, Hitler's words are addressed directly to France. However, Father Chaillet sought to shock and awaken the French by highlighting the unequivocal nature of Hitler's hatred of and desire to destroy France. Hitler wrote:

> France's activities in Europe to-day, spurred on by the French lust for vengeance and systematically directed by the Jew, are a criminal attack against the life of the white race and will one day arouse against the French People a spirit of vengeance among a generation which will have recognized the original sin of mankind in this racial pollution.[21]
>
> I shall never believe that France will of herself alter her intentions towards us, because, in the last analysis, they are only the expression of the French instinct for self-preservation.... Only when the Germans have taken all this fully into account will they cease from allowing the national will-to-life to wear itself out in merely passive defense, but they will rally together for a last decisive contest with France. And in this contest the essential objective of the German nation will be fought for. Only then will it be possible to put an end to the eternal Franco-German conflict which has hitherto proved so sterile. Of course, it is here presumed that Germany sees in the suppression of France nothing more than a means which will make it possible for our people finally to expand in another quarter.[22]

The third edition, *Racists: A Self-Portrait*, analyzes and denounces the content of *Mein Kampf* and *The Myth of the Twentieth Century*. The previous edition, *Our Combat*, expresses Father Chaillet's compassion toward his people, but at the same time does not exempt them from their duty. His message cries out with ardent conviction: France needs to spiritually combat this Nazi religious force; its spiritual survival depends on it.

> For being *patriotic, humane*, and *Christian*, France does not have to be inspired by the inhuman and anti-Christian counterfeits of Germanism, racism not of Hitler's neo-propaganda.... *The French*, who suffer today in body, more still in their souls, who aspire to save what is more precious to them than life, *the honor and the freedom of their homeland, with the honor and freedom of humanity*, wage the same fight as the Christians who, at the same time, fight for the testimony of their Faith, for the *safeguard of the highest and most universal values*, threatened, like France itself, by the triumph of Hitler. Our fight brings us together today to the great battleground of Spiritual Resistance against Hitler's dictatorship, the invisible and invincible battleground of souls.... This *Witness*, which translates our confidence and our resolution, will fix it in our heart and in our memory.[23]

We will return to this second volume when we deal with Chaillet's theme of Christian unity, but for the moment, our attention is drawn to the volume titled *Antisemites*. Obviously, one of the threads of the spiritual struggle is anti-Semitism, and it is in this context that Chaillet addresses this essential element of the Nazi menace. In this edition, subtitled "Antisemitism and the French Consciousness," and framed by quotes from the esteemed French writers, Jacques Maritain and Charles Péguy, Father Chaillet enters the battle with a clear strategy and insight of the problem, bolstered by his spiritual training and respect for the past of his homeland.

> Anti-Semitism is not in the National Socialism system an extension of opportunity, linked by the sole arbitrary will of Hitler, linked in turn to the body of doctrine. On the contrary, it is at its heart. . . . That we have some difficulty in explaining the importance attached by the German National Socialists to this question . . . it is in fact impossible to deny and which is imposed on us to judge, from the point of view of French loyalty, the anti-Semitism which is sweeping over enslaved France. . . . To admit anti-Semitism . . . is to admit indeed that there is a human group, defined by its ancestry . . . that it is truly outside of humanity, that Christianity itself would not be enough to make it enter there and that the action of grace would fail before racial difference. . . . *All the work of the French nation, in the course of history, is it not a defense of human dignity based on the possession and use of reason, and is it not true that racial anti-Semitism is the very negation of this dignity?*[24]

Father Chaillet continues with quotes from Pascal, Descartes, and Montaigne to awaken the French conscience, stemming from its intellectual heritage. However, it is toward the spiritual domain that Chaillet aims true when he evokes the French Christian heritage. It refers to the great French philosophers, to their intellectual heritage, while recalling the source of their inspiration:

> And this very spirit, they did not invent or find within themselves by chance: the source is easy to discover. Where then is it, if not in this Christianity with which the whole of France is imbued. . . . Is it not in fact the essence of the Christian Message that the call of Jesus is addressed to all men, and that to pretend to exclude, even without anger and by deliberate decision, a human group from the common law, is to break this unity that is sought above all by divine love?[25]

This search for Christian unity to which Chaillet refers in this quotation will be the subject of the following brief study.

The Christian Unity Theme in Chaillet's Texts: Möhler's Influence

It is of primary importance here to mention the quarrel between the official Church of France and the "dissident" priests of *The Christian Witness*, especially in the matter of ecumenism and the publication's inclusion of both Catholic and Protestant authors. The two most reiterated accusations of the hierarchy toward the dissident priests were the clandestine nature of the newspaper (we will deal with that complaint in the next section) and the common cause of all Christians (Catholic and Protestant alike) against Hitler's power. This last criticism of *The Christian Witness* relates to the ecumenical and international character of its content.

The Christian Witness recognized and declared itself entirely ecumenical in the articles which it published and in the volumes it disseminated. It recognized that Hitler's ideology—even if it hated the Catholic Church specifically in *Mein Kampf* and in *The Myth of the Twentieth Century*—was an essentially anti-Christian ideology, whatever the differences in doctrine or faith. Some members of the French episcopate, however, did not appreciate this publicity given to the letters and testimonies from pastors and bishops from Germany, Austria, Alsace, and Holland. They believed that *The Christian Witness* published them as an indirect criticism of their silence.[26] Father Chaillet was not unaware of their reaction, but faithful to his principles and devoted to Möhler's idea of Christian unity, he was going to pursue strict ecumenism in *The Christian Witness*.[27] His call for Christian unity was not long in coming, and was published in the second volume, *Our Fight*:

> To all French people, concerned about human dignity and the future of France, *The Christian Witness* will stand for the inevitable urgency of forming a *single common battle front*, which engages us all in solidarity in the fraternal communion of a stronger truth than the contagion of transient triumphant lies.[28]

Chaillet demonstrates the existence of this unity by publishing in the same volume an extract from a letter and a speech by Protestant theologian Karl Barth, parallel to the letters of the German and Dutch bishops. In the fight against Nazi hatred of Jews, the edition titled *Antisemites* professes the same Christian solidarity of denunciation:

> It is hardly necessary to add that Christians—Catholic or Protestant—belonging to spiritual communities both national and supranational, have no trouble recognizing the legitimacy of this spiritual link uniting the Israelites, without prevent them from being loyally and fully incorporated into their nation.[29]

Christian unity is also evident in the volume *Christian and Human Rights*, but in the context of a defense against accusations of hiding.

> The Catholics and Protestants of France, who decided to bring to the attention of their co-religionists and the French in good faith, authentic texts and controlled facts testifying to the Christian resistance to Hitlerism, are not naive enough to believe themselves heroes by the mere fact of being condemned, by the presence of the occupying or controlling authority, to use clandestine means.[30]

The most frequent accusation against *The Christian Witness* by the French episcopate also concerned its clandestine nature. To this objection the editors replied that it was censorship which obliged it to remain in the shadows. Renée Bédarida describes the infringements of censorship and quotes Pierre Chaillet in the foreword to the publication of the compiled volumes of *Les cahiers et courriers clandestins du Témoignage Chrétien*:

> Didn't it forbid everything unfavorable to the occupier? Didn't it refuse to publish pontifical declarations? Had it not had the encyclical *Mit Brennender Sorge* removed from commerce and libraries? As for Radio Vatican's French broadcasts, systematic interference prevented their transmission. "Our work should be done in broad daylight," writes Father Chaillet in 1942; "it is not our fault if the censorship and Hitler's police force . . . us to prepare it in secret. The Church has often known such hours since the first century of its history."[31]

This example, referring to the primitive Church, was written in the grave hours of the winter of 1942. After the roundups of the Jews in Paris during the previous summer, the occupation of the southern zone in autumn, the creation of the militia and the introduction of the STO (the *Service du travail obligatoire*—Compulsory Work Service) in the winter of 1942–1943, everything seemed dark and desperate. In the article "Undertaking of the Nazification of France," Chaillet rallies the Christian spirit.

> This domination of Nazi Paganism, for more than two years, has fallen on France, which was not sufficiently prepared. . . . It is urgent that Christian thought in France regroups, warns and is vigilant; that she learns to distinguish under the disguises, with which he covers his maneuvers, this current of Nazi paganization—and that she finally dares to denounce it.[32]

Chaillet's article in this edition is long and dense. The content brings out the lucid nature of this theologian enamored of the vision of Christian unity and of the dedication of the early Church in combating Nazism.

We will end this section with an example of this lucidity, this zeal, and this love of France which characterized Pierre Chaillet's own writings published in *The Christian Witness*.

> We do not limit collaboration with Nazism. The reason is simple: it is that Nazism is much more than a temporal regime, an institution or a political constitution with which one could compromise politically. Nazism is a religious revolution, a pagan Myth; it is the racist religion of the German deity. It is not limited, cannot compromise, cannot be divided. . . . It's all or nothing. . . . He wants to annex spiritual man and spiritual France.[33]

GASTON FESSARD'S IRREPLACEABLE CONTRIBUTION TO *THE CHRISTIAN WITNESS*

Some contributors to *The Christian Witness* in France were extraordinary—by their theological training, of course, but also by their knowledge of German culture and character, which helped them to penetrate in-depth the Positive Christianity of National Socialism. We have just studied the writings of the intrepid Jesuit, Father Pierre Chaillet. We meet another in the person of fellow Jesuit Gaston Fessard. These are the key theologians who served as prophets to a Church already embarked on a far too equivocal path toward such a formidable power as Hitler's Nazism.

Why use the word "prophet"? These few theologians fought Nazism on the spiritual plain, never compromising their convictions, even in the face of exclusion from their own Church and Jesuit order. The religion of National Socialism, embedded in the Nazi political program, led to the engagement of these two priests from before the beginning until the end of the war. If Pierre Chaillet engaged in the fight by creating an environment for ecumenical expression in *The Christian Witness* and in the field of active social engagement aimed at saving the Jews, we will see here that Gaston Fessard took the initiative in the intellectual field, where his prophetic message is characterized by its systematic analysis. This is evident in his warning to his compatriots in *France, Beware of Losing Your Soul*, the first of fifteen volumes of *The Christian Witness*. Obviously, they did not accomplish all the victories of the Christian resistance alone, but they engaged against everything: Nazism from across the Rhine, the Vichy regime, and even more importantly as regards the Jesuit fathers, they were obliged to go against the hierarchy of their own congregation. They remained faithful to their mission, which consisted of fighting together with their Christian brethren to help save the Jews in France.

The years of observing the disastrous events of Hitler's rise to power in the early 1930s had passed, and when Poland was invaded, France went to war against Germany in September 1939. After "the phony war" from September 1939 to May of 1940—so called because of the lack of any military engagement—France found herself defeated, occupied in the north, cut into zones, and under the new collaborationist regime of Vichy in the south. This small group of Jesuit Fathers of the Fourvière Scholasticate, all Germanists, theologians, and fierce anti-Nazis, led the spiritual and ideological struggle against Nazism during this period.

A serious controversy broke out within the clergy itself as soon as the Assembly of Cardinals and Archbishops (ACA) document came out in July 1941, followed by its implementation among the Jesuits. Just before these events, in the spring of 1941, Henri de Lubac wrote his well-known "letter to my superiors." It has become one of the most famous documents in French Christian resistance literature for its humility, sincerity, and content.[34] Father de Lubac, who was part of the small nucleus of resistant theologians in Fourvière, was a great friend of Pierre Chaillet[35] and Gaston Fessard. This letter served as an important precedent for Gaston Fessard's seminal text, *France, Beware of Losing Your Soul*, published the following year in *The Christian Witness*.

A brief look at this letter will serve as an introduction to Fessard's text. Its form, however, reflects a different audience: the hierarchy of the French episcopate. If Father de Lubac's focus is the end of ignorance in the French episcopate, the goal of Gaston Fessard is "to open the eyes of *all French people* still concerned with human Christian values."[36]

Written in April 1941, seven months before the official document of the Church's collaboration, de Lubac's letter exudes an air of naive concern, that of a subordinate who fears the consequences of the ill-advised decision of his superiors. The humble and sincere tone is imbued with the idea "If only they knew!" His humility emerges from the fact that de Lubac knows more than his superiors about the Christian persecution by the Nazis. This is reflected as well in the sincerity of his expression, because he knows that the same fate awaits France if the Church does not recognize the inherently anti-Christian character of Hitler's regime. De Lubac writes:

> It seems that we have become, to a large extent, the dupes of the necessity in which we find ourselves to participate in the official lie. . . . Many priests are in extreme ignorance of the situation. . . . Our spiritual leaders, would they share, however little, such a state of mind? This is the question that it is impossible not to ask oneself today, in the depths of your soul, and that to humbly ask permission to ask, in all simplicity and with all respect. We hear some of them congratulate themselves publicly . . . they speak readily of "providential defeat," "of a miracle," etc. . . . But from none of them has yet reached us, even the most timid reminder of doctrine, the most modest of warnings.[37]

At the end of his letter, Father de Lubac continues to express his fear that the hierarchy of the Church is in dangerous ignorance, which could have serious repercussions on the spiritual salvation of French Catholics:

> I do not expect or desire any political activity from our spiritual leaders, no impossible "crusades." What it is that I would like is that they are more fully informed so that they can better give to those who ignore the knowledge of the danger, that they are better able to encourage our faith and to help us to save our souls; the impression is that, faced with the terrible upheaval of the world, Catholicism is resigning. . . . After all, should they not have reason to complain, absorbed as they are necessarily by the daily worries of their charge, if they were to find later that they had been able to remedy the evil when there was still time, because those of their inferiors who had the means did not take the initiative to inform and alert them?[38]

If the tone and the character of the letter tried not to insult or to go beyond the orders of the hierarchy, its content resembles that of Gaston Fessard's in *The Christian Witness*. In his letter Father de Lubac speaks of the religious situation in Germany and Austria. He refers to the encyclical, *Mit Brennender Sorge*.[39] He presents examples of the ruins of Catholic heritage in these countries,[40] recognizing that France is not immune. He cites examples, including the concentration camps on French soil, a leaning toward the cult of the State, and the propagation of anti-Semitism. He also unequivocally denounces the ideology of the Nazi Religion: "Because it is at the same time a formidable pagan push, which has at the same time the most powerful means of seduction and of constraint that have ever been found together."[41]

Since the recipient of his letter is the French episcopal hierarchy, this letter also touches on a subject absent from Father Fessard's famous first volume: the suppression of communications between the French episcopate and the Vatican. Father de Lubac emphasizes this attack on Catholic unity and declares it an element of the systematic application of the Hitler method.[42] After having carefully drafted this letter, the sad reality is that it remained without an official response. Father de Lubac was summoned by his superiors to talk about it, but no action followed the interview. However, as previously indicated, the research, the documentation, and the content of this letter were not in vain. On the contrary, this letter supported the birth of *The Christian Witness*, which, for its part, would have an important impact not only in the milieu of the Catholic hierarchy, but in the very consciousness of a large number of French people. This describes the goal and scope desired by Gaston Fessard in the first volume of The *Christian Witness*.

Gaston Fessard, a well-known Parisian Jesuit, editor of the journal *Études*, and expert on Hegelian philosophy, had already published, before the war, vigorous comments on communism and Nazism.[43] This knowledge base would serve as an irreplaceable precedent when he was approached in the spring of 1941 by two priests, François Varillon and Jean Daniélou, who asked him to write a fairly brief text to be distributed on the sly during the festivities of Bastille Day, July 14. Their request arose from their fear of the threat of the Nazi Religion and Hitler's ideology on the Catholic youth of Lyon.[44]

If this fear for the youth served, a priori, as a common inspiration for Father Fessard and the two priests, the final result would show two different priorities. For clandestine distribution during the festivities on July 14, a short text that was easy to mimeograph was needed. This requirement would not turn into reality, since the final version was far too long, but little did it matter in the short term, because it served as the inspiration for the final text, which is a masterpiece of the literature of Christian spiritual resistance. "Father Fessard wanted to write a text which would disclose the sinister character of Nazism, would present an in-depth, systematic, detailed analysis of Nazi doctrine and methods, such as Hitler expected to impose on France through the intermediary of the government of Vichy."[45]

Obviously, such a priority was not going to be limited to the length of a clandestine tract, and the result would be an extraordinary analysis of about fifty pages.[46] But what to do with it? This precious document would serve as the first edition of *The Christian Witness*. Its title, *France, Beware of Losing Your Soul* (*France, prends garde de perdre ton âme*) is scandalous and provocative. Yet, from the contents of the document, it is evident that it was written for an educated and engaged elite, or at least for those who were ready to engage. This text leaves no doubt about the religious aspirations of Nazism. In this context, we will analyze the components of this ideological exposure of Nazism by this systematic and prophetic theologian.

In this document Fessard denounces National Socialism by presenting three essential points. First, like Tillich, he notes that National Socialism is not just a political regime. In fact, it is a *Weltanschauung*—that is to say, a vision of the world based on a mystique. To justify himself, Fessard quotes Hitler in passages from *Mein Kampf*. Here are some examples which show us the sinister and Machiavellian ideas of Hitler.

> Any conception of the world is intolerant by its nature. . . . This law applies exactly to religions. Christianity, too, was not content, and could not content itself with raising its own altars. A logical necessity led it to tear down the altars of paganism. Doctrinal faith could only be born against this background of fanatic intolerance.[47]

Next, Fessard approaches the writings of Rosenberg, which we studied in part I. Rosenberg was, as we know, the main ideologue of the Nazi Party and inspirer of all anti-Christian measures in German public schools.[48] Author of *The Myth of the Twentieth Century*, considered "the book in which Hitler best recognized his own conceptions,"[49] Rosenberg gives a racial justification to this neopagan mystique of National Socialism. Fessard emphasizes a fairly clear synopsis of Rosenberg's racial ideas with respect to religion in the following passage:

> The Germans being the only racial nucleus that has remained pure, it is up to them to regain awareness of their racial value and of their cultural mission to regenerate Europe through the cult of race. Regeneration which requires a total purification of the Germanic blood by measures which will be able to be accepted only if the blood and the race give birth to a true worship and to a religious myth which will take the place of the old religions.[50]

Even more theologically insightful regarding the Nazi idea of Christianity, Fessard could not be clearer in his explanation of the distinction between Positive Christianity and Negative Christianity in Nazi ideology:

> From Christianity, it is necessary to keep all that, in it, is the exaltation of life, of strength, of honor and of freedom: this is *"Positive Christianity,"* and to eliminate all that, on the contrary, is humility, asceticism, acceptance of death and suffering, love and grace: this is "negative Christianity," that which the Churches inherited from Judaism through Saint Paul.[51]

The following two quotes from Rosenberg's *The Myth of the Twentieth Century*, chosen by Fessard, divulge the essence of what Nazism considers "Christian":

> Jesus appears to us today as the master conscious of himself, in the best and highest sense of the word. It is his *life* which has meaning for Germanic man and not his painful *death*, which has ensured his success among the Alpine and Mediterranean peoples. The powerful preacher, inflamed with anger in the temple, the man who led the crowds and whom everyone followed: this is the formative ideal which, for us, emerges like a light from the Gospels. But not the lamb of the sacrifice of Jewish propaganda, nor the crucified. And if this ideal cannot be derived from the Gospels, then the Gospels are also dead.[52]
>
> The doctrine of Saint Paul constitutes until our days, in spite of all the attempts at justification, the Jewish spiritual basis, so to speak the Talmudic and Eastern side of the Roman church and the Lutheran church. What will never be granted in ecclesiastical circles is that Saint Paul gave international significance to a Jewish national insurrection which had been suppressed: and thus he opened an even wider path to the racial chaos of the old world.[53]

Finally, Fessard addresses Hitler's resolution to dominate the world by force and by the vision of National Socialism. He arrives at the same conclusion as Tillich—that Hitler did not envisage any coexistence of Christianity and Nazism because "one of the two must disappear."[54] This intention could not be clearer than in the following passage from *Mein Kampf*:

> Any attempt to combat a moral system with material force ultimately fails, unless the combat takes the form of an attack for a new spiritual position. It is only in the mutual struggle between two philosophical conceptions that the weapon of brute force, used stubbornly and ruthlessly, can bring about the decision in favor of the party it supports.[55]

On the ideological level, Fessard is one of the first to suggest a study of previous persecutions in Germany and Austria in order to reveal the processes of systematic application of Hitler's National Socialism. This is an extraordinary element in this first volume of *The Christian Witness*. It is a veritable "macabre treasure map" to the inner thought that gives a morbid comprehension of what these exclusively trained Jesuits understood. In the course of his study, he noticed a fundamental difference between Hitler's persecution and that of Bolshevism. "As much as the persecution of Bolshevism is simple, brutal and obvious to all eyes, as that of National Socialism is underhanded, concealed and treacherous."[56] Even more profound is his analysis of the Nazi processes which took place in the same way, according to a sinister logic in Germany, in Austria, and, obviously, in France. Of what does this process of National Socialist ideology consist? Fessard, in a text worthy of fame, divides the method into three stages: a period of seduction, of compromise, and finally, of perversion or destruction.

> First, to *seduce*, by opposing with force promises, a common goal of action, the ambiguous nature of which is hidden under honest words and appearances. Then *compromise* by taking action in concert for this common and apparently good goal. Finally, *pervert* everything that has . . . abandoned itself [in a cowardly way] to these goals, or *destroy* everything that courageously resists. Indeed, when, during this common action, the dishonesty of the real goal is revealed, then blackmail and terror are employed to force all that there is of cowardice in man, to be silent in the resultant ambiguity and to persevere in common action. In this way, the compromise becomes *perversion*. The ally—the attractive and first of all honest collaborator—is transformed into a perverted accomplice and linked to the criminal by his very participation in the common crime. If, on the contrary, honesty rebels, false and slanderous accusations will convince it of disloyalty, duplicity, immorality, and after an infinity of small police measures have gagged all the voices of conscience and tied up any resistance of the will,

the most brutal violence will reduce to impotence and if necessary destroy all opposition.[57]

This lucid analysis evokes Tillich's ideas in his study, titled *Le démonique*. Tillich, we may remember, explains in the introduction to his study why absolute lucidity was needed when dealing with Nazism:

> This article, I wrote reluctantly. True knowledge is always love, the union of oneself with its object, which thereby ceases to be only its object. But the union with the demonic comes at the cost of the destruction of oneself: either we awaken this demon who lives in each one, always ready to lose him; or else we bring to light the creative aspect in the demonic, which alone allows us to speak of it; we bring it up from the depths and at the same time strip it of its substance. It is a strange experience: the discourse on the demonic succeeds savage violence or emptiness, or even both at the same time; the devil takes revenge for being identified. Only the prophet can name him without suffering, because he defeats him.[58]

The remarkable text by Gaston Fessard, *France, Beware of Losing Your Soul*, engages this creative aspect in *the demonic*. His analysis systematically exposes the substance of the creative force of *the demonic* within Nazism. The revenge Tillich speaks of manifests itself through the Third Reich's multiple persecutions. Indeed, Fessard's systematic method facilitates the transition to concrete examples of the warning signs of the dangers to come. They are already abundant in the religious persecutions in Germany, in Austria, and the beginnings of those of the French religious communities since the Armistice.

Fessard, after presenting this analysis of the systematic persecutions perpetrated by National Socialism, wastes no time in giving direct examples of this Nazi technique. It starts, of course, with Germany. As shown in part I, the German Catholic Church had fallen victim to this method. The Catholics, who initially distrusted much more than the Protestants the Nazi promise of a restoration of "German greatness," were finally seduced by the promise of reward. The German Church signed the Concordat of 1933, which later appeared as a compromise when Hitler's oppression began. The perverse Nazi interpretation of what "political Catholicism" meant was cited as an excuse to accuse priests and bishops of actions against the German nation.[59]

Regarding Austria, Fessard notes an accelerated application of the technique of seduction, compromise, and perversion. Von Papen, who succeeded in negotiating the Concordat with the Holy See, served also as the Reich's ambassador in Vienna in 1938. His seduction, based on innuendo as to the common ideal of Germanism, quickly bore fruit, and from March 1938, the swastika found its place in Vienna. The compromise of the clergy was also rapid. "We obtain the unreserved immersion of the Austrian bishops in the new order of things. Cardinal Innitzer goes so far as to address a letter to the Führer which he signs with the ritualistic 'Heil Hitler'!"[60] This same cardinal, whom we have cited before, in the face of the destruction and perversion that followed, repented of his cowardice, which became complicity. "The seminaries are closed, the convents dispersed. . . . The hatred of National Socialism, equal to that of Communism, is unleashed here without restraint against the Church."[61] Speaking of Austria, we must not forget, of course, Father Chaillet's book, *Suffering Austria,* which served as a chronicle of the persecution to come in the event of compromise with Nazism.

If these two French priests, Fessard and Chaillet, tried to warn the French by examples taken from abroad, the time would be short before French examples of Nazi persecution emerged. Renée Bédarida refers in her book, *The Weapons of the Spirit,* to the results that Father Fessard predicted in the first volume of *The Christian Witness,* which cites the first Vichy restrictions on the freedom of faith. Fessard explains:

> Catholics, and not the least, slide down the slope of compromise, such as Cardinal Baudrillart; monks write in the collaborationist press and thus lend their support to the enemy's work; right-wing Catholics like Xavier Vallat agree to "carry out the dirty works of Nazism." In contrast, we have closed the mouths of Christians who, in *The New Times* and in *Spirit*, were trying to take a stand. All honest and impartial information has become impossible. The encyclical *Mit Brennender Sorge* has disappeared from bookstores and libraries, Vatican Radio broadcasts are systematically scrambled, censorship is spreading everywhere. Vichy policy keeps citizens in the dark.[62]

However, the most obvious example is that of Alsace and Lorraine. The autumn of 1940 had not even arrived when the Reich annexed Alsace and Lorraine, in flagrant violation of the Armistice agreements. These provinces would be administered throughout the war as part of the Third Reich, and the Nazi regime would do with them as it saw fit.

The same method of systematic persecution revealed by Gaston Fessard was imposed on these two former French provinces from the first months of the annexation. The list of closures and censures expectedly resembled those that affected the German and Austrian Catholic churches, as we cited earlier with references from Renée Bédarida's book, *Les catholiques dans la guerre, 1939–1945.*[63]

Faced with the fait accompli of the annexation, Alsatians and Lorrainians must have felt bitterness and deep disgust at the "National Revolution" of the Pétainist regime and the Hitler–Pétain meeting in Montoire on October 24, 1940. This is evident in the saddened reflections of an Alsatian priest, Father Flory: "It seems that the French have blithely sacrificed Alsace. It would still have been a comfort to hear the Head of State say a word of regret. So here I am again, and perhaps until my death, a stateless person and an exile."[64]

After studying these attempts to warn against the dangerous history of religious persecution abroad and in France, one might conclude that the French population should have known that any Nazi collaboration was going to have a disastrous effect on the country. However, this was not the case, and these warnings affected only a small part of the population who, for the most part, wanted only to see an end to hostilities at all costs. The warnings to the French against collaboration with the Reich were only heard by an elite few. As Renée Bédarida makes clear, with regret: "But, in spite of these warnings—which hardly touch more than the elite—the majority of Catholics are more concerned with the German danger than the Hitlerian danger."[65]

A significant part of this elite included ecclesiastics, members of the hierarchy of the French Catholic Church who, as we have already seen, did not appreciate dissident priests refusing to collaborate with the Vichy regime. It was essential to the editors of *The Christian Witness* that its scope quickly increase. Because of the limited edition of five thousand copies for this first volume,[66] and given the importance of its content, the trilogy of lucid theologians from Fourvière, Fathers Chaillet, Fessard, and de Lubac, wrote the edition titled *Collaboration and Fidelity* one year later, in November 1942. Its goal was to provide another presentation of Fessard's analysis of Nazism, but updating it with the terrible recent persecutions on French soil. With a circulation of thirty thousand, *Collaboration and Fidelity* included the French protests in the occupied and unoccupied zones of the horrifying roundups of the Jews on July 16 and 17, 1942, in Paris. A description of these events introduces the letters of the religious authorities. A report of the terrible reality was provided by one of the major French assistance agencies:

> The families were concentrated at the Winter Velodrome [Vélodrome d'Hiver] Stadium. About nine thousand people, including children, stayed more than a week at the Vél d'Hiv while waiting to be transferred to the Pithiviers and Beaune-la-Rolande camps. After a few days, the children were separated from the parents and they were deported to the East.... Horrible scenes of separation: numerous suicide attempts, mothers gone mad, brutalized to make them let go of their young.... Place of deportation unknown, steps taken by the International Red Cross without results. One would have thought that the children would not be deported. Vain efforts. The departures of children from 2 to 12 years old took place under the same dreadful conditions: how many will arrive alive at the end of their journey into the unknown?[67]

Letters of protest to Marshal Pétain followed this poignant report, from pastors, cardinals, and archbishops, including Pastor Marc Boegner of the

National Council of the Reformed Church of France; Archbishop Saliège of Toulouse; and Cardinal Gerlier, archbishop of Lyon.

It is important to note that a turning point took place in *The Christian Witness* in 1942. Its desire to remain in the spiritual field of struggle spills over more and more into the political field because of the events of 1942 and 1943. Marcel Ruby summarizes the volumes published in 1942 and 1943 and comments on their contribution, which contrasts with the apolitical objective of *The Christian Witness* of the past. It begins with the foreword to the volume *Défi* (*The Challenge*), which is dedicated to the martyrdom of Poland.

> Faced with the frightening picture of the "New Europe" produced in Poland during the three years of the Hitler invasion, every Frenchman . . . will resolve to keep in check the odious blackmail of propaganda in defense of European civilization. Shame will perhaps seize the hearts of the accomplices of this propaganda. . . . This time, it is the Vichy Government which is indicted. Little by little, and especially since the occupation of the free zone on November 11, 1942 . . . this spiritual Resistance is indeed a national Resistance and therefore, at the same time, a political act. Patriotic concerns and properly spiritual concerns will therefore be intimately involved: this is the case for the positions taken against *Collaboration et Fidélité*, October and November 1942.[68]

This stand against collaboration engages a conflict of conscience on several levels for all French people. Father Fessard is the author of several works in this regard that decipher this crisis. In particular, they are found in his theories of *Le Prince-esclave* (*The Slave Prince*) and of *Le Bien Commun* (*The Common Good*), where he astutely clarifies the reality of the threat of a French civil war. In the volume of *The Christian Witness* with the title *Collaboration and Fidelity*, he touches briefly on the topic of collaboration when addressing the element of Hitler's methodical hold on a people through deception:

> *Compromise*: Because here is where the ambiguity lies: "collaboration" is in fact only a slavery that the winner exercises over the vanquished, measuring his constraint, his "generosity" and his punishments, depending on whether the slave returns more or less and accepts more or less willingly his de facto situation.[69]

A better synopsis of the spiritual and political state of occupied France would be hard to find.

NOTES

1. Duquesne, *Les Catholiques français sous l'occupation*, 148.

2. Bédarida, *Pierre Chaillet*, 61.
3. Jacques Maritain, "Avant-propos" to *France, prends garde de perdre ton âme* (New York: Les éditions de la Maison Française, 1943), 8–9.
4. Bédarida, *Les catholiques dans la guerre*, 124.
5. Bolle, "*Les chrétiens et la résistance*," 228.
6. Ibid., 125. Once again it is clarified here that for the ease of reading, the English translation of *Les Cahiers du Témoignage Chrétien* will be used, that is to say, *The Volumes of The Christian Witness*.
7. "*Puissance des Ténèbres*" in French.
8. Duquesne, *Les Catholiques français sous l'occupation*, 154.
9. Bédarida, *Les catholiques dans la guerre*, 127.
10. Jean-Pierre Gault, *Histoire d'une fidélité: Témoignage chrétien, 1944–1956* (Paris, France: Éditions du Témoignage Chrétien, 1963), 28.
11. Duquesne, *Les Catholiques français sous l'occupation*, 149.
12. Ibid., 149.
13. Ibid., 153.
14. Bédarida, *Pierre Chaillet*, 113.
15. Marcel Ruby, *La Résistance à Lyon* (Paris, France: *Les hommes et les lettres*, 1979), 255.
16. Bédarida, *Les armes de l'esprit*, 172, 285.
17. Ruby, *La Résistance à Lyon*, 262.
18. Appendix C contains a list of the fifteen volumes of *Témoignage Chrétien* cited in Marcel Ruby's book, *La Résistance à Lyon*.
19. Chaillet, *Les racistes peints par eux-mêmes*, 86.
20. Ibid., 111.
21. Ibid., 112, citing Adolf Hitler, *Mein Kampf*, 621. This textual reference to *Mein Kampf* may be found in the version cited in part I: Hitler, *Mein Kampf* (London: Hurst and Blackett Ltd., 1942), 343.
22. Ibid., 370–71.
23. Pierre Chaillet, "*Notre combat*," in *Les cahiers et courriers du Témoignage Chrétien* (Paris, France: Editions du Témoignage Chrétien, 1979), 46–47.
24. Pierre Chaillet, "*Antisémites*," in *Les cahiers et courriers du Témoignage Chrétien* (Paris, France: Editions du Témoignage Chrétien, 1979), 133–34.]
25. Ibid., 134.
26. Renée Bédarida, foreword, *Les cahiers et courriers du Témoignage chrétien* (Paris, France: Editions du Témoignage Chrétien, 1979), 13.
27. Bédarida, *Pierre Chaillet*, 155.
28. Chaillet, "*Notre combat*," 47, note 23.
29. Chaillet, "*Antisémites*," 147.
30. Chaillet, "*Droits de l'homme et du chrétien*," *Les cahiers et courriers du Témoignage chrétien*, 152–53.
31. Bédarida, *Pierre Chaillet*, 153.
32. Pierre Chaillet, "*Les voiles se déchirent*," in *Les cahiers et courriers du Témoignage chrétien*, (Paris, France: Editions du Témoignage Chrétien, 1979), 258.
33. Ibid., 260.

34. It is reproduced in the appendix of Jean Chélini's book, *L'Église sous Pie XII*.
35. Bédarida, *Pierre Chaillet*, 144.
36. Ibid. Italics added for emphasis.
37. Chélini, *L'Église sous Pie XII*, 303–5.
38. Ibid., 310.
39. Ibid., 299.
40. Ibid., 298.
41. Ibid., 299.
42. Ibid., 303.
43. Duquesne, *Les Catholiques français sous l'occupation*, 15–16.
44. Bédarida, *Pierre Chaillet*, 144.
45. Ibid.
46. Duquesne, *Les Catholiques français sous l'occupation*, 15.
47. Hitler, *Mein Kampf*, 452–53, quoted by Gaston Fessard, *France, prends garde de perdre ton âme*, *Témoignage Chrétien*, vol. 1 (Paris, France: Editions Témoignage Chrétien, 1979), 31.
48. Reymond, *Une église à croix gammée*, 86.
49. Ibid.
50. Rosenberg, *The Myth of the Twentieth Century*, 119, quoted by Fessard, "*France, prends garde de perdre ton âme*," 31.
51. Fessard, *France, prends garde de perdre ton âme*, 32.
52. Rosenberg, *The Myth of the Twentieth Century*, 604, quoted by Fessard, *France, prends garde de perdre ton âme*, 32.
53. Ibid.
54. Fessard, op. cit., 35.
55. Hitler, *Mein Kampf*, 171–172, quoted by Fessard, op. cit., 33.
56. Fessard, op. cit., 35.
57. Ibid., 35–36. The italics are from the original text.
58. Tillich, *Le démonique*, 123.
59. Ibid.
60. Ibid., p. 37.
61. Ibid.
62. Bédarida, *Les armes de l'esprit*, 59–60.
63. Bédarida, *Les catholiques dans la guerre*, 42–43.
64. Joseph Ball, *L'Abbé Flory (1886–1949): Documents et Témoignage recueillis par Joseph Ball images de Jean Garneret* (Besançon, France, 1978), 207, cited by Bédarida, *Les catholiques dans la guerre*, 43–44.
65. Bédarida, *Les catholiques dans la guerre*, 14.
66. Ibid., 286–87.
67. "*Collaboration et fidélité*," in *Témoignage Chrétien* (Paris, France: Éditions du Témoignage Chrétien, 1979), 208.
68. Ibid., 261–62.
69. Ibid., 197.

Chapter 11

L'Amitié chrétienne (Christian Friendship)

After writing *Suffering Austria*, Chaillet decided to take concrete action in aiding German and Austrian victims seeking refuge from the Nazi regime. He established a "Relief Committee for Christian Refugees" with Cardinal Gerlier as honorary president and Pastor de Pury as vice president. Thanks to Catholic and Protestant cooperation, this ecumenical committee was able to establish itself in Lyon, find interpreters, provide work for these refugees, and give them needed funds.[1] This collaboration represented the philosophy of the Protestant and Catholic editors of *The Christian Witness*. François Delpech comments in a colloquium in Lyon, "Churches and Christians in the Second War":

> It is significant that the Christian Friendship and *The Christian Witness* were founded jointly by simple Catholics, by great Jesuits and by Protestants of various orders. It is not only a circumstantial rapprochement, but a common return to the sources. In the history of ecumenism, this is a decisive step.[2]

Chaillet was able to implement the theology of unity of the Church of Möhler while enlarging and modifying it in an unexpected way. What would have happened if the Catholic Church in France had recognized the threat of Nazism and understood the advantage of an ecumenism based on a common faith? It is all the more regrettable that such blindness was in fact translated into the French Church's criticisms of the ecumenical efforts of *The Christian Witness*, which cited both Catholic writers and Protestant pastors from France and across the Rhine. Despite these criticisms, the success of *The Christian Witness* was manifested in two areas, each meriting a brief study.

Firstly, the assistance provided to the victims of National Socialism in French concentration camps was provided by Christians, thanks to the efforts of Protestants, and later helped by L'Amitié chrétienne (Christian Friendship), a group of ecumenical composition. Pierre Chaillet was involved in both mobilizing efforts. The two organizations would work together to fight for more humane conditions in a country where the right of refuge had always been a national asset, but which, during this dreadful war, had been abandoned.

The second subject of study will deal with the continuous efforts of the Christian resistance to appeal to the Church of France and remind it of its duty in the face of victims being hunted down. It is indeed thanks to this relentless pressure from the Christian resistance that the Church finally, in 1942, addressed from the pulpit the Catholic congregations, urging them to provide haven to the fleeing Jews.

Furthermore, in the conclusion, we will laud the positive reactions of the French people to this late call, affirming that it succeeded in saving many French Jews. As a final word, an important and surprising hypothesis will be presented.

The internment camps on French territory were opened by decrees of Daladier's government in May and November of 1938, creating "special centers" to accommodate the waves of refugees from Nazism and the Spanish Civil War. After the repatriation of most Spaniards, 70 percent of the internees were foreign Jews.[3] The situation worsened as time went on, noted by Renée Bédarida in her biography of Chaillet:

> At the end of 1940, there were therefore nearly forty thousand foreign Jews locked up in the various camps of the southwest, southeast and from Limousin, the best known of which are Rivesaltes, Le Vernet, Rieucros, Argelès, Gurs, Noé, Récébédou, les Milles, camps which sadly deserved the name of concentration camps.[4]

From the French Protestant milieu emerged the CIMADE (Comité Inter-Mouvements Auprès des Évacués) (Inter-Movement Committee for Assistance to Refugees), an organization which, when it was created, was meant to help refugees from Alsace-Lorraine to reach the interior of the country in 1939. After this initial activity, it became involved in assisting interned Jews.[5] As for the efforts of Catholics, they had been only a small minority compared to those of Jewish and Protestant organizations.[6] Chaillet had already been engaged since the summer of 1938 helping refugees from National Socialism. He founded the new "Aid Committee for Refugee Christians," formed before the war in Lyon, which we spoke of earlier. When he was sent to Nîmes by Cardinal Gerlier in 1941 to head a new committee charged with organizing the various mutual aid efforts in the camps, Father Chaillet realized the absence of Catholic representation in these efforts. Amazed, he wrote a report, "Foreign Refugees and the Catholic Assistance Effort," from which Renée Bédarida included an excerpt from a private archive:

Up to now, in spite of some meritorious, but very dispersed and uncoordinated, efforts on the part of the Catholic Church, we have painfully observed that the work of material, social and moral assistance, in the numerous "camps of accommodation" and with isolated refugees in the cities, is almost completely accomplished by the large Protestant and Israelite committees in conjunction with the foreign refugee assistance committees. . . . Nothing can be done effectively as long as the episcopate of the unoccupied zone will not have decided on the creation of a central body.[7]

His appeal would remain unanswered, with no action taken by any part of the hierarchy, and aid in the camps in the two zones would be carried out primarily by laymen and religious volunteers, except for a few official chaplains.[8]

L'Amitié chrétienne (Christian Friendship), as mentioned above, was born in Lyon in the last months of 1941. Chaillet was involved in this interfaith initiative, which originally aimed to ensure the protection of Jewish property, but very quickly this initial intention was overwhelmed by the need to bring together various Christian teams faced with the advent of governmental persecution, such as the Jewish statute of October 3, 1940, the discriminatory ordinances of Vichy, and the new Commissariat-General for Jewish Affairs. François Delpech explains this in his article, "The Persecution of the Jews and Christian Friendship":

> The idea of bringing these various teams together and creating a Christian [net]work, which would work in close collaboration with Jewish organizations, but which would benefit from the official patronage of Cardinal Gerlier and Pastor Boegner, sprang spontaneously together in the last months of 1941. It was proposed by two liberal Protestants . . . Gilbert Beaujolin and a young student . . . Olivier de Pierrebourg. Pierrebourg launched the idea and proposed the name of Christian Friendship. . . . André Weil, who ensured the link between the Consistory and the Christians, found it a good idea and arranged its acceptance by Jewish efforts, with the only condition [that] of dealing with Father Glasberg and Father Chaillet and Pastor de Pury, who saw the possibility of sheltering their illegal activities under an official cover.[9]

Indeed, *Christian Friendship* was able to continue until November 1942 with relative tolerance on the part of the Lyon authorities.[10]

If this limited freedom proved to be useful, the reality of the clandestine activities which the Christian Friendship accomplished was a greater reason for creating this new organization. As for the underground actions of CIMADE, the official status of the organization with Vichy also served as a cover.

Of what did these clandestine activities consist? For the hunted, whether they were Germans, Alsatians, or Jews, the needs were invariably the same: accommodation, camouflage, escape, and a supply of identity papers.[11] An example here of the aid given to foreign Jews by Christian Friendship proves useful, to emphasize the seriousness and the danger of their work. Specifically, it is the heartrending example of Christian Friendship's liberation of 108 Jewish children from the transitional camp of Vénissieux, and the parallel calamitous reality of parents having to give up their children. Two sources will be cited. The first is found in Renée Bédarida's book *Pierre Chaillet*:

> This constant worry to preserve the lives of the children brought, [during] the last days of August 1942, [the] team of Christian Friendship to an audacious adventure.... In the suburbs of Lyon, the abandoned fort of Vénissieux was ... serving as a holding camp [for] several thousand foreign Jews who were to be transported subsequently in convoy to Drancy. Christian Friendship was able to pass several benevolent workers into the fort as social assistants. They had [a] list of certain refugees that could be exempt from deportation ... and they then had to participate in the selection process, in particular for children under sixteen.[12] "And so, J. M. Soutou tells the story of how the team of Christian Friendship began this necessary tragedy that ... consisted of separating the children from their parents. It took two days and three nights."[13]

The second reference to this tragic event was published in *Les Collections de l'Histoire* magazine in its October 2007 issue. Annette Wieviorka explains in her article "In the Name of the Just":

> It seems that the first veritable network was begun by "Christian Friendship." At the end of 1940, in Lyon, there was functioning a Catholic organization for [aiding] Jews and foreigners directed by Pierre Chaillet.... The role of *The Christian Witness*, founded by Father Chaillet in Lyon at the start of 1941, seems both precarious and exemplary.... The fight against antisemitism was placed centrally to the struggle, which was not only Christian, but concerned France itself. The small group of writers, printers and distributors was, however, very much alone.... In August 1942 when the deportations began in the free zone, Christian Friendship, not thinking of themselves, communicated secretly to those that were threatened. August 26th the Jews were taken to a detainment center in Vénissieux.... Christian Friendship succeeded in rescuing 108 children. The rescue at Vénissieux was to serve as a model of what was to follow elsewhere.[14]

To end this section on the active engagement of the Christian spiritual resistance, and, more specifically, on its extraordinary founder, Pierre Chaillet, we will focus on an incident that could be straight from a World War II movie;

in fact, it should be made into one, if there were a filmmaker today astute enough to see the need to tell Chaillet's story. It will be recounted by Renée Bédarida here, who, in her own right, deserves to be lauded as an engaged and dedicated woman, a rarity at the time for her unwavering dedication to the Christian resistance.

The scene is set at the clandestine headquarters of Christian Friendship in Lyon, as Chaillet, hiding in the countryside after the occupation of the southern zone by the Nazis, attempts a meeting with some of the core staff:

> The work had become more and more dangerous since the arrival of the Germans. In actuality, the Gestapo had become suspicious at what was happening at this "small Christian office," and decided on a raid at the HQ, Constantine Street, at dawn January 27, 1943. Unlucky timing for Father Chaillet. . . . He arrived that very morning at the address to find a German soldier opening the door.[15]
>
> The Germans had invaded the locale and assembled all the personnel present in the only heated office. . . . Donoff [one of the staff on-site] begins a conversation with the police in perfect German, which gains their confidence, and they let him stoke the fire with the aid of some "old papers," and in that way disappeared under their noses the majority of compromising documents . . . in his corner and against the wall, Father Chaillet had begun to chew and swallow all that he had in his pockets that would be susceptible to suspicion. Then, he tries to get himself passed off as a simple priest from the north, finding refuge in Lyon, coming to simply borrow blankets. The police end up taking them all to Gestapo headquarters. . . . Finally, in the afternoon, Father Chaillet is ejected outside with force, slaps and kicks.[16]

As part III concludes, what some may call an audacious claim will nevertheless be the topic of a hypothesis proposed to serve as the conclusion to the work of *The Christian Witness*, Christian Friendship, and the dedication of a truly unsung hero, Pierre Chaillet.

CONCLUSION

Provocative hypothesis: Thanks to the pressure applied by *The Christian Witness* on the Church of France, the Christian resistance was greatly responsible for the high survival rate of French Jews, equaling three-quarters of their total number, who did not perish under Hitler's occupation.

To conclude part III, testimony and fact join together in substantiating that the Christian resistance played the decisive role in the tardive decision made by the Catholic hierarchy to finally encourage Catholics to hide the Jews. It came at the "better late than never" date following the terrible roundups of the mostly foreign Jews in Paris during the summer of 1942. This hypothesis explains the large percentage of Jews saved in France,[17] cited at three-quarters of the French Jewish population.[18] This fact is due directly to the intervention of CIMADE and to Christian Friendship in the camps, and, indirectly, to the indomitable pressure exerted by the Christian resistance on the French Catholic hierarchy. This pressure was demonstrated clearly in November 1941 when the first edition of *The Christian Witness* came out. Father Fessard, in his famous text, denounced Hitler's anti-Semitism and warned France "to beware of losing her soul" to the Nazi menace.

It is important to also remember that Louis Cruvillier, risking his life as did any other courier caught with copies of the publication, ensured the delivery of every edition of *The Christian Witness* to every bishopric of the Catholic hierarchy of the French Church. The delivery of the thirty-two-page volume, *Antisemites*, could not have had a more timely arrival. This text appeared the month before the horrible roundups in Paris, in June 1942. Renée Bédarida explains:

> During 1942, anti-Jewish persecutions fell on both sides of the dividing line: a relentless process by which occupants, collaborators, German and French police attacked men, women, and children. In response to this monstrous hunt, this new volume [of *The Christian Witness*], the fourth, applies the power of speech. This is a doctrinal denial which claims to be both a manifestation of "French common sense" and "Christian wisdom." It is a question of responding to a triple goal: to inform, to break the silence, [and] to demonstrate that anti-Semitism and anti-Christianity are one. Faithful to the method followed in the previous issues, the volume begins by summarizing, based on a considerable mass of texts, the arguments of the Nazi thinkers. The choice of quotations makes it possible to understand how far Hitler's hatred goes . . . [It extends] up to the "final solution" of the Jewish question.[19]

Despite the effort made by this volume of *The Christian Witness* to break the silence of the Catholic hierarchy, there was no reaction from them until the sordid progress of the raids in the summer of 1942, and the release of the fifth volume, *Human and Christian Rights*, published in August. Two sentences from Father Chaillet's notebook are chosen by Renée Bédarida in her book to underscore the tone of indignation. "We must cry out to the ignorant or indifferent world around us our disgust and our indignation that we can practice on our soil such a manhunt. . . . Where are the prophets who will thunder over their bent backs?"[20]

Some letters of protests against the roundups appeared before the release of the fifth volume of *The Christian Witness*, in particular that of Cardinal Suhard to the cardinals and archbishops of the occupied zone, dated July 22, 1942.[21] Yet one can wonder about the possibility of pressure on the hierarchy in the occupied zone, caused on the one hand by the roundups, and on the other, by the release of twenty thousand copies of the fourth volume, *Antisemites*. Did *The Christian Witness* play the role of prophet, thundering over the "bent backs," as Chaillet exclaims in the same volume? Renée Bédarida wonders about this:

> Is this just a coincidence, or have the bishops heard the call of the collected volumes? Can we speak of an influence of *The Christian Witness* on the judgment of those who, in the unoccupied zone, have decided to break the silence? Honesty requires that this question be formulated. But there are no decisive elements for an answer. Obviously, all the bishops of France regularly received a copy of each of the editions of *The Christian Witness*.[22]

There is also another reason to believe this hypothesis. It is linked to a favorable visit of Father de Lubac to Monsignor Saliège in the first fortnight of August, on the initiative of Father Chaillet. This is according to testimony from Father de Lubac in his book, *Christian Resistance to Anti-Semitism, Memoirs, 1940–1944*, published in 1988. Father de Lubac recounts his visit to Monsignor Saliège. He finds him in a pitiful physical state, almost paralyzed, unable to speak and barely able to write. Despite these limitations, they understood each other and succeeded in formulating an outline of the approach to take. Each of the two prelates, along with other members of the Toulouse episcopate, were going to prepare a written speech, the text of which would be transmitted clandestinely to all the priests of the diocese. It would be a solemn pastoral letter read from the pulpit on the same Sunday—a fait accompli, meaning the police would be unable to resort to censorship. This is in fact what happened shortly thereafter.[23]

It is important to add a cultural element here. Many French middle schools, when studying the World War II era, read a famous autobiography, *Un sac de billes* (*A Bag of Marbles*), written by a young French Jewish boy, Joseph Joffo, who was on the run with his brother, Maurice. In the final section of his book, "*Dialogue avec mes lecteurs*" ("Dialogue with My Readers"), Joffo quotes part of the solemn pastoral letter that was read on that critical and decisive Sunday, giving accolades to Monsignor Saliège without knowing the background story cited above:

> I would like to give homage to certain French people of this era. For example, to Mgr. Jules-Gérard Saliège, archbishop of Toulouse, for his courageous message to the people of France and for his cry of revolt: "Jews are men, Jews are women, all is not permitted against them, against these men, these women, these fathers and mothers of families. They are part of the human race. They are our brothers like so many others. A Christian cannot forget this." This message circulated in France in September 1942.[24]

Returning to Father de Lubac (later a cardinal), we note an active intervention of the main characters of *The Christian Witness* bringing spiritual pressure upon two archbishops of the unoccupied zone, certainly favoring our hypothesis.

In the end, this is not an easy hypothesis to prove, because it depends above all on the testimony of members of the episcopate as to the true extent of the influence of *The Christian Witness* on the French Church's direction, coming late in 1942, to hide the Jews. One thing is certain: This is the real turning point in a commitment of the French people to come to the aid of the French Jews. In her 1998 book, *Catholics in the War*, Renée Bédarida comments:

> It is undeniable that, for the majority of the Catholics of France, it was the episcopal declarations of August and September which served as the detonator. Because they led thousands of priests, religious men and women, laypeople, to carry out acts of charity which, at the same time, were very often acts of disobedience toward their spiritual leaders, and especially toward the orders of the government of Vichy and those of the occupier.[25]

Whether Protestants or Catholics, early or tardive, these rescue efforts by French Christians represent a victory of a united Christian conscience that defied the French historical animosities and religious wars, bringing an awakening of Christian solidarity unprecedented in its scope. Such was one of the major motivating themes of Pierre Chaillet's vision in *The Christian Witness*, and in the variety of ecumenical groups that were created in this dark time in France during World War II. A more in-depth study on the influence of *The Christian Witness* on the official Catholic and Protestant churches in France remains to be done. Recognition of the extraordinary accomplishments of these dissident Jesuits also remains unaccomplished. These future research efforts will certainly have the purpose of bringing to light and celebrating the courageous actions of all the valiant participants in the Christian resistance.

NOTES

1. Bédarida, *Pierre Chaillet*, 80–82.
2. François Delpech, "La persécution des Juifs et l'Amitié chrétienne," in *Églises et chrétiens dans la seconde guerre mondiale, la région Rhône-Alpes* (Actes du Colloque de Grenoble: Les Presses universitaires de Lyon 1976), 216.
3. Lucien Lazare, *L'Abbé Glasberg* (Paris, France: Éditions du Cerf, 1990), 47–48.
4. Bédarida, *Pierre Chaillet*, 122–23.
5. Bédarida, *Les armes de l'esprit*, 128.
6. Bédarida, *Pierre Chaillet*, 123.
7. Ibid., 125.

8. Ibid.
9. Delpech, "*La persécution des Juifs et l'Amitié chrétienne,,*" 164.
10. Bédarida, *Pierre Chaillet*, 129.
11. Bédarida, *Les armes de l'esprit*, 131.
12. Bédarida, *Pierre Chaillet*, 131–33.
13. J. M. Soutou, "*Souvenirs des années noires*," *Cahiers de L'Alliance Israélite universelle,* no. 201 (October–November 1979), 12. For the history of Christian Friendship, see François Delpech, *Sur les Juifs: Études d'histoire contemporaine* (Lyon, France: Presses Universitaires de Lyon, 1983), 240 et suiv., et Bédarida, *Les armes de l'esprit*, op.cit., "*Le combat contre le racism.*"
14. Annette Wieviorka, research director at Le Centre national de la recherche scientifique (CNRS) (French National Center for Scientific Research), "*Au Nom des Justes*" ("In the Name of the Just"), in *Les Collections de l'Histoire* (October 2007), 87.
15. Bédarida, *Pierre Chaillet*, 136.
16. Bédarida, *Les armes de l'esprit*, 136.
17. Serge Klarsfeld, *Les enfants d'Izieu: une tragédie juive* (Paris, France: Éditions Az Repro, 1984), 12.
18. Ibid., 86.
19. Bédarida, *Les armes de l'esprit*, 116.
20. Ibid., 123–24.
21. Ibid., 126.
22. Ibid., 124.
23. Ibid., 157–58
24. Joseph Joffo, *Un sac de billes* (Paris, France: Hachette Livre, 2001), 410.
25. Bédarida, *Les catholiques dans la guerre*, 179.

Afterword: What Needs to Be Done?

WHY SHOULD WE CARE TODAY?

My book, *Le Nazisme comme religion: Quatre théologiens déchiffrent le code religieux nazi (1932–1945)*, was published in French by Laval University Press in Quebec, Canada, in 2006. It was my doctoral thesis in theology. After this initial publication, which was of course more theological and academic in nature, my goal was to publish a version of the content in English, written for the general educated public. While this goal has always remained the same, much has happened in the interim. It remains a fascinating yet unknown story with discoveries to pursue and further exploration to be done. Granted, the audience reflects a certain hybrid of interest: religious topics, the enigmatic nature of Nazism, and World War II in France. However, "Good things come to those who wait," and exciting events have transpired that make this version of the book even more relevant today.

Rosenberg's diary was discovered in 2013, and it was published by the United States Holocaust Memorial Museum in Washington, DC, in 2015. This discovery has been pivotal in substantiating what are now three solid references to the irrefutable proof of the cornerstone contents in Hitler's Sports Hall, still standing in Nuremberg. This story would intrigue anyone. The diary provides viable historical references to the two volumes of the Third Reich—that is, *Mein Kampf* and *The Myth of the Twentieth Century*—stating that they may be waiting to be discovered in Nuremberg as proof of the vital role that Positive Christianity was to play in the thousand-year Reich.

Even more interesting is Nuremberg's contemplation, since 2016, of what to do with Hitler's Sports Hall, which represented his "field of dreams" but today is crumbling away. The investigation must be done soon on this particular cornerstone, as well as other Nazi buildings, before they are destroyed unwittingly by city officials.

Added to this "right time and right place" scenario is the fact that for the first time in history there is a Jesuit pope, Pope Francis, who would certainly express interest in the Jesuits of *The Christian Witness* and to their ecumenical accomplishments. It can be hoped that, in particular, the founding vision of Pierre Chaillet would finally be recognized by his own Church. The 1997 repentance of the Church of France swayed the actions of the Holy See one year later. Now, nearly a quarter of a century later, a fresh look at the Concordat of 1933 by the Vatican and a greater appreciation of the Christian resistance in France by the Church of France is called for. With a vantage point based on this book, the new discovery of Rosenberg's diary, and the yet-to-be-discovered contents of the cornerstones, a new perspective is necessary. The importance given by Hitler to the religion of Positive Christianity, first by enshrining it in the original 25 points of the Nazi Party, and second, by interring it in the cornerstones of Nazism's greatest buildings, must be made known. Once this is verified, the four points below will follow, bringing not only clarity to the self-defined religion of Nazism, but also to the French Christian resistance that successfully united Protestant and Catholic in a common purpose and together succeeded in saving the lives of Jewish people in France.

WHAT NEEDS TO BE DONE?

Usually, the afterword of a nonfiction book addresses work that has been accomplished since its publication. That is not the case here, however. As a matter of fact, this afterword is really more of a call to action, or at least a call to attention, which will bring clarity where there was obfuscation and recognition where there was none. The hypothesis is the same: Nazism contained, from its inception and in its scope, a religious objective which was to bring about the disappearance of traditional Christianity, replacing it with Positive Christianity, which was to serve as the spiritual guiding light of the Third Reich. A hypothesis begs to be proven. The proof is now here, and Nazism becomes more understandable in its sinister core.

There are four major actions to be taken and much research to be done, laid out in the sections that follow.

Point One: Positive Christianity Exposed, Understood, Studied, and Debunked

As was mentioned in the preface and again in part I, the proof of the importance of Rosenberg's *The Myth of the Twentieth Century* may be hidden in plain sight. Its content and dissimilarity to traditional Christianity must be made clear. It is a priority action to be undertaken posthaste. The cornerstone contents of Hitler's architectural buildings of the Third Reich may have long contained the two foundational writings of *Mein Kampf* and *The Myth of the Twentieth Century*. An interesting update from *The Art Newspaper* in an article by Catherine Hickley, dated May 20, 2019, reports Nuremberg's decision to preserve Hitler's decaying Sports Hall. An opportunity for verification may be forthcoming. To have found only one copy of Rosenberg's book in the Yale library system, and that was a bound photocopy, was certainly sobering. After exposing the existence of such a historical find dating from the era of the huge Nazi rallies of Nuremberg, there is the need to clearly review the Nazi period with this discovery in mind, and the sooner the better.

Point Two: Recognition for Pierre Chaillet and the French Christian Resistance

A call for the recognition of the extraordinary work of Pierre Chaillet has been a motivational element to my vision for this publication in English since I began to learn of his heroic efforts. He should be as well-known to the French as Jean Moulin, the French hero of the Resistance. Indeed, the two French heroes knew each other and respected each other's calling, the former in military and espionage engagement, the latter in the spiritual battle and the rescue of the Jews in France.

A call to recognition here is twofold. The first should come from the Holy Father himself. Pope Francis is the first Jesuit to become pope. The hero of the French Christian resistance was also a Jesuit, along with others from their small entourage in Lyon, but it was Pierre Chaillet that led, organized, and risked his life on many an occasion, to give birth and nurture *The Christian Witness* and the French Christian resistance. Through these two sources of information, pressure was constantly put upon the French episcopate, and through their mobilizing ecumenical efforts, three-quarters of French Jews survived. Chaillet deserves recognition from the Church of France, from his Jesuit order, and from the first Jesuit Pope. It is regrettable that he has remained an unsung hero in his own Mother Church, in his own order of the Jesuits, and in his own nation. It is only the exceptional gratitude of the Jewish people at the Yad Vashem memorial in Israel that has shown him this honor.

Point Three: A New Vatican Perspective: Christian Suffering Caused by the Concordat of 1933

In 1998 the Roman Catholic Church followed the lead of the Church of France, who in 1997 offered words of contrition for their inadequate efforts in rescuing Jews from the Holocaust. These sincere gestures could be updated today with the new information available, including the ramifications of the Concordat of 1933. Pope Pius XII was certainly not Hitler's pope, and he certainly was not an anti-Semite. However, the former secretary of state for the Holy See under the aging Pope Pius XI possessed, as we have seen, a long and revelatory experience of what the Nazis were, what they believed, and what they wanted to accomplish.

Eugenio Pacelli helped to draft the Concordat of 1933, and he liaised with the Nazi Reich, moving forward in an expeditious manner a treaty that, for many, should never have been signed. Without succumbing to the pressure of a hurried Hitler, the unique nature of his life, his accomplishments, and his experience would have better served the papacy by waiting to see the progress of the Nazi ideology in action. The Reich wanted to tie the hands of the Catholic hierarchy from the top down as soon as possible.

Without the Vatican-signed Concordat of 1933, the Christian shield would have emanated from the Holy See and, in like fashion of the humble Jesuit Chaillet, a combined Christian effort with Protestants and Catholics together would have held, and the threat of the Nazi Religion could have been averted. By signing a treaty with the Nazi regime, the Vatican neglected both the protection of the Catholic hierarchies of Europe and their congregations. This left them enfeebled from 1933 on, as persecution of Christian and Jew alike began right after the Concordat was signed. Furthermore, by forcing clear-minded visionary Jesuits of France to be obliged to go against their order and the French Catholic Church, choosing the Resistance to show the way forward, crippled their efforts and delayed what could have been achieved.

While regrettable, it is necessary to understand all of this in order to clarify the reality of the sordid Nazi vision.

Point Four: Recognition for the Publications of the Friends of Europe

This is a call to research and recognize the valiant efforts of the information disseminated by the Friends of Europe in England. Still obscure and unknown today, their seventy-five publications, spanning the entire crucial period of the 1930s, brought vital information regarding the religious ideology of Positive Christianity as the new faith base of the Third Reich in Germany.

Who was receiving and reading all of these publications that documented the aberrations of these new religious tenets being forced upon the German populace? Winston Churchill, during these crucial years of the 1930s, published in this collection. Was he so well informed by their up-to-date and in-depth content that it may have helped to inspire him in his warning of the threat to the demise of "Christian civilization"?

These questions must be answered to provide a global picture of the religious ramifications that were in play during the tumultuous years of the 1930s in Germany and the ensuing dark years of World War II. All has not been explained. All has not been understood. To see the whole picture of the enigmatic puzzle of Nazism, we need one more puzzle piece, and that is the Nazi Religion.

Appendix A:
The Program of the National Socialist German Workers' Party

In Arthur C. Cochrane, *The Church's Confession Under Hitler*
(Philadelphia: Westminster Press, 1962)

The program of the German Workers' Party is a program for the times. The leaders have no intention, once the aims announced in it have been achieved, of setting up ones merely in order to ensure the continued existence of the party through artificially stimulated discontent of the masses.

1. We demand the union of all Germans to form a Great Germany on the basis of the right of self-determination of nations.
2. We demand the equality of Germany with other nations, and the abolition of the Peace Treaties of Versailles and Saint-Germain.
3. We demand land and territory [colonies] for the sustenance of our people and for settling our superfluous population.
4. None but members of the nationality may be citizens of the State. None but those of German blood, irrespective of religion, may be members of the nationality. No Jew, therefore, is a member of the nationality.
5. Anyone who is not a citizen of the State may live in Germany only as a guest and must be subject to the law for aliens.
6. The right to determine the leadership and laws of the State is to be enjoyed only by citizens of the State. We demand, therefore, that all public offices, of whatever kind, whether in the Reich, in the States, or in the municipalities, shall be filled only by citizens of the State. We oppose the corrupt parliamentary system of filling posts merely with a view to party considerations and without reference to character or ability.
7. We demand that the State shall make it its first duty to promote the industry and the livelihood of the citizens of the State. If it is not possible to

maintain the entire population of the State, then the members of foreign nations (noncitizens) must be expelled from the Reich.
8. All further immigration of non-Germans must be prevented. We demand that all non-Germans who entered Germany subsequent to August 2, 1914, shall be forced to leave the Reich forthwith.
9. All citizens shall enjoy equal rights and duties.
10. The primary duty of every citizen is to work either intellectually or physically. The activities of the individual must not clash with the interests of the community but must be realized within the frame of the whole.

We therefore demand:

11. Abolition of incomes unearned by either work or effort.
12. In view of the enormous sacrifices of property and life demanded of a people in every war, personal enrichment through war must be regarded as a crime against the nation. We demand, therefore, ruthless confiscation of all war profits.
13. We demand nationalization of all trusts.
14. We demand profit sharing in large concerns.
15. We demand the extensive development of old-age pensions.
16. We demand the creation and maintenance of a healthy middle class, immediate communalization of department stores and their lease at cheap rates to small merchants, and extreme consideration for all small merchants in purchases by the Federal Government, states, and municipalities.
17. We demand land reform adapted to our national needs, the enactment of a law for confiscation without compensation of land for public purposes, abolition of land interest, and prevention of all speculation in land.*
18. We demand a most ruthless struggle against those whose activities are injurious to the public interest. Base crimes against the nation, usurers, profiteers, etc., irrespective of creed or race, must be punished with death.
19. We demand the substitution of a German common law for the materialistic cosmopolitan Roman law.
20. In order to make it possible for every talented and diligent German to acquire a higher education and thus be able to occupy leading positions, the State must carry out a thorough reconstruction of our entire

---

*The following statement is necessary to clear up the false interpretations given by our opponents to point 17 of the program of the NSDAP: In view of the fact that the NSDAP holds to the view of private property, it is self-evident that the phrase "confiscation without compensation" refers only to the creation of legal means whereby land which was acquired in illegal ways or which is not being administered to the best interests of the nation's welfare might be expropriated if necessary. This is directed primarily against Jewish land-speculation companies.

Munich, April 11, 1928
[signed] Adolf Hitler

educational system. The curriculums of all educational institutions must be adapted to the needs of practical life. The comprehension of political ideas, from the beginning of a child's understanding, must be the goal of the school (through civic education). We demand the education of intellectually gifted children of poor parents without regard to class or occupation, and at the expense of the State.

21. The State must take care of improvement in public health through protection of mothers and children, through prohibiting child labor, through increasing physical development by obligatory gymnastics and sports laid down by law, and by the extensive support of all organizations concerned with the physical development of young people.
22. We demand the abolition of mercenary troops, and the formation of a national army.
23. We demand a legal battle against deliberate political lies and their dissemination by the press. In order to make possible the creation of a German press we demand:

    a. All editors and contributors of newspapers appearing in the German language must be members of the German nationality.
    b. Non-German newspapers must require express permission of the State before they appear. They must not be printed in the German language.
    c. Non-Germans must be forbidden by law to participate financially in German newspapers or to influence them. As punishment for violation of this law we demand that such a newspaper be immediately suppressed and the non-German participating in it be immediately expelled form the country. Newspapers that give offense to the national welfare must be suppressed. We demand legal battle against any tendency in art and literature that exercises a disintegrating influence on our national life. Institutions that violate the abovementioned demands must be shut down.

24. We demand liberty for all religious confessions in the State, in so far as they do not in any way endanger its existence or do not offend the moral sentiment and the customs of the Germanic race. The party as such represents the standpoint of "positive Christianity" without binding itself confessionally to a particular faith. It opposes the Jewish materialistic spirit within and without, and is convinced that permanent recovery of our people is possible only from within and on the basis of the principle of: General Welfare Before Individual Welfare.
25. In order to carry out all these demands we call for the creation of a strong central authority in the Reich with unconditional authority by the

political central parliament over the entire Reich and all its organizations, and the formation of chambers of classes and occupations to carry out the laws promulgated by the Reich in the various individual States of the federation. The leaders of the party promise that they will fight for the realization of the abovementioned points and if necessary even sacrifice their lives.

Munich, February 24, 1920

After due consideration, the general membership of the party decided on May 22, 1926, that "This program is never to be changed."

Appendix B:
Paul Tillich's "Ten Theses on National Socialism"

In *Écrits contre les nazis* (*Writings against the Nazis*)
(1932–1935), Paris: Editions du Cerf; Geneva, Labor
and Fides; Quebec, Laval University Press, 1994

1. A Protestantism that opens up to National Socialism and rejects socialism is about to betray once again its mission to the world.
2. By obeying apparently in principle according to which the kingdom of God is not of this world, Protestantism shows itself, as often already in its history, obedient to the victorious powers and moving toward their demonism.
3. By justifying nationalism and the ideology of blood and race by the divine order of creation, Protestantism abandons its prophetic foundation for a new paganism, either overt or hidden, and betrays its mission to witness for the one God and for the one humanity.
4. By granting to the form of feudal and capitalist rule, to which National Socialism serves effectively as protection, the dignity of one authority willed by God, Protestantism helps to perpetuate the class struggle and betrays its mission to bear witness against violence and for justice as a model of any social order.
5. Protestantism is in very serious danger of embarking on this path which will lead it in all respects to ruin. Since its debut, it lacks the support of a group independent of worldly powers and national divisions. It lacks a principle prophetically grounded and critical of society. In Lutheran lands, it lacks the will to mold reality in the image of the kingdom of God. In Germany, it is no longer defined sociologically except by the group of those who line up behind National Socialism, and find themselves so bound ideologically and politically.

6. The official declarations of the neutrality of ecclesiastical bodies do not change anything in the actual attitude of wide circles of theologians and laypeople. They lose all value when socialist pastors and parishes are affected by ecclesiastical sanctions and when theologians who oppose heathen nationalism do not find protection in the Church.
7. Protestantism must preserve its prophetic and Christian character opposing the paganism of the swastika's cross from the Christian cross. It must testify to the fact that, on the cross, the sanctity of nation, race, blood, and power is severed and submitted to judgment.
8. According to its essence, Protestantism does not have the possibility of subscribing to a determined political orientation. It must keep, with regards to its freedom, that which allows Protestants to affiliate with any political party, even to the parties which fight Protestantism in its ecclesiastical reality, but he must submit all undertakings, whether human or ecclesiastical, to the judgment and hope of the kingdom of God announced by the prophetic preaching of primitive Christianity.
9. In this way, Protestantism can indicate to the political will of the groups united in National Socialism a true and just goal, responding to the expectation of their social distress, and liberate this demonism of the movement to which it is submitted and which destroys the people and humanity.
10. An alliance, patent or secret of Protestant churches with the National Socialist Party in order to suppress socialism and combat Catholicism, would lead necessarily, after the increase in power of which benefit presently the Churches, to the collapse of German Protestantism.

Appendix C:
Friends of Europe Publications

The following is a list of Friends of Europe publications arranged according to subject.

1. HITLER STUDIES

No. 9   One Year of Hitlerism: *The Times* Correspondent in Berlin, with a foreword by Sir Edward Grigg, MP
No. 29   Hitler's Thirteen Points: Adolf Hitler
No. 30   Hitler's Thirteen Points: A Criticism by Sir Malcolm Robertson, GCMG, KBE
No. 34   Hitler the Man: Adolf Hitler, with a preface by Henry W. Nevinson
No. 37   The Racial Conception of the World: Adolf Hitler, with a foreword by Sir Charles Grant Robertson
No. 38   Germany's Foreign Policy: Adolf Hitler, with a foreword by the Duchess of Atholl, MP
No. 41   The Nazi Party, the State and Religion: Adolf Hitler, with a foreword by Dr. Hugh Dalton, MP
No. 60   Adolf Hitler's Reichstag Speech, February 20, 1938
No. 61   The End of Austria: The Speeches of Dr. von Schuschnigg and Adolf Hitler
No. 70   The Redistribution of the World: Adolf Hitler's Reichstag speech, with a foreword by Viscount Cranborne, MP

2. NAZI POLITICS

No. 2   Hitler, Germany, and Europe: a German Diplomat
No. 3   The Future in Europe: Wickham Steed

No. 4	Europe's Danger, Europe's Hope: Professor Albert Einstein
No. 7	Speeches on Germany, with a foreword by Sir Austen Chamberlain, KG, PC, MP
No. 14	Hindenburg's "Political Testament"
No. 16	German Foreign Policy before the War: The 1907 Memorandum of Sir Eyre Crowe, with a foreword by Hilaire Belloc
No. 32	The German Refugees and the League of Nations: James C. McDonald, with a foreword by Viscount Cecil
No. 58	The Action of the Party on State and Nation in Germany, with a foreword by Professor Gilbert Murray
No. 69	The Nazi International, with a foreword by Sir John Murray, KCVO, DSO
No. 72	Holland, Nazi Germany and Great Britain: Philip Debock, with a foreword by Colonel C. E. Ponsonby, MP

3. RELIGION AND CHRISTIANITY

No. 12	Protestantism in the Totalitarian State
No. 13	Germany's National Religion, with a foreword by G. K. Chesterton
No. 20	Confessions: The Religious Conflict in Germany, with a foreword by the Rev. A. E. Garvie, MA, DD, DTh
No. 21	The Church–State Struggle in Germany: the Rev. Henry Smith Leiper, MA, D.D., New York, with a foreword by the Rev. W. Stuart Macgowan, MA, LLD, London
No. 22	Hitlerism: Why and Whither; Some Aspects of a Religious Revolution: Professor George Norlin, president of the University of Colorado, with a foreword by the Rt. Hon. H. A. L. Fisher, Oxford
No. 26	Rosenberg's German "Mythus": An Evangelical Answer by Pastor Heinrich Hüffmeier, Berlin, with a foreword by Rev. Sidney M. Berry, MA, DD, Secretary, Congregational Union of England and Wales
No. 27	Rosenberg's Positive Christianity, with a foreword by Rev. Richard Downey, Archbishop of Liverpool
No. 28	Cross and Swastika: the *Manchester Guardian* special correspondent, with a foreword by the Rev. John S. Whale, MA, Cambridge
No. 31	The Creed of the Nordic Race: Dr. Wilhelm Kusserow, Berlin with a foreword by the Rev. Henry Sloane Coffin, DD, LLD, New York
No. 35	Outline of a Nordic Religion: Felix Fischer-Dodeleben, with a foreword by the Rev. A. G. Fraser, CBE
No. 39	The 25 Theses of the German Religion: Professor Ernest Bergmann, with a foreword by the Rev. F. W. Norwood, DD

No. 41	The Nazi Party, The State and Religion: Adolf Hitler, with a foreword by Dr. Hugh Dalton, MP
No. 44	"Mythus" II. The Character of the New Religion: Dr. Alfred Rosenberg, with a foreword by the Rev. John Arendzen, MA, DD (London)
No. 46	"Mythus" I. The Worship of Race: Dr. Alfred Rosenberg, with a foreword by Professor Charles A. Beard (USA)
No. 47	"Where is God!": Graf E. Reventlow, with a foreword by the Rev. H. Emerson Fosdick, DD (New York)
No. 48	"Mythus" III. International Implications of the New Religion: Dr. Alfred Rosenberg, with a foreword by the Rt. Hon. Josiah C. Wedgwood, DSO, MP
No. 50	Getting Rid of Jesus Christ: Dr. Mathilde Ludendorff, with a foreword by the Hon. Lady Maxse
No. 51	The Completion of the Protestant Reformation: Dr. Arthur Dinter, with a foreword by the Rev. Dr. James Parkes
No. 54	Immorality in the Talmud: Dr. Alfred Rosenberg, with a foreword by the Rev. Herbert Danby, DD
No. 55	The Protestant Opposition Movement in Germany, 1934–1937, with a foreword by Dr. Reinhold Niebuhr, DD, Union Theological Seminary, New York
No. 56	Germanic Vision of God: Professor Wilhelm Hauer, with a foreword by Dr. Edwyn Bevan
No. 64	The Germanisation of the New Testament: Bishop Ludwig Müller and Bishop Weidemann, with a foreword by the Rev. Dr. H. C. Robbins
No. 65	Church, Volk and State: German Protestant Leaders, with a foreword by Atkinson Lee, MA
No. 66	Protestant Pilgrims to Rome: The Betrayal of Luther by Alfred Rosenberg, with a foreword by the Rev. Nathaniel Micklem, DD
No. 67	Protestantism Between Rome and Moscow: Matthes Ziegler, with a foreword by the Rev. Eric Fenn
No. 68	The Poisonous Mushroom: Ernst Hiemer, with a foreword by the Bishop of Durham

4. NAZI MILITARISM

No. 1	Hitler and Arms: J. L. Garvin
No. 5	Germany Re-arming
No. 6	The Military Preparedness of German Industry

No. 10   The Military Science of Professor Banse, with a foreword by Admiral Sir Herbert Richmond

No. 36   The "Total" War: General Ludendorff, with a foreword by General The Hon. Sir Herbert

5. DR. ALFRED ROSENBERG

No. 26   Rosenberg's German "Mythus": An Evangelical Answer by Pastor Heinrich Hüffmeier, Berlin, with a foreword by the Rev. Sidney M. Berry, MA, DD, Secretary, Congregational Union of England and Wales

No. 27   Rosenberg's Positive Christianity, with a foreword by Dr. Downey, Archbishop of Liverpool

No. 44   "Mythus" II. The Character of the New Religion: Dr. Alfred Rosenberg, with a foreword by the Rev. John Arendzen, MA, DD (London)

No. 46   "Mythus" I. The Worship of Race: Dr. Alfred Rosenberg, with a foreword by Professor Charles A. Beard (USA)

No. 48   "Mythus" III. International Implications of the New Religion: Dr. Alfred Rosenberg, with a foreword by the Rt. Hon. Josiah C. Wedgwood, DSO, MP

No. 49   The Future of German Foreign Policy: Dr. Alfred Rosenberg, with a foreword by Sir Bernard Pares, KBE

No. 54   Immorality in the Talmud: Dr. Alfred Rosenberg, with a foreword by the Rev. Herbert Danby, DD

No. 66   Protestant Pilgrims to Rome: The Betrayal of Luther: Dr. Alfred Rosenberg, with a foreword by the Rev. Nathaniel Micklem, DD

6. NAZI EDUCATION

No. 11   A Nazi School History Textbook (1914–1933), with a foreword by Prof. Ernest Barker

No. 15   Youth on the Rhine. The Problem of the Saar: William Teeling

No. 17   Education under Hitler: Vivian Ogilvie, with a foreword by Dr. G. P. Gooch

No. 25   The New Spirit of Military Education: Professor Dr. Ziegler, with a foreword by Major-General Sir Charles Gwynn, KCB, CMG, DSO

No. 40   Race, Mind and Soul (An example of the New Racial Science of Germany): Dr. L. G. Tirala, with a foreword by Sir Grafton Elliot Smith, late London University

No. 42	History on a Racial Basis: Dr. Johann von Leers, with a foreword by Julian Huxley, MA, DSc
No. 52	An Exchange of Letters: Thomas Mann, with a foreword by J. B. Priestley
No. 53	From the World War to the National Revolution, 1914–1933: Dr. W. von Kloeber, with a foreword by E. L. Woodward, MA
No. 57	The Teaching of History: Its Purpose, Material and Method: Wilhelm Rödiger, with a foreword by T. S. R. Boase, MA
No. 63	A Nazi View of German History: Erich Czech-Jochberg, with a foreword by Professor David S. Muzzey (New York)

7. COLONIAL QUESTIONS

No. 43	Nazi Activities in South West Africa, with a foreword by Lord Lugard
No. 59	Germany Without Colonies, with a foreword by the Rt. Hon. L. S. Amery, MP

8. BRITISH POLICY

No. 8	The Prevention of War by Collective Action: Lord Howard of Penrith
No. 18	International Law or International Chaos: Lord Howard of Penrith
No. 19	The House of Commons and German Re-armament: Stanley Baldwin, MP, Winston Churchill, MP
No. 23	The House of Commons and the German Situation: J. Ramsey MacDonald, MP, Winston Churchill, MP, and other members
No. 24	Germany, Great Britain and the League of Nations: the Rt. Hon. Anthony Eden, MP
No. 33	The Principles of British Foreign Policy: the Rt. Hon. Anthony Eden, MC, MP
No. 45	British Foreign Policy after the League of Nations Crisis: the Rt. Hon. Anthony Eden, MP
No. 62	The Austrian Crisis and British Foreign Policy: Speeches by the Rt. Hon. Anthony Eden, MP, the Prime Minister (the Rt. Hon. Neville Chamberlain, MP), and the Rt. Hon. Winston Churchill, MP

Index

Page numbers in italics refer to illustrations.

ACA. *See* Assembly of Cardinals and Archbishops
Aid Committee for Refugee Christians, 166
Alsace, 160, 168
L'Amitié chrétienne, xiii. *See also* Christian Friendship
Amorite people, 34–35
Ancient Rome, 17
Anschluss, 74
anti-Christian persecution, 139–41, 151
Antisémites (Chaillet), 147, 150, 151, 170
anti-Semitism, 49–50, 74, 103, 138–39; Barmen Declaration on, 104; Barth on, 107; Chaillet opposed to, 150; *The Christian Witness* attacking, 146–47; in France, 155; of Hitler, 13–14; Pius XI opposing, 117; Roman Catholic Church on, 104–5; on 25-point platform, 106–7
Ariosophy, 24
Aryan race: origins of, 15; purity of blood of, 15–16. *See also* Germanic race

Asmussen, Hans, 49, 100; Barth and, 107–8
Assembly of Cardinals and Archbishops (ACA), 120–22, 154
L'Aube, 144
Austria, 117, 158; Bédarida on, 136; Chaillet on, 135–41; Fessard on, 159–60; Jewish people in, 139; National Socialism in, 159–60

A Bag of Marbles (Joffo), 171
Barmen Declaration, 95, 124, 127; on anti-Semitism, 104; Barth on, 100–101; Christocentrism in, 100; history of, 99–111; on Jesus Christ, 101–2; on Jewish question, 102–4; Reymond on, 100, 102; shortcomings of, 102–3
Barth, Karl, xiii, 66, 76, 92, *96*; on anti-Semitism, 107; Asmussen and, 107–8; on Barmen Declaration, 100–101; Christocentrism of, 95; on common front, 101; Feige on, 102, 105–6; French Protestants influenced by, 124–25; on God, 99–100; Maury and, 124; *Mein Kampf* read by, 107; on National Socialism, 105, 108–9; on Nazi Party, 107; on Nazi Religion, 110; on Positive Christianity, 108–9; on socialism, 96–97; in SPD, 96–97;

theology of, 97–98, 103–4; Tillich and, 95–97, 105, 109–10; turning point of, 105, 109–10; on unity, 103
Baudrillart, Alfred, 117
Bavaria, 69–70
Bédarida, Renée, 119, 120, 121, 125, 129, 160; on Austria, 136; on Chaillet, 134, 146, 166; on Christian Friendship, 168–69; on *Christian Witness*, 170–71; on unity, 133
Beer Hall Putsch, 6, 12, 72
Bérard, Léon, 120
Bernanos, Georges, 147
Berning, Wilhelm, 28
Berry, Sydney M., 56
The Bible of a Political Church (Dodd), 2–3
Binion, Rudolf, 42
Blut und Ehre (Rosenberg), 23
Boegner, Marc, 123–24, 161–62; Pétain supported by, 126
Bolshevism, 73, 158; *Myth of the Twentieth Century* on, 18–19
Bonhoeffer, Dietrich, 76
Bonus, Artur, 7
Boozer, Jack, 104
Borkenau, Franz, 63; Stone on, 64
de Boynes, Norbert, 121
Bracher, Dietrich, 3
Braune, Walter, 81
Bürckel, Gauleiter, 140
Busch, Eberhard, 99–100, 104, 107

Caen, ix–x
Les Cahiers du Témoignage Chrétien. See *The Volumes of The Christian Witness*
carrot and stick, 47
Casalis, Georges, 101, 125, 127
The Catholic Church and Nazi Germany (Lewy), 71
Catholicism. See Church of France; French Catholics; German Catholic Church; Roman Catholic Church

Catholics in the War (Bédarida), 160, 172
Les catholiques dans la guerre, 1939–1945. See *Catholics in the War*
Chaillet, Pierre, xiii, xiv, 74, 75, 101, 116, 122, *130*, 161; on anti-Christian persecution, 139–41; anti-Semitism opposed by, 150; on Austria, 135–41; Bédarida on, 134, 146, 166–67; with Christian Friendship, 169; in *The Christian Witness*, 131, 147–53; on Concordat of 1933, 140; Debré on, 129, 131, 143; ecumenism of, 132; on freedom, 137; on French Christian Resistance, 149–50; on German Catholic Church, 132; on Hitler, 140, 148–49; on Holy Spirit, 132–33; on *Mein Kampf*, 148–49; Möhler and, 132–35, 151–53; Mounier and, 145–46; Nazi Party fought by, 131–35; on political murder, 138; on *prophetic voice*, 148–50; on racism, 138–39; recognition for, 177; Tillich and, 134; unity desired by, 132–33, 150, 151–53, 165
Chappoulie, Henri, 126
Chélini, Jean, 118, 126
Childers, Thomas, 2–3
Christendom, 109
Christian Friendship: Bédarida on, 168–69; Chaillet involvement with, 169; clandestine activities of, 166–68; Jewish people aided by, 168
Christianity, Tillich on, 89
Christian Resistance to Anti-Semitism, Memoirs, 1940–1944 (de Lubac), 171
The Christian Witness, xiii, 11, 75, 110, 120, 122–23, 138; anti-Semitism attacked in, 146–47; Bédarida on, 170–71; birth of, 144–45; Chaillet at, 131, 147–53; Church of France pressured by, 169–70; ecumenism in, 151; Fessard in, 153–62; Maritain on, 143–44; Nazi Religion

combated by, 116; page counts in, 147; *prophetic voice* in, 148–50; recognition for, 177
Christocentrism, 92, 99, 105, 110, 133; in Barmen Declaration, 100; of Barth, 95
The Church and the Political Problem of Our Day (Barth), 105–6, 107, 109–10
The Church Confronts the Nazis (Locke), 45–46
"Churches and Christians in the Second War" (Delpech), 165
Churchill, Winston, xiii, 60, 178–79
Church of France, 115–23, 166; *Christian Witness* pressuring, 169–70; Pétain and, 117–18; in Vichy regime, 120
The Church's Confession Under Hitler (Cochrane), 43, 77
CIMADE. *See* Inter-Movement Committee for Assistance to Refugees
clandestine publications, 144–45
Cochrane, Arthur C., 43; on Positive Christianity, 77
Coffin, Henry Sloane, 56, 61; on German Christian Movement, 62
Collaboration and Fidelity (Chaillet and Fessard), 146, 161
Combat, 147
Comité Inter-Mouvements Auprès des Évacués. *See* Inter-Movement Committee for Assistance to Refugees
The Common Good (Fessard), 162
Concordat of 1933, 29, 30, 45, 104–5, 117, 133, 159; Chaillet on, 140; Hitler on, 51–52, 70; Pius XII and, 178; suffering caused by, 177–78
Confessing Church, 59, 77, 127; death of, 104; extreme members of, 103; history of, 99–111
Contributions to the Germanization of Christianity (Bonus), 7

Les Courriers du Témoignage Chrétien. *See Letters of The Christian Witness*
"The Creed of the Nordic Race" (Kusserow), 61
Cruvillier, Louis, 170

Daim, Wilfried, 24
Daladier, Édouard, 166
Dalin, David G., 24, 27, 71–72, 116–17; on *Mein Kampf*, 61; on *Myth of the Twentieth Century*, 61
Dalton, Hugh, 60
Daniélou, Jean, 156
Darlan, 126
Dawidowicz, Lucy, 50
Debré, Michel, 135–36; on Chaillet, 129, 131, 143
Delpech, François, 165, 167
the demonic: Fessard on, 159; nationalism and, 84; National Socialism and, 88; in Positive Christianity, 102; Tillich on, 80–84, 88–89, 97, 102
Le Demonique (Tillich), 159
The Devil's Diary (Wittman and Kinney), xiv, 11, 60
d'Harcourt, Robert, 144
divide and conquer, 48, 127
Divini Redemptoris, 73
Dodd, William, on Nazi Party, 2–3
Downey, Richard, 57–58
Droits de l'homme et du chrétien. *See Human Rights and the Christian*
Duden German Dictionary, 30
Duquesne, J., 120, 145

Eckart, Dietrich, 24, 41; on Hitler, 25
Écrits contre les nazis, 1932–1935 (Tillich), x
ecumenism, 101–2; of Chaillet, 132; in *Christian Witness*, 151
education program, Third Reich, 17–18
Une Église à croix gammée? (Reymond), 75
L'Église sous Pie XII (Chélini), 118, 122

Esprit, 145–46
Études, 155–56
Evangelical Church, 99–100

Faith and Life, 123
Federation of Protestant Churches, 76
Feige, Franz, 92, 95; on Barth, 102, 105–6; on Tillich, 89
Fessard, Gaston, 27, 75, 122, 136–37, 146; on Austria, 159–60; in *Christian Witness*, 153–62; on the demonic, 159; on Hitler, 156, 158; National Socialism attacked by, 156–57, 158–59; on Positive Christianity, 157–58; on Rosenberg, 157
La Feuille, 144
FFACE. *See* French Federation of Christian Student Associations
Final Solution, 50
Fleming, Gerald, 50–51
Foi et vie, 144
Fouilloux, Étienne, 74, 119
France: anti-Semitism in, 155; Hitler on, 149; internment camps in, 166; Jewish people in, xiii, 152; in World War II, 153–54. *See also specific topics*
France, Beware of Losing Your Soul (Fessard), 136, 153–54, 156
La France Continue, 144
Francis (Pope), 176
freedom, Chaillet on, 137
"The Freedom of the Church" (Chaillet), 134
Frenay, Henri, 45, 147
French Catholics, 115–23; de Lubac on, 155; Pétain supported by, 119. *See also* Church of France
French Catholics under the Occupation (Duquesne), 120
French Christian Resistance, xiii, 55, 129; Chaillet on, 149–50; intellectual heritage of, 150; Jewish people aided by, 169–70; recognition for, 177; relief provided by, 165–66

The French Christians Between Crisis and Liberation (Fouilloux), 119
French Federation of Christian Student Associations (FFACE), 124
French National Assembly, *20*
The French Protestant (Léonard), 125
French Protestantism, 123–27; Barth influencing, 124–25
Friends of Europe, 26–27, 55–56, 59; publications of, 56, 187–91; recognition for, 178–79

von Galen, Clemens, August Graf, 73, 75
de Gaulle, Charles, 60
Gerlier (Cardinal), 65, 166
German Catholic Church, 52, 69–70, 122; Chaillet on, 132
German Christian Movement, 6–8, 102; Coffin on, 62; flag, *76*
Germanic race: belief in, as chosen people, 13–15; as origin of civilization, 15–18; Rosenberg on, 16–17
German National Price for Art and Science, 59
German Social Democratic Party (SPD), Barth in, 96–97
Gestapo, 136
God: Barth on, 99–100; unconditional love of, 84
Göring, Herman, 12

Hegel, G. W. F., 155–56
von Hindenburg, Paul, 48
A History of Hitler's Empire (Childers), 3
Hitler, Adolf, x, xii, 1; action plans, 77; anti-Semitism of, 13–14; Chaillet on, 140–41, 148–49; as chancellor, 49; on Concordat of 1933, 51–52, 70; Eckart on, 25; Fessard on, 156, 158; on France, 149; on Jewish people, 50; Kershaw on, 43; on *Myth of the Twentieth Century*, 9–10, 11–12,

28–29; on parliamentary system, 51–52; on Positive Christianity, 87; propaganda genius of, 44–47; on Protestant Church, 77; religious policy of, 40–41, 61; Roman Catholic Church opposed by, 47, 70–71, 133; Rosenberg and, 25–30, 41–42; on Third Reich establishment, 40; Vatican and, 27–28, 52, 69–70
Hitler among the Germans (Binion), 42
Hitler and Nazi Germany (Spielvogel), 24, 49
Hitlerist approach, 50
The Holy Reich (Steigmann-Gall), 65
Holy See, 27–29, 70, 72, 117, 159
Holy Spirit, 35; Chaillet on role of, 132–33
Homeland Security, xiv
Hoyer, Hermann, 6
Hüffmeier, Heinrich, on Rosenberg, 56–57
Huguenots, 19–20
Human Rights and the Christian (Chaillet), 147, 152

Innitzer (Cardinal), 140, 160
Inside the Third Reich (Speer), 1
Inter-Movement Committee for Assistance to Refugees (CIMADE), xiii, 166, 167, 170
internment camps, in France, 166
In the Beginning Was the Word (Hoyer), 6
In the Garden of Beasts (Dodd), 2
Israel, 104

Jesuits, 121, 140, 153
Jesus Christ, 58; Barmen Declaration on, 101–2; Jewishness of, 107; in Positive Christianity, 34–35
Jewish people, 46, 49–50, 62; in Austria, 139; Christian Friendship aid to, 168; in France, xiii, 152; French Christian Resistance aid to, 169–70; history of, 104; Hitler on, 50; Jesus Christ and Jewishness, 107; Rosenberg on, 33–34. *See also specific topics*
Jewish question, 95; Barmen Declaration on, 102–4; Tillich on, 104
Joffo, Joseph, 171–72

kairos moment, 79, 89; defining, 85; Tillich on, 85–87
Kershaw, Ian, 39, 40, 42; on Hitler, 43; on Nazi Party, 3–4
Kinney, David, xv, 11, 60
Kirchenkampf, 102
Kolnai, Aurel, 63; Stone on, 64–65
Krause, R, 46
Kristallnacht, 74
Kusserow, Wilhem, 61

de Lagarde, Paul, 7
Länder political system, 27, 29, 69
Larson, Erik, 2
Laval, Pierre, 126
Laval University, x–xi, 9, 175
Lebensraum, 17
Léonard, Emile, 125
Letters of The Christian Witness, 147
Lewy, Guenter, 71
Liebenfels, Lanz von, 24
Locke, Hubert, 45–46
Lorraine, 160
de Lubac, Henri: on French Catholics, 155; letter of, 154–55; on Saliège, 171
Luther, Martin, x, 45–46
Lyon, 145

Machiavellianism, 40, 43, 156
Mandouze, André, 147
Der Mann, der Hitler die Ideen Gab (Daim), 24
Maritain, Jacques, 116, 150; on *Christian Witness*, 143–44
Marxism, 59
masses, indoctrination of, 86–87

Maury, Pierre, 123; Barth and, 124
Mein Kampf (Hitler), x–xii, xiv, 3, 24, 39, 158; Barth on, 107; Chaillet on, 148–49; conquest strategies rooted in, 47–50; Dalton on, 61; parliamentary system criticized in, 51; religious references in, 40
Micklem, Nathaniel, 58
middle class, 45
miscegenation, 148
Mit Brennender Sorge, 48, 73–74, 122, 140, 155
Möhler, Johann Adam, 131; Chaillet and, 132–35, 151–53; on Church and State, 134; theology of, 132; unity as conceived by, 137
Monod, Jacques, 124
monotheism, 104
moralism, 3–4
Moulin, Jean, 177
du Moulin de Labarthète, Henry, 126
Mounier, Emmanuel, 145–46; Chaillet and, 145–46
Müller, Ludwig, 46, 52, 76
Munich mentality, 137
My Search for Absolutes (Tillich), 81
myth, defining, 13
The Myth of Hitler's Pope (Dalin), 27, 71–72, 116–17
The Myth of the Twentieth Century (Rosenberg), x–xv, 6, 47, 57, 99; on Bolshevism, 18–19; on chosen people, 13–15; on civilization, 15–18; in cornerstones, 9–11; Dalton on, 61; on France, 19–21; Hitler on, 9–10, 11–12, 28–29; importance of, 176–77; Positive Christianity in, 31, 35–36; printings of, 28; publication of, 26; Roman Catholic Church attacked in, 27; Roman Catholic Church on, 70; Speer on, 11–12; Tillich on, 86–87; title of, 13; translation of, 9

National Art Crime Team, 60

nationalism, 85; the demonic and, 84; Tillich on, 84
National Revolution program, 119, 124, 160–61
National Socialism, 6, 106; in Austria, 159–60; Barth on, 105, 108–9; the demonic and, 88; Fessard attacking, 156–57, 158–59; formation of, 24; program of, 181–84; Protestantism and, 90–91; refugees from, 166–67; systematic application of, 158; theology of, 97; three-stage process of, 158–59; Tillich on, 88–89
Nazi Party, xii, 26; Barth on, 107; Chaillet fighting, 131–35; Dodd on, 2–3; education program of, 17–18; Kershaw on, 3–4; Positive Christianity of, 6–7, 30; Program of 1920, 30; rallies, 59; religious dimension of, 43–47; Roman Catholic Church and, 27–28; on socialism, 97; Speer on, 1–2; 25-point platform, 39, 42–43, 60–61, 181–84. *See also* National Socialism
Nazi propaganda, 30; biblical content of, 5
Nazi Religion, xi, xii, 43–47, 60, 176; Barth on, 110; *The Christian Witness* combating, 116; Tillich on, 79–81, 83. *See also* Positive Christianity
Le Nazisme comme religion, quatre, théologiens déchiffrent le code religieux nazi (1932–1945) (Burton), xi, 175
Negative Christianity, 12; disappearance of, 51–53; Positive Christianity distinguished from, 157; Rosenberg on, 31–35
New Deal, 72
The New German Empire (Borkenau), 64
new paganism, 85–86, 104
Niemöller, Martin, 46, 76
Night of Long Knives, 74
Nobel Peace Prize, 59

Nordic Creed, 61–62
Normandy, x
Notre Combat. See *Our Fight*
Le nouvelle echo, 144
Nuremberg Congress Hall, *10*, 55, 175–76; Rosenberg on, 10–11
Nuremberg trials, 1

Operation Barbarossa, 19, 29–30
original sin, 84, 138; Positive Christianity on, 33
von Ossietzky, Carl, 59
Our Fight (Chaillet), 147, 148, 149, 151

Pacelli, Eugenio. *See* Pius XII
Pastors' Emergency League, 46, 48, 59, 76
Paul of Tarsus, 46; Rosenberg on, 31–33
Paxton, Robert, 119
Péguy, Charles, 150
Pétain, Philippe, 145; Boegner support for, 126; Church of France and, 117–18; collaborationism of, 120, 122, 125, 160–61; French Catholic support for, 119
Petit, Paul, 144
Pierre Chaillet (Bédarida), 168
Pius XI (Pope), 27, 48, 73, 116, 178; anti-Semitism opposed by, 117; death of, 122
Pius XII (Pope), 71, 73, 117; Concordat of 1933 and, 178
Poland, 162
The Political Diary of Alfred Rosenberg and the Onset of the Holocaust, xiv
political murder, Chaillet on, 138
Pomeyrol Theses, 101, 124, 126
Positive Christianity, xi, xiii, 39–40, 43, 48, 99; Barth on, 108–9; Cochrane on, 77; debunking, 176–77; defining, 35–36; the demonic in, 102; Fessard on, 157–58; Hitler on, 87; implementation of, 51–53; Jesus Christ in, 34–35; in *Myth of the Twentieth Century*, 31, 35–36;
of Nazi Party, 6–7, 30; Negative Christianity distinguished from, 157; on original sin, 33; Protestant Church reacting to, 75–77; Roman Catholic Church critiques of, 57–58; Rosenberg on, 12, 28; salvation in, 14; Third Reich and, 70–71
Positive Christianity (Rosenberg), 26–27
Power of Darkness (Chaillet and d'Harcourt), 144
prophetic preaching, 90
prophetic voice, 79; Chaillet on, 148–50; in *Christian Witness*, 148–50; Tillich on, 84–85, 88
prophetic way, 91; in Protestantism, 89–90; Tillich on, 89–90
Protestant Church and Protestantism, 30, 36, 45, 185–86; Hitler on, 77; National Socialism and, 90–91; on Positive Christianity, 75–77; prophetic way in, 89–90; Rosenberg on, 58–59; Tillich and, 79–80, 88–90. *See also* French Protestantism
Protestant Pilgrim to Rome (Rosenberg), 58
The Protocols of the Elder Men of Zion and Jewish World Politics (Rosenberg), 23–24
Psychopathic Got (Waite), 49
publications, clandestine, 144–45
de Pury, Roland, 123, 125, 145
Putz, Eduard, 103

racism, 17; Chaillet on, 138–39; of Third Reich, 138–39
Racists: A Self-Portrait (Chaillet), 11, 117, 138, 147, 149
Raymond, Bernard, 7–8
refugees, from National Socialism, 166–67
Reichstag, 45
Relief Committee for Christian Refugees, 165
The Religious Dimension of Culture, 83
religious socialism, of Tillich, 92

La Résistance à Lyon (Ruby), 146
Responses to Nazism in Britain, 1933–1939 (Stone), 63
Reymond, Bernard, 27, 40, 42, 46, 75, 88, 107; on Barmen Declaration, 100, 102
Richard, Jean, x–xi, 83; on Tillich, 91
Roman Catholic Church, 8, 16, 36, 45; on anti-Semitism, 104–5; in Germany, 52; Hitler opposed to, 47, 70–71, 133; on *Myth of the Twentieth Century*, 70; *Myth of the Twentieth Century* attacking, 27; Nazi Party and, 27–28; Positive Christianity critiqued by, 57–58; Rosenberg, 14
Roosevelt, Franklin Delano, 72
Rosenberg, Alfred, x, xii, xv, 23, 46, 61; on Catholic Church, 14; diaries of, xiv–xv, 175–76; Fessard on, 157; on Germanic race, 16–17; Hitler and, 25–30, 41–42; Hüffmeier on, 56–57; influence of, 28; on Jewish people, 33–34; Negative Christianity critiqued by, 31–35; on Nuremberg Congress Hall, 10–11; on Paul of Tarsus, 31–33; political career of, 23–26; on Positive Christianity, 12, 28; on Protestant Church, 58–59; on Russian literature, 18–19; surname of, 23
Ruby, Marcel, 146
Russian literature, Rosenberg on, 18–19

Saliège, Jules-Géraud, 116; de Lubac on, 171
salvation, 122; in Positive Christianity, 14; universality of, 14, 32
satanic force, 82–83
Sept, 144
The Slave Prince (Fessard), 162
social Darwinism, 47
socialism: Barth on, 96–97; Nazi Party on, 97; religious, 92
Soviet Union, invasion of, 29–30
Spanish Civil War, 166

SPD. *See* German Social Democratic Party
Speer, Albert, 6, 9; on *Myth of the Twentieth Century*, 11–12; on Nazi Party, 1
Spielvogel, Jackson, 24, 42, 49
Sportpalast Scandal, 45–46
the State, Church and, 136; Möhler on, 134
status confessions, 105
Steigmann-Gall, Richard, 65–66
Sterling Memorial Library, 9
Stone, Dan, 63; on Borkenau, 64; on Kolnai, 64–65
Suffering Austria (Chaillet), 135–41, 160, 165; publication of, 137
Synod, 103, 124

Taylor, Myron C., 72
Témoignage Chrétien. *See The Christian Witness*
Le Temps, 52
Le temps des illusions (Moulin de Labarthète), 126
Temps nouveau, 144
Ten Theses against the Nazis (Tillich), xiii, 61
"Ten Theses on National Socialism" (Tillich), 79–81, 87–92, 131; text of, 185–86
Theologian or Prophet (Reymond), 110
"Theological Declaration of the Confessional Synod of Barmen," 76
Third Reich, x, xv, 6; buildings constructed by, 9; educational system of, 17–18; foundation of, 27; Hitler and establishment of, 40; Hitlerist approach to history of, 50; mass indoctrination by, 86–87; Positive Christianity and, 70–71; propaganda of, 44; racism of, 138–39; on revolution of mentalities, 3; Vatican and, 70
Three Republics for One France (Debré), 129–30

Thule Gesellschaft, 24
Tillich, Paul, x, xiii, 61, 66, *80*, 185–86; Barth and, 95–97, 105, 109–10; Chaillet and, 134; on Christianity, 89; Church defined by, 134–35; on the demonic, 80–84, 88–89, 97, 102, 159; exile of, 99; Feige on, 89; on Jewish question, 104; on *kairos moment*, 85–87; on *Myth of the Twentieth Century*, 86–87; on nationalism, 84; on National Socialism, 88–89; on Nazi Religion, 79–81, 83; ontological base of, 84; on *prophetic voice*, 84–85, 88; on prophetic way, 89–90; Protestant Church and, 79–80, 88–90; religious socialism of, 92; Richard on, 91; theology of, 97; 25-point platform attacked by, 106
totalitarianism, 105
The Trace of the Jews in World History (Rosenberg), 23–24
Treaty of Versailles, 52
the Trinity, 35
25-point platform, 39, 42–43, 60–61; anti-Semitism on, 106–7; text of, 181–84; Tillich attacking, 106
The Twilight of Civilization (Maritain), 143

Ukraine, 29–30
unconditional love, of God, 84
Union Theological Seminary, 61
L'Unité de l'église. See Unity in the Church
United States Holocaust Memorial Museum, 175
unity: Barth on, 103; Bédarida on, 133; Chaillet desiring, 132–33, 150, 151–53, 165; Möhler conceiving, 137
Unity in the Church (Möhler), 132, 133
universality, of salvation, 14, 32
University of Caen, ix

The Varieties of Protestantism in Nazi Germany (Feige), 92, 95
Varillon, François, 156
Vatican, 177–78; Hitler and, 27–28, 52, 69–70; Third Reich and, 70. See also Holy See
The Veil Rips Apart (Chaillet), 147
Vélodrome d'Hiver Jewish roundup, xiv
Vérités, 145
Vichy and the Jews (Paxton), 119–20
Vichy France (Paxton), 119
Vichy National Council, 126
Vichy regime, 117–18, 127, 153–54; Church of France in, 120; religion in, 160
La Vie intellectuell, 133, 134
Völkischer Beobachter, 24–25
Volksgemeinschaft, 43, 48, 64
The Volumes of The Christian Witness, 144–45, 152
von Trotha, Thilo, 23

Wagner, Richard, 7
Waite, Robert, 49
The War against the Jews (Dawidowicz), 50
The War against the West (Kolnai), 64
The Weapons of the Spirit (Bédarida), 160
Weltanschauung, 40
What Is Nazism? (Kershaw), 3–4
Wieviorka, Annette, 168
Wilhelm (Kaiser), 76
Wittenberg, 2
Wittman, Robert, xv, 11, 60
Word of God, 124
World Church Conference, 58, 59
World War I, 52, 92, 117
World War II, ix, xiv; France in, 153–54
Writings against the Nazis (Tillich), 85

Yale, 9

About the Author

Kathleen Burton has a PhD in theology from Laval University (L'Université Laval, in Québec), which she earned on a full-tuition scholarship. She also has an MA degree in French from Central Connecticut State University and a BA degree in political science from the University of California, Los Angeles. She studied at the Institut d'Études Politiques de Bordeaux, in France, during her undergraduate years and studied international law at the Sorbonne University in Paris.

This book is based on her doctoral thesis, which was published in French in 2006 by Laval University Press. The title (in English) is *Nazism as Religion: Four Theologians Decipher the Nazi Religious Code (1932–1945)*. Because English is Dr. Burton's first language, she has translated the work herself, expanded the research, included recent discoveries, and targeted the general educated public for this book.

Dr. Burton has twenty-five years of experience teaching French at the university level, the last fifteen at Yale University.

www.ingramcontent.com/pod-product-compliance
Lightning Source LLC
Chambersburg PA
CBHW052041300426
44117CB00012B/1921